"The rediscovery of Thomas Cranmer's vision for worship, enshrined in the Book of Common Prayer, is one of the exciting developments of recent years. Zac Hicks takes us to the source of Cranmer's inspiration in the great doctrine of justification by faith alone, which he expressed in timeless prose. A must-read for everyone who wants to worship God in spirit and in truth."

Gerald Bray, research professor at Beeson Divinity School of Samford University and author of *Doing Theology with the Reformers*

"Worship and trust go together, for good or ill. Zac Hicks shows how the *Book of Common Prayer* was shaped brilliantly by Thomas Cranmer to commend a deep trust in the sufficiency of Jesus Christ, in whom is all comfort and eternal life. *Worship by Faith Alone* shows us the richly Protestant nature of Cranmerian Anglicanism. Even more so, Hicks shows us how worship can convey Jesus Christ to us."

Michael Allen, John Dyer Trimble Professor of Systematic Theology at Reformed Theological Seminary, Orlando

"In an era obsessed with questions of worship style or the worshiper's positive experience, Zac Hicks's study of Thomas Cranmer reminds us that the more critical issue is how worship proclaims and participates in the gospel of Jesus Christ. I have long been concerned that much of the worship in this contemporary era has been ashamed of this gospel, not by overt rejection but by a more subtle—and equally disastrous—omission. *Worship by Faith Alone* through Cranmer's historical example shows how to avoid this drastic error."

Lester Ruth, research professor of Christian worship at Duke Divinity School

"In *Worship by Faith Alone,* Zac Hicks brings together analysis of Cranmer's thought and Reformation liturgy with a deep concern for the health of modern worship. Useful to church leaders and students of worship and liturgy, *Worship by Faith Alone* offers readers a vision of worship that is gospel centered in word, action, and atmosphere, exemplifying the belief that history has relevance for the contemporary world."

Matthew Laube, assistant professor of church music at Baylor University

WORSHIP BY FAITH ALONE

THOMAS CRANMER, THE BOOK OF COMMON PRAYER, AND THE REFORMATION OF LITURGY

ZAC HICKS

FOREWORD BY ASHLEY NULL

Academic

An imprint of InterVarsity Press
Downers Grove, Illinois

InterVarsity Press
P.O. Box 1400 | Downers Grove, IL 60515-1426
ivpress.com | email@ivpress.com

InterVarsity Press® is the publishing division of InterVarsity Christian Fellowship/USA®. For more information, visit intervarsity.org.

Scripture quotations, unless otherwise noted, are from The Holy Bible, English Standard Version, copyright © 2001 by Crossway Bibles, a division of Good News Publishers. Used by permission. All rights reserved.

Published in association with the literary agency of Wolgemuth & Associates.

The publisher cannot verify the accuracy or functionality of website URLs used in this book beyond the date of publication.

Cover design and image composite: David Fassett
Interior design: Daniel van Loon

ISBN 978-1-5140-0522-4 (print) | ISBN 978-1-5140-0523-1 (digital)

Printed in the United States of America ♾

Library of Congress Cataloging-in-Publication Data
A catalog record for this book is available from the Library of Congress.

29 28 27 26 25 24 23 | 8 7 6 5 4 3 2

For Joel, Jesse, Brody, and Bronwyn.

Praising God, with you, that his property is always to have mercy.

זֶבַח וּמִנְחָה לֹא-חָפַצְתָּ אָזְנַיִם כָּרִיתָ לִּי

Θυσίαν καὶ προσφορὰν οὐκ ἠθέλησας, σῶμα δὲ κατηρτίσω μοι.

Ps 40:6 / Heb 10:5

CONTENTS

LIST OF FIGURES

FOREWORD

ASHLEY NULL

I GREW UP IN WESTERN KANSAS, amid horizon-wide fields of wheat and countless clusters of grazing cattle scattered across seemingly endless acres of slightly undulating plains. One of my most favorite things to have ever written is a contribution to a collection of essays entitled *150 Years of Kansas Beef.* My chapter was "Cowboys, Cowtowns and Cattle Trails of Kansas." Why did I explore something so far afield from my academic interest in Cranmer and the English Reformation? Frankly, I wanted to write something my family would read. In short, I think it is accurate to say that I grew up in rural America. Yet, in all my years in Kansas, I never saw a horse pushing a cart. Pulling, yes, but pushing? I never saw that happen, not even once. After all, a horse's head is not really designed to efficiently push a cart, but its body is so effective at pulling that even after human society made the transition from work animals to machines, we still refer to the energy required to move things in units of "horsepower." However, when it comes to Christianity, this inversion of horse and cart seems to happen all the time.

Let me explain. One of the most basic principles in Christianity to get straight is which comes first: the cart or the horse. Do we initiate and God's responds? Or does God initiate and we respond? Do we take a step towards God and, consequently, he takes a step towards us? Or does God come to us, embrace us, hugging us tight with his love so that we find ourselves instinctively drawn to put our arms around him in return, receiving the fullness of that love which he is imparting to us?

Or, rather, do we try to do something in-between these two diametrically opposite approaches? Do we start with the horse first, but then switch to the cart? Are we saved by Christ's gift on the cross, but expect afterwards to be sanctified by our own efforts? Is our will bound before salvation, but afterward it must choose to initiate godliness? Or worse, do we think that our choices after salvation earn God's further blessings? In short, are we saved by grace, but sustained by our own sweat? Or do we keep the horse in front of the cart from the beginning of our Christian lives to its consummation in the age to come? Philippians 1:6 teaches us that God will complete the good work he has begun in us, and Philippians 2:13 goes ever further, telling us that our desire and power to choose God instead of sin is actually his work in us. In short, do we long for God to lead us, or do we expect, or at least hope, that he will get behind what we are already doing and push us along our own way?

Of course, we are not the first generation of Christians to put the cart before the horse in matters of faith. These essential questions were the same ones which the sixteenth-century Protestant Reformers were asking of their church and of themselves. Like Martin Luther before him, Thomas Cranmer found the definitive answers in Scripture, namely, the grace and gratitude theology outlined by Saint Paul in his Epistles: "not I, but Christ"; "not by my works, but by his promised gift of faith"; "not just for my salvation only, but for my salvation, sanctification and glorification"; in short, "Christ in me, the hope of glory."

However, it was one thing for Cranmer to establish how the English church defined the true Gospel in the *Articles of Religion* (1553). It was quite another to insert justification and sanctification by grace alone through faith alone into the daily rhythms of English life, let alone to make it the heartbeat of Christian discipleship within every English believer. For these enormous tasks, Cranmer relied on the church's liturgy. As his first step, he used the Sunday morning service, initially still in Latin, as an opportunity to preach the Reformation's biblical message through the English sermons in the newly mandated *Book of Homilies* (1547). After having established the theological content for corporate prayer, Cranmer then devised two successive prayer books in English for divine service: daily, weekly, and on special occasions (1549 and 1552). He trusted that regular biblical preaching would help the English people understand their prayers, but he also expected that the liturgy's scriptural readings and prayers would deepen their understanding of the faith and inflame their hearts with more love for God and his Gospel.

Clearly, Cranmer saw liturgy as an essential means for him to shape the piety of the nation in a new, more authentically ancient direction. Hence, determining the rationale for his editorial decisions is absolutely crucial not only for correctly interpreting his prayer books in their contemporary context but also for accurately describing how Cranmer understood mission to the people of his era. Yet, arriving at a satisfactory answer is not a straightforward matter. To borrow a common sixteenth-century humanist analogy, Cranmer was a very busy bee indeed who gathered pollen from a vast garden of liturgical flowers. Ever since, scholars have spent much effort in trying to distinguish the various flavors within the resultant liturgical honey and to promote as the most important that strain which tasted best to them.

Zac Hicks is to be commended for his close reading of Cranmer's writings, which has permitted him to provide a convincing account. In the midst of all the other influences and sources for Cranmer's liturgical work, Hicks marshals much evidence to show that the Reformation's recovery of Paul's message—"not I, but Christ"—was Cranmer's plumb line in shaping his liturgical legacy for the Anglican Communion. Hicks confirms the fact, so often overlooked, that Cranmer designed the *Book of Homilies*, the Book of Common Prayer and the *Articles of Religion* to be a three-stringed cord which strongly proclaims the Gospel message: Christ is the horse which pulls the cart of our Christian salvation and discipleship. May he enable us to recover this abiding truth in our era as well!

PREFACE

THE WORK OF this book matters because the gospel matters. If we are eager to see the transformation of the world, or even just the transformation of our own lives, we have to come to grips with the fact that the good news of Jesus Christ is the only thing that can do this. Our trying harder, being more clever, or implementing better structures or strategies—none of these things can do it. Only the gospel can. Writing to the first-century church in Galatia, Paul passionately expresses how he longs for their transformation "until Christ is formed in you" (Gal 4:19). The apostle had spent the previous chapters belaboring the fact that the only way Christ can be formed in us is when we abandon the idea that we can do it on our own and instead live every day by saying, "The only way I'm going to be able to do this is by trusting that you've already done it for me." The gospel, all by its naked self, does this formational work.

This book is attempting to build a cumulative case for how this vision of the formational power of the naked gospel can be unleashed in the worship services of the people of God. The book will therefore sometimes sound like a broken record when words and phrases like *grammar*, *faith alone* (*sola fide*), *justification*, and, yes, *gospel* keep coming up. Stay with it. Along these lines, some readers who wish for the book to take on a more measured and scholarly objectivity may be disappointed by my occasional editorializing, especially in footnotes. For better or worse, nearly twenty years of pastoral ministry biases me toward verbalizing the "so what" a little more often than strict academic scholarship typically does. Therefore, for some this editorializing may be a liability. But for others straining for implication and application, such interjections will be a lifeline. Either way, my hope for this book is that, in its historical-theological inquiry, it might establish enough categories for what we now refer to as gospel-centered worship so that people who care about all of this, in their own areas of influence in Christ's church, might be given more imaginative runways to launch into the same kind of work Cranmer did.

> *Lord, we beseche thee to kepe thy Churche and housholde continually in thy true*
> *religion; that they whiche do leane onlye upon hope of thy heavenly grace may*
> *evermore bee defended by thy mightie power; through Christ our lorde.*
> Collect for the Fifth Sunday after the Epiphany (Book of Common Prayer, 1552)

ACKNOWLEDGMENTS

I THANK GOD for many things throughout this process. I'm grateful first for Mike Allen, who encouraged me to do my doctoral work at Knox Seminary and not somewhere else, and I'm doubly grateful that as I began, unbeknownst to me, Knox was architecting a short-lived but perfect-for-me track called "The Theology and Worship of the English Reformation." It's not an overstatement to say that this coursework has changed the trajectory of my life.

I'm grateful to David McNutt and the team of editors who helped make this book significantly better than it started. In particular, two scholars under David's supervision shed incredible light on many weaknesses of argumentation and even some significant errors. This process elevated the quality of scholarship, and I am humbly appreciative. I also give thanks to the advisory board of the Dynamics of Christian Worship series who had the generosity and vision to see this as a valuable contribution to this great lineup of books and authors.

This book wouldn't have seen the light of day if it were not for significant mentors, friends, and dialogue partners. Ashley Null's teaching, conversations, and correspondence have greatly shaped and sharpened this work. Dialogues in the in-between moments inside and outside the office with Gil Kracke have impacted my thinking, and I'm thankful that Gil graciously took the time to read an early version of my manuscript and provide critical feedback. Andrew Pearson, whether he knew it or not, was always providing fresh angles, new insights, and untapped scholarship in our many dialogues. Sheri Herum found nonexistent gaps in the rearing of five small children to read and edit my manuscript, providing not only some forehead-wiping saves, but also some great questions and comments that sharpened my argumentation and line of thinking. Lisa Yeager graciously lent her expertise in Latin to ensure that my quotations and translations were accurate. Brenda and Leon Hicks, my parents, led me to Christ and his gospel, and gave me a writer's genetics. Finally, I thank God for my friend, mentor, and doctoral supervisor, Jonathan Linebaugh. This book is the fruit of nearly a decade of meaningful conversation, shared life experiences, supportive friendship, and international gallivanting.

Throughout the process, I had two families who supported my work more than any other. First, my spiritual family at the Cathedral Church of the Advent cheered me on, provided financial assistance to complete this work, and gave me real-time feedback as I repeatedly taught on these concepts and attempted to apply them in our weekly worship in downtown Birmingham. My time at the Advent was proof that this kind of scholarship isn't ivory-tower work but meaningful on the ground, for real life and real concerns. Second, and most importantly, my immediate family—my tribe—has supported me by suffering through long stretches of my typing away with big piles of books around me, buried and inattentive. Abby has shouldered extra work, and there were a few "fatherless" times in the fall of 2019 for Joel, Jesse, Brody, and Bronwyn, which they all accepted without complaint. I couldn't have done this without their support and grace.

PEERING OVER THE ARCHBISHOP'S SHOULDER

Christianity has embedded in it the germ of antireligion
that fights its own tendency to become a religion
that is based in works-righteousness.

ESTHER ACOLATSE

PROTESTANTISM AND GOSPEL-CENTRALITY

We have apparently arrived at a moment in Western evangelicalism where gospel-centrality is a thing. In the grand scheme of worldwide Christianity, it might not be a very popular or widespread thing, but it is a thing. Gospel-centered, gospel-shaped, gospel-driven, and the like have all but become brands in certain tribes and subcultures.[1] Responding cries have challenged that all this talk has diluted the clarity of what the gospel is and what the gospel does. The longer I live and move and have my being in the realm of gospel-centered worship,[2] the more I am sympathetic to these cries for clarity.

---

[1] See, for instance, the Gospel Shaped Church DVD series and book released a few years ago by The Gospel Coalition: *Gospel Shaped Living* by Vermon Pierre (2015), *Gospel Shaped Worship* by Jared Wilson (2015), *Gospel Shaped Outreach* by Erik Raymond (2015), and *Gospel Shaped Mercy* by Stephen Um (2017), published by the Good Book Company; and the Gospel-Centered book series: *The Gospel-Centered Life, The Gospel-Centered Community,* and *The Gospel-Centered Life for Teens,* by Robert H. Thune and Will Walker (2016), *The Gospel-Centered Parent* by Rose-Marie Miller, Deborah Harrell, and Jack Klumpenhower (2015), published by New Growth Press.

[2] This conversation for me is twenty years strong. My own awakening to gospel-centrality started back in 2002 with some wonderful bootleg materials handed through what at the time felt like an

In the first chapter of his epistle to the Romans, Paul headlines his letter by describing the gospel as the "power" of God (1:16). The apostle then goes on to unpack that power over the next ten chapters. At the center of that enterprise is a stark antithesis: no one can be justified by works of the law, but instead justification is a gift, received by faith (3:20-25). This antithesis appears in Paul's letters again and again as the *way* the gospel is made clear (e.g., 1 Cor 15:9-10; Gal 2:16; Eph 2:8-9; Phil 3:9). In other words, the gospel is proclaimed in all its power precisely when it is recognized and received by faith, apart from works. Paul speaks elsewhere of paradoxical instances where that power is absent even while its fruit is still apparent, albeit in counterfeit form. In his words, such people are caught "having the appearance of godliness, but denying its power" (2 Tim 3:5).[3] I have begun to wonder whether the landscape of Western worship is not dotted, if not significantly fortressed, with expressions and practices which have the appearance of godliness—of worshipfulness, of piety, of passion, of zeal, of truthfulness, of even the right words and the right "biblical elements"—and yet deny the power that animates them all. I long for the kind of zealous, fiery worship marked by a "demonstration of the Spirit and of power," and I believe, with Paul, that this demonstration happens best when worship has "decided to know nothing . . . but Jesus Christ and him crucified" (1 Cor 2:1-5).

This book seeks to clarify the Scripture's vision for gospel-centered worship with the hope that such clarification might lead us toward a daring confidence that the very power that stands at the center of Christianity—the good news of Jesus Christ for sinners—is sufficient to withstand all contenders and lead the church into the uncharted waters of the future. But instead of directly surveying the Scriptures or overtly developing a liturgical theology of gospel-centrality, we might do well to come at this from the side.

Those of us who stand in the Reformation tradition of evangelicalism (before it was tarnished by cultural and political overtones, an *evangelical* was

---

underground railroad of pathways cut by church planters in the Presbyterian Church in America (PCA). I am ever indebted to pastors Jim Talarico and Steve Sage for introducing me to those early church planting manuals and manuscripts from Tim Keller and Redeemer Presbyterian Church in New York. Those materials, combined with the mentorship of Jim and Steve, effected for me a kind of second conversion from which, thank God, I have yet to recover.

[3] All scriptural quotations are from the English Standard Version (ESV), unless otherwise noted; ©2001 by Crossway Bibles, a publishing ministry of Good News Publishers.

simply a "gospel-person") have to admit that our commitment to *sola scriptura* is prone to being bastardized into a kind of strict biblicism which in turn closes our ears to other faithful Christians of the past who have read and interpreted the same Bible we prize. In other words, something in our Protestant DNA causes us to almost instinctively bristle at listening to the Great Tradition.[4] Tradition, to say the least, is complicated, but in the best of light it is merely that repository of previous generations of Christians wrestling with what the Word of God was saying to them and then living out the work of that Word in their given time and place. If those of us in Protestant traditions would lift our heads for a second, we might be able to look back and notice that the question of what the Bible has to say about gospel-centered worship is not a new one. This was, in fact, my own far-too-late discovery. There I had been on my own for over a decade as a pastor and worship leader grappling with the Scriptures about what it meant for the gospel to govern and guide the worship service. Then one day, someone lifted my head, and I encountered a Christian who five hundred years ago asked those very same questions I was asking and answered them with far more knowledge, far more depth, far more work, and far more clarity. I had met the reformer, Thomas Cranmer.

If people are aware of Thomas Cranmer, they are likely acquainted with the *fruit* of his labor—the Book of Common Prayer, and the broad and global legacy of English-speaking worship that traces its history back to it. However, far fewer are aware of the *labor* itself. The goal of this book is to expose that labor in order to learn. This effort is nothing more than an attempt to transport ourselves five centuries back and stand over the shoulder of England's greatest reformer as he sits bent over his candlelit desk, surrounded by hundreds of books, manuscripts, notes, and liturgies contemporaneous and historic.[5] We

---

[4]"Great Tradition" generally means that body of knowledge, wisdom, and practice, chiefly acquired through scriptural reflection, originating out of apostolic and patristic eras, faithfully passed down across regions, cultures, and expressions, with varied continuity and discontinuity throughout the history of the church. From my Protestant perspective, I like to more simply define Great Tradition as how the church wrestled through the meaning and application of Scripture in their time and place. I have heard the term used in places like D. H. Williams, *Retrieving the Tradition and Renewing Evangelicalism: A Primer for Suspicious Protestants* (Grand Rapids, MI: Eerdmans, 1999); Williams, *Evangelicals and Tradition: The Formative Influence of the Early Church* (Grand Rapids, MI: Baker Books, 2005), 49; Jim Belcher, *Deep Church: A Third Way beyond Emerging and Traditional* (Downers Grove, IL: InterVarsity Press, 2009).

[5]This picture of the solitary Cranmer is admittedly idyllic. Alongside the Archbishop's own work was a small army of secretaries and researchers who were doing the same thing, which is why it is

will observe the Archbishop at work with these liturgical sources.[6] When we do so we will see he is not only translating, but transposing. We will see him making decisions. And we will try to ask, on what basis is he making those decisions? Can we observe an undergirding set of criteria or a rationale behind what he chooses to keep, what he chooses to omit, what he chooses to move, and what he chooses to remain in place?

This book makes the claim that Cranmer indeed had such a rationale and that this rationale, though not exclusive and singular, so overwhelmed the Archbishop in its importance[7] that it dominated all other criteriological motivations for liturgical redaction. Getting right to it, what overwhelmed Cranmer was God's love for him in Christ, and once that love seized him, the Archbishop became fiercely committed to the clear proclamation of that good news.[8] In other words, Cranmer's vision for liturgical renewal was intensely fixated on the gospel. His evangelical convictions drove his liturgical decisions.[9] If this is true, then I would suggest that as we look over the Archbishop's

---

probably more proper to refer to Cranmer, as many have done, as the architect, rather than the author, of the Book of Common Prayer.

[6]In those moments Cranmer was not only surrounded by those physical publications and notes but was also encircled by countless friends and colleagues who through correspondence, conversation, and co-labor filled his mind with influential thoughts.

[7]There is perhaps a no more gripping firsthand account of Cranmer's apprehension of God's love in Jesus Christ than in the reports of his principal secretary, Ralph Morice, published in John Gough Nichols, ed., *Narratives of the Days of the Reformation* (London: Camden Society, 1859), esp. 246-247, where Morice relays how Cranmer's understanding of the gospel led him to treat his enemies.

[8]This maps very well onto Diarmaid MacCulloch's observation that the sixteenth-century movement in England was not necessarily "Protestant" at its inception, perhaps unlike what was taking place on the Continent. Rather, "A description more true to the period would be 'evangelical.'" Gospel centrality is what united reform in England. See Diarmaid MacCulloch, *Tudor Church Militant: Edward VI and the Protestant Reformation* (London: Penguin, 1999), 2.

[9]Despite centuries of biographical sketches and theological outlines of the Archbishop which have attempted to cast Cranmer in the molds of wildly disparate theological images (often suspiciously coinciding with whatever vision of Anglicanism was in vogue), the relatively recent work of Diarmaid MacCulloch and Ashley Null has perhaps once for all laid the question of Cranmer's Protestantism to rest. This book assumes such work, namely, that by the early 1530s, most likely connected with his ambassadorial trip to Germany in 1532, Cranmer's soteriology was firmly and decidedly Protestant, even as his sacramentology would take longer to arrive at its eventual Reformed resting place. See Diarmaid MacCulloch, *Thomas Cranmer: A Life* (New Haven, CT: Yale University Press, 1996), esp. 59-78; and Ashley Null, *Thomas Cranmer's Doctrine of Repentance: Renewing the Power to Love* (Oxford: Oxford University Press, 2000). A more contested idea, but one that I support, is that while Cranmer's mature sacramentology was Reformed, his soteriology remained more distinctively Lutheran where such theology diverges from Zurich and Geneva. On this, see the work of Gil Kracke, "Cranmer's *Häuptartikel*: Revisiting Thomas Cranmer's Theology Through a Lutheran Understanding of Justification" (DMin diss., Knox Theological Seminary, 2017).

shoulder, we will discover that he provides, among all sixteenth-century Reformers English and Continental,[10] a most exemplary model of what it might mean to be gospel-centered in our worship today.

I want to be careful to recognize that gospel-centered is modern speak, and it is therefore terminologically anachronistic to refer to Thomas Cranmer's gospel-centered theology. Still, the argument of this book is that it is not *theologically* anachronistic to view Cranmer's work as an attempt at gospel-centered worship. In fact, I'm hoping Cranmer will provide for us a much more theologically rich and biblically faithful definition for what it

---

[10]To be sure, Reformers like Luther and Calvin were equally committed to a gospel-centric vision for liturgical revision, but there were methods and strategies unique to Cranmer that make him a supreme example for emulation. Forty years ago, Bryan Spinks convincingly argued that because Luther's "chief article" of justification by faith alone governed his theology, it likewise governed his liturgical reform. Spinks quotes Luther at length, and in particular cites the German reformer's *Taufbüchlein* as a case study in how *sola fide* became Luther's primary filter for his reform of the baptismal liturgy (Spinks, *Luther's Liturgical Criteria and His Reform of the Canon of the Mass* [Bramcote: Grove Books, 1982]). A generation before Spinks, liturgical theologian Vilmos Vajta convincingly critiqued nineteenth-century interpretations of Luther's liturgical motivations: "They could not grasp Luther's liturgics adequately because they had lost contact with the center of his theology" (Vajta, *Luther On Worship: An Interpretation* [Minneapolis: Fortress, 1958], 20). Calvin was no doubt as committed, but he seems simply to have been less interested in the whole project of liturgical revision, as his liturgical work appears to more slavishly republish the liturgical work of Bucer, whereas Cranmer was far more selective and discerning with his employment of Bucer and the other Reformed and Lutheran *Kirchenordnungen* (see Bryan Spinks, "German Influence on Edwardian Liturgies," in *Sister Reformations* [*Schwesterreformationen*], ed. Dorothea Wendebourg [Tübingen: Mohr Siebeck, 2010], 186). The Reformed liturgies took less interest in the received liturgical tradition than did Cranmer, and were therefore constructed more simply, with a two-fold objective of emphasizing preaching and reconstructing liturgies from the patristic witness. Spinks observes that Cranmer's employment of the liturgical tradition was far more rich than that of Luther or Calvin, who, by comparison, were not given to consult material from anything other than their "immediate Catholic antecedents" (see Bryan Spinks, "Renaissance Liturgical Reforms: Reflections on Intentions and Methods," *Reformation and Renaissance Review* 7, no. 2–3 [2005]: 275). After comparing Cranmer's liturgical agenda to that of the Continental Reformers, another scholar concludes that because the latter relied more heavily on the sermon to catechize, they spent less time thinking about how their liturgical revisions would do that same kind of work (see Mark Lindsay, "Thomas Cranmer and the *Book of Common Prayer*: Theological Education, Liturgy, and the Embodiment of Prosper's Dictum," *Colloquium* 47, no. 2 [2015]: 206-7). Still, we should be cautious in too quickly comparing pan-European liturgical reform as a kind of apples-to-apples enterprise. Each region had their own cultural context and their own unique skirmishes and sticking points with Rome and local politics. Even with that caution, however, I do believe that Cranmer among the Reformers stands at the top of successful and thorough application of the doctrine of justification by faith alone to liturgical content and shape. He should therefore be given a much more in-depth hearing. It may be true that, as Diarmaid MacCulloch puts it, Cranmer "was rarely an original thinker" when it came to his *theological* work (MacCulloch, *All Things Made New: The Reformation and Its Legacy* [Oxford: Oxford University Press, 2016], 119), but what we hope to show is that when it came to *liturgical* work, the Archbishop was *uniquely* creative in editing and placing multitudinous source-fragments into a cruciform mosaic of gospel-proclamation.

looks like for worship services to be centered on Christ's gospel. Nevertheless, I will attempt to use the phrase sparingly with reference to Cranmer's work.

I further recognize the boldness of the claim that Cranmer's evangelical convictions drove his liturgical decisions. Indeed, much ink has been spilled, including Cranmer's own, about what his motivations were behind the choices made in the formation of the Book of Common Prayer. It will be helpful to briefly recount what has been said about Cranmer's criteria for liturgical redaction, both to affirm their truth and to expose why they fall short of accounting for his great doxological obsession.

CRANMER'S CRITERIA FOR REDACTION

The Archbishop's preface to the 1549 Book of Common Prayer states his methodological intentions plain enough, and we want to observe these stated reasons alongside some unstated ones that centuries of liturgical analysis make equally clear. Our goal here is to better understand Cranmer's criteria for liturgical redaction and to set the stage for the argument that they inadequately account for all his liturgical moves. Cranmer's criteria in eight broad categories are catechesis, affective persuasion, missional intelligibility, participation, unification, simplification, antiquity, and scripturality.

1. Catechesis. In Cranmer's mind, the Scriptures themselves are the bedrock of the liturgy. Therefore, Scripture reading would be front and center in liturgical reform. Cranmer advocates this reform precisely so that believers and ministers can "be more able . . . to exhort other[s] by wholesome doctrine, and to confute them that were adversaries to the truth."[11] In short, one of Cranmer's aims with the liturgy was to catechize the people. In the sixteenth century the average believer possessed limited biblical knowledge.[12] The liturgy

---

[11] Cranmer, "The Preface," in Joseph Ketley, ed., *The Two Liturgies, A.D. 1549, and A.D. 1552* (Cambridge: Parker Society, 1844), 17.

[12] Relatively recent studies have challenged the long-held belief that medieval England was predominantly illiterate (cf. esp. Katherine Zieman, *Singing the New Song: Literacy and Liturgy in Late Medieval England* [Philadelphia: University of Pennsylvania Press, 2008]). Not only do such works urge us to redefine literacy, but they also show how literacy was deeply connected with liturgy. Furthermore, it is true that across late medieval Europe *biblical* literacy, though limited, was not entirely absent. We have enough evidence of pre-Reformation vernacular Bibles, lay mass books, and other devotional resources in England and on the Continent to demonstrate that especially upper classes had access to the Scriptures in versions beyond the Latin. We know

would serve as a primary place where this widespread biblical vacuum could be filled. And even though we will classify simplification as a separate criterion, we acknowledge with Bryan Spinks that simplification and catechesis for Cranmer went hand in hand: "In terms of his main Latin source, the Sarum rite, he simplifies *for the purpose of education*."[13]

2. Affective persuasion. As a descendant of medieval affective piety, as a humanist in the school of Erasmus, and as a Protestant persuaded by

---

that possessors of such books would invite others to read in small groups, opening up the reality of even the illiterate achieving some measure of biblical knowledge (Wim François, "Vernacular Bible Reading in Late Medieval and Early Modern Europe: The 'Catholic' Position Revisited," *The Catholic Historical Review* 104, no. 1 [2018], 26). For biblical literacy in England in particular, see Richard Marsden, "The Bible in English in the Middle Ages," in *The Practice of the Bible in the Middle Ages: Production, Reception, and Performance in Western Christianity*, ed. Susan Boynton and Diane J. Reilly (New York: Columbia University Press, 2011), 272-95; and Hilary M. Carey, "Devout Literate Laypeople and the Pursuit of the Mixed Life in Later Medieval England," *Journal of Religious History* 14, no. 4 (Dec 1987), 361-81. Still, studies such as these are focused on the nobility and knightly classes. Far less can be certain about the biblical knowledge and literacy of the lower classes.

[13]Spinks, "Renaissance," 282. This emphasis on the liturgy's catechetical power appears to have helped shape a unique feature of American Episcopalianism and Anglicanism—namely, the perspective that Anglican unity is found not in the tradition's biblical summaries in the creeds, homilies, or doctrinal statements like the Thirty-Nine Articles, but in fidelity to the Prayer Book. This emphasis on unity around the Prayer Book was present in the beginning, as the Articles and homilies never carried the kind of official authority in the US as in England, evidenced in the preamble to the Constitution of the Episcopal Church, which states that it is "upholding and propagating the historic Faith and Order as set forth in the Book of Common Prayer" (*Constitution and Canons, Together with the Rules of Order* [New York: Office of the General Convention, 2018], 1). Often, this is where the lauded and loathed liturgical axiom *lex orandi lex credendi* (whose historical and theological ambiguities appear to be not surprisingly moldable to the viewpoint of whoever is marshaling it) is summoned (see Maxwell Johnson, "Liturgy and Theology," in *Liturgy in Dialogue*, ed. Paul Bradshaw and Bryan Spinks [London: SPCK, 1993], 202-25). Leading Episcopalian Prayer Book authority, Leonel Mitchell, expressed this quite clearly when he said in his original preface that there is a "dependence of theology upon worship" (Leonel Mitchell and Ruth Meyers, *Praying Shapes Believing: A Theological Commentary on the Book of Common Prayer* [New York: Seabury, 2016], xviii). And as another writer says unequivocally, "The Prayer Book serves as our greatest pedagogical source" (J. Barrington Bates, "On the Search for the Authentic Liturgy of the Apostles: The Diversity of the Early Church as Normative for Anglicans," *Journal of Anglican Studies* 12, no. 1 [2012]: 46). In some cases, this perspective is expressed even in terms of strict adherence to the rubrics in such a way that, according to some, violation of the rubrics is grounds for ecclesiastical discipline. This is no doubt the fruit of believing that the Prayer Book alone is sufficient to bind Anglicans doctrinally (and that *lex orandi lex credendi* is a one-way street—our theology never governs or informs our prayer), untethered from the original formularies of the Church of England, and unaccompanied by faithful preaching and teaching of the Scriptures. It makes complete sense, therefore, that the revisers of the 1979 American Prayer Book (The Episcopal Church, The Book of Common Prayer and Administration of the Sacraments and Other Rites and Ceremonies of the Church [New York: Church Publishing Incorporated, 1979]; hereafter BCP 1979) would bury the Thirty-Nine Articles deep in the publication, subsumed under the heading, "Historical Documents."

Melanchthon's Lutheran interpretation of Augustine's affective theology,[14] Cranmer was committed to the idea that a good liturgy did more than provide a framework for worship. The liturgy's aim was to cause the worshiper's heart to, in his words, "be the more inflamed with the love of [God's] true religion."[15] The liturgy would primarily do this affectively persuasive work through its use of language and rhetoric. By "affective," we mean "a mode of experience that is tethered to physical bodies and that encompasses emotion, feeling, and desire."[16] With these objectives in mind, we observe the Archbishop not merely translating the received liturgies, but instead, as a "connoisseur of English,"[17] he would "stamp them with his own style,"[18] transposing the language into more rich and expressive keys. Cranmer's Prayer Books are famous for their excessive doublets, triplets, and even occasional quadruplets: "Humble and hearty"; "direct, sanctify, and govern"; "read, mark, learn, and inwardly digest."[19] Certainly, these expansions of single Latin and English words betray his training as an Erasmian humanist as he employs affectively charged rhetoric, using language to evoke and provoke the senses. Compared with other preexisting English translations of prayers, Cranmer's translations consistently exhibit a superior felicity of style. Take for instance this Collect for Whitsunday, alongside its predecessors, exposing Cranmer's strong affective style (see fig. 1.1).[20]

---

[14]See the summary of this in Ashley Null, "The Power of Unconditional Love in the Anglican Reformation," in *Reformation Anglicanism: A Vision for Today's Global Communion*, ed. Ashley Null and John Yates III (Wheaton, IL: Crossway, 2017), 45-76.

[15]Cranmer, "Preface," 17.

[16]Simeon Zahl, *The Holy Spirit and Christian Experience* (Oxford: Oxford University Press, 2020), 3.

[17]Diarmaid MacCulloch, "Cranmer's Ambiguous Legacy," *History Today* 46, no. 6 (June 1996): 31.

[18]E. C. Ratcliff, "The Liturgical Work of Archbishop Cranmer," *Journal of Ecclesiastical History* 7, no. 2 (October 1956): 191.

[19]C. S. Lewis observes other doublets that expanded on single Latin words: *peccata* is doubled as "sins and wickednesses"; *mortifica*, "mortify and kill"; *videant*, "perceive and know"; *tradi*, "to be betrayed and give up." He says that doublings like these produce "great rhythmical benefits" that have produced a Prayer Book which is, in Lewis's estimation, "the one glory of the Drab Age" of English literature. See his *English Literature in the Sixteenth Century Excluding Drama* (New York: Oxford University Press, 1944), 204, 217-18.

[20]The prayers from Joye and *The King's Primer* are recorded in Geoffrey Cuming, "Thomas Cranmer: Translator and Writer," in *Language and the Worship of the Church*, ed. David Jasper and R. C. D. Jasper (New York: St. Martin's Press, 1990), 110-11. The Collect from the Prayer Book is from Ketley, *Liturgies*, 58. The original Latin from the Gregorian Sacramentary reads, "*Deus qui hodierna die corda fidelium sancti spiritus illustratione docuisti: da nobis in eodem spiritu recta sapere, et de eius semper consolatione gaudere. Per . . .*" (from F. E. Brightman, *The English Rite: Being a Synopsis of the Sources and Revisions of the Book of Common Prayer*, vol. 1 [London: Rivingtons, 1915], 442).

GEORGE JOYE'S HORTULUS ANIMAE, 1530	THE KING'S PRIMER, 1545	THE BOOK OF COMMON PRAYER, 1549
O God, which has instructed the hearts of faithful men with the lightening of thy Holy Ghost;	O God, which by the information of the Holy Ghost, hast instructed the hearts of thy faithful,	God, which as upon this day hast taught the hearts of thy faithful people by the sending to them the light of thy Holy Spirit;
grant us to savour aright in the same Spirit,	grant us in the same Spirit to have right understanding,	grant us by the same Spirit to have a right judgment in all things,
and to rejoice evermore of his holy consolation,	and evermore to rejoice in his holy consolation.	and evermore to rejoice in his holy comfort;
	Through Christ our Lord.	through the merits of Jesus Christ our Saviour;
which livest and reignest in the same Spirit ever.		who liveth and reigneth with thee in the unity of the same Spirit, one God, world without end.

Figure 1.1. The Collect for Whitsunday and its sources

At the same time, these kinds of translational moves may also be an attempt to slow down the liturgy to allow for a meditative rumination in prayer, or, in the words of Cranmer's Homily on Scripture, a chewing on "the heavenly meat of our souls" in order "that we may have the sweet juice, spiritual effect, marrow, honey, kernel, taste, comfort and consolation of them."[21] The net effect of all these observations is that Cranmer freely translated out of a desire to see people *moved* by the liturgy. Cranmer's criteria included facilitating a "hearty" encounter.[22] In fact, the verbal statistics in his 1552 Holy Communion

---

[21]Cranmer, "A Fruitfull Exhortation to the Reading and Knowledge of Holy Scripture," in *Certain Sermons or Homilies (1547) and A Homily Against Disobedience and Wilful Rebellion (1570): A Critical Edition*, ed. Roland B. Bond (Toronto: University of Toronto Press, 1987), 62, 67. English in this and all subsequent quotations from the *Homilies* has been modernized. For more on Cranmer's expansion of words and phrases for the purpose of meditative rumination on Scripture, see Ashley Null, "Thomas Cranmer and Tudor Church Growth," in *Towards a Theology of Church Growth*, ed. David Goodhew (New York: Routledge, 2016), 209-10.

[22]On Cranmer's liturgy and the heart, see especially Stephen Sykes, "Cranmer on the Open Heart," in *This Sacred History: Anglican Reflections for John Booty*, ed. Donald S. Armentrout (Cambridge: Cowley, 1990), 1-20.

and Morning Prayer liturgies speak for themselves, as Cranmer's translations of those liturgies significantly increase the use of "heart" language.[23]

3. *Missional intelligibility*. Cranmer further articulated that his liturgical redaction was motivated by an emphatic desire that worship be "plain and easy to be understanded."[24] The Archbishop even summons Paul's own admonitions, presumably from 1 Corinthians 14, regarding foreign tongues and making gathered worship intelligible: "St. Paul would have such language spoken to the people in the Church as they might understand and have profit by hearing the same."[25] Certainly the great missionary passage from Cranmer's preface to the Great Bible of 1540 could be easily applied to his liturgy, to the end that all kinds of people such as "publicans, fishers, and shepherds may find their edification." Tempering the above comments about felicity of style, Cranmer would not sacrifice intelligibility on the altar of artistry, unlike "the writings of the Gentile philosophers and rhetoricians, to the intent the makers should be had in admiration for their high styles and obscure manner of writing, whereof nothing can be understood without a master or an expositor."[26] Diarmaid MacCulloch notes that Cranmer was linguistically conservative with his use of English Latinisms and

---

[23]In Morning Prayer (1552) "heart" and its cognates appear eleven times: Opening Sentences (3); exhortation to Confession (2); Confession (1); Venite (3); Benedicite (1); and Suffrages (1). In 1549, Matins only mentions "heart" once. In Holy Communion (1552) "heart" and its cognates appear twenty-eight times: the Collect for Purity (2); Decalogue (10); Prayers for the king and his "heart" (3); Offertory sentences (1); optional Collects for the closing of the service if Communion is not celebrated (2); Prayers of the People (1); second Exhortation to communion (1); third Exhortation (2); Confession (1); Absolution (1); Sursum Corda (1); Words of Administration (1); Post-Communion Prayer (1); Peace (1). An additional mention is in the liturgy's opening rubrics about a reconciled person who has forgiven "from the bottome of hys hearte" (see Ketley, *Liturgies*, 265). In 1549, Holy Communion mentions "heart" only thirteen times. Prior to that, *corda* and its Latin cognates appear only seven times in the Sarum eucharistic rite.

[24]The term *missional* is another admitted anachronism. It is a twentieth-century word, and a concerted effort toward what we now call missions and evangelism did not develop until the turn of the eighteenth century. Still, what we are arguing is that some of the emphases of the modern missions movements—emphases such as inculturation, intelligibility, and hospitality to the outsider—are present in Cranmer's reasoning. As we will see, it is not simply that Cranmer desired a more intelligible liturgy, but intelligible for the sake of reaching more people. See Ketley, *Liturgies*, 18. Cranmer actually makes this statement three times.

[25]Ketley, *Liturgies*, 17.

[26]Cranmer, "Preface" to the Great Bible (1540, being the second edition of the 1539 Great Bible), in John Edmund Cox, ed., *The Works of Thomas Cranmer*, vol. 2 (Cambridge: The University Press, 1846), 120. One of the great ironies for those still using older forms of the Prayer Books is that properly engaging such liturgies now *requires* a "master or an expositor."

Greekisms, preferring instead wording and phraseology of Anglo-Saxon vocabulary and style.[27] This apparently conscious choice seems to flow naturally from his missionary impulse to contextualize liturgy and prayer to the native tongue of the common person. Cranmer desired the Prayer Book not to be high art, but to have a plain[28] and simple kind of beauty, so that the liturgy might be apprehended by all kinds of people. Though this missionary impulse toward contextualization and inculturation is not unique to Cranmer or even the Reformation era,[29] this criterion of intelligibility certainly drove Cranmer further in his editorial decisions than most up to that point.

4. Participation. Hand in hand with intelligibility was a desire for greater congregational participation. Cranmer's redaction of the liturgy sought to move more things out of the mysterious and private words and actions of the priest and into the public language and movements of the people. Behaviors that might appear surprising to twenty-first-century Christian worshipers were quite common in Cranmer's day. For the congregation, this included walking around during the sermon, engaging in gossip or small talk with one's neighbor during the service,[30] or simply doing one's own thing throughout the liturgy, such as privately praying, or entering and exiting at random. In preparation for a visit to the diocese of Norwich, Cranmer sent ahead a list of injunctions including this: "That every minister do move his parishioners to come diligently to the church,

---

[27]MacCulloch points this out near the 37:30 mark in "The Book of Common Prayer," *In Our Time* podcast, produced by the BBC, released October 17, 2013.

[28]In his annotations on Henry's corrections of the Bishops' book, Cranmer squabbles with Henry over the use of the word *cure* versus the use of *charge* when referring to pastoral ministry. His stated reason for preferring the latter is thus: "It is a small difference between 'cure' and 'charge,' but that the one is *plain English*, and the other is deducted out of the Latin" (Henry Jenkyns, *The Remains of Thomas Cranmer*, vol. 2 [Oxford: The University Press, 1833], 77; emphasis added). See also Thomas A. Krosnicki, "How Dark the Night: The 'Inlumina' Prayer," *Worship* 85, no. 5 (September 2011): 449, who points out that in Cranmer's translation of a particular prayer, "Rather than a verbatim or obsequious Latinized English translation, the Anglican genius took the text and tailored it for the community of his day and the vernacular of his time. In the language of today, we could argue that he worked according to the principle of 'dynamic equivalence.'"

[29]Besides the most obvious example of Wycliffe and the Lollards, Eamon Duffy points out that the desire for the vernacular predates the Reformation and was a broadly felt impulse in medieval England generations before Cranmer: "More than a century before Mirk had used parish clergy to encourage their parishioners to say their prayers in English" (Duffy, *The Stripping of the Altars: Traditional Religion in England 1400–1580* [New Haven, CT: Yale University Press, 1992], 80).

[30]See Zieman, *Singing the New Song*, 86.

and when they come not to talk or walk in the sermon, Communion, or divine service time, but rather at the same to behave themselves reverently, godly and devoutly in the church."[31] Clerical custom aided and abetted this behavior, as it was quite common to mumble or quietly speak the liturgy and quickly work through the mass, which is why Cranmer's liturgies contain rubrics for the minister to lead the liturgy "with a loud voice." We therefore find Cranmer making liturgical decisions based on this desire for greater participation.

5. Unification. In line with the political agenda of the day,[32] Cranmer's preface clearly states that the Prayer Book was redacted with the specific purpose such that "all the whole realm shall have but one use."[33] Top on Henry's agenda was nationwide obedience and submission.[34] Certainly this demand was the fruit of his egomania,[35] but it was also because Henry believed that a well-ordered society full of loyal subjects would produce peace, stability, and cultural flourishing. Cranmer believed in these endgame virtues as well, even if he did not share Henry's conviction of the means.[36] For Henry, the virtues of England's unity were the fruit of loyalty and submission to the king. For Cranmer, those virtues were the fruit of the gospel. Therefore, unifying the disparate liturgies of England to "but one use" was simultaneously political and theological, with the latter being more toward Cranmer's motivation for liturgical conformity.

---

[31]See Paul Ayris, "The Public Career of Thomas Cranmer," *Reformation and Renaissance Review* 4 (2000): 124-25.

[32]Some liturgiologists call this criterion "conformity." See J. Barrington Bates, "Expressing What Christians Believe: Anglican Principles for Liturgical Revision," *Anglican Theological Review* 92, no. 3 (Summer 2010): 458.

[33]Cranmer, "Preface," in Ketley, *Liturgies,* 19.

[34]See Richard Rex, "The Crisis of Obedience: God's Word and Henry's Reformation," *The Historical Journal* 39 (1996): 863-94.

[35]David Evett calls this "hegemonic legitimation," namely that it was Henry's chief agenda to legitimize his crown and see to it that all of England be his loyal subjects. Interestingly, Evett posits that this is why the language of "servant" and "service" is so strongly featured in the Prayer Book (see Evett, "Luther, Cranmer, Service, and Shakespeare," in *Centered on the Word: Literature, Scripture, and the Tudor-Stuart Middle Way,* ed. Daniel W. Doerksen and Christopher W. Hodgkins [Newark: University of Delaware, 2004], 89).

[36]Cranmer, of course, did believe in the divine right of kings (i.e., the royal supremacy), which, "from about 1531 until literally the last morning of his life, remained Cranmer's guiding principle" (MacCulloch, *All Things,* 120), but the question for the Archbishop here was one of whether a well-ordered society could be produced simply by a forceful submission of the will, or by something else, namely, the gracious, forgiving love of God in Jesus Christ.

6. *Simplification.* Tied to unification[37] was the idea that the liturgy should pare down "the number and hardness of the rules" and "the manifold changings of the service." With a hint of sarcasm, Cranmer expressed concern "that many times, there was more business to find out what should be read, then to read it when it was found out."[38] Both leading and following the liturgy had become cumbersome for clergy and laity alike, and Cranmer felt that it was time to demolish many of the rickety additions that had been built onto the liturgical house over the years. And so we find across the board, chiefly exhibited in the Daily Offices and the Holy Communion liturgy, Cranmer's liturgical agenda included condensing all material into one simple volume.

7. *Antiquity.* Of all the criteria of Cranmer pointed out by the history of liturgical scholarship, it is antiquity that continually comes to the fore as one of Cranmer's chief editorial motivators. In the preface, Cranmer clearly desires to put forth a liturgy "agreeable to the mind and purpose of the old fathers,"[39] whom he sets in contrast again and again to the liturgy of his present. This is not surprising. As a humanist, Cranmer would be predisposed to appeal to the "primitive" sources over against more recent iterations of liturgical formulation. And, especially as the preface opens with ominous pessimism about how "the continuance of time" ends up corrupting what was once pure, it is clear that antiquity is a primary value. We might stress here that while modern liturgical scholars have pointed out that Cranmer's access to patristic liturgies was perhaps limited and piecemeal,[40] what they often overlook is that his access to and study of the Fathers' *theological outlook* was vast and comprehensive. Even if he did not possess the widest array of ancient liturgies, he was saturated with ancient Christianity's "mind and purpose." And especially if, as this book will argue, Cranmer's motivations were more fundamentally theological, for him the Fathers' theological writing

---

[37]Marion Hatchett, "The Anglican Liturgical Tradition," in *The Anglican Tradition*, ed. Richard Holloway (Wilton: Morehouse-Barlow: 1984), 51: "From a practical standpoint this establishment of uniformity was made easier and cheaper by pulling the various rites and directions that had been scattered through a number of volumes . . . into one book which, with the Bible, would provide all the necessary texts and be within financial reach of parishes and of individuals."

[38]Cranmer, "Preface," in Ketley, *Liturgies,* 18.

[39]Cranmer, "Preface," in Ketley, *Liturgies,* 18.

[40]E.g., Hatchett, "Anglican Liturgical Tradition," 49-50.

would be just as useful (even perhaps more useful) as liturgical sources as the ancient liturgies themselves.

8. Scripturality. The broadest consensus, though, is that fidelity to the Scriptures was Cranmer's chief criterion. In fact, most liturgical scholars argue that the Archbishop's commitment to antiquity is actually grounded in his commitment to the Bible. As one historian notes, "What the witness of Christian antiquity contributes, as Cranmer sees it, is a confirmation of a correct interpretation of the scriptures."[41] Another liturgiologist rightly observes that Cranmer

> was not beholden to any notion that the ancient codified liturgical texts enjoyed the privileges ascribed to the inspired scriptures; they were not rendered untouchable in light of their respected and accepted historical pedigree. They had no more objective, intrinsic theological value than newly minted, theologically correct orations penned and articulated in his day. Intuitively he seemed to have understood the difference between idol and icon.[42]

By far and away, scriptural fidelity takes centerstage in the Prayer Book's preface. Cranmer strongly criticizes how little Bible was read and how much the liturgy was instead unnecessarily filled with "uncertain stories, Legends, Responds, Verses, vain repetitions, Commemorations," and other "such things, as did break the continual course of the reading of scripture."[43] Instead, what is to be read and prayed should be nothing "but the very pure word of God, the holy Scriptures, or that which is evidently grounded upon the same."[44] In short, as Cranmer was evaluating liturgical sources for use in England, his first evaluative question seems to have consistently been, "Is it biblical?"[45]

---

[41]K. J. Walsh, "Cranmer and the Fathers, especially in the Defense," *Journal of Religious History* 11 (1980): 236.

[42]Krosnicki, "How Dark the Night," 451-52.

[43]Cranmer, "Preface," in Ketley, *Liturgies,* 17, 18.

[44]Cranmer, "Preface," in Ketley, *Liturgies,* 18.

[45]What Cranmer would understand as biblical or scriptural certainly needs to be clarified. The Church of England divided along these lines not long after Cranmer's death in what would eventually be known as the "normative" and "regulative" principles, though the seeds of the debate were sown in Cranmer's lifetime. The flashpoint that seemed to formalize the debate occurred among the Marian exiles in Frankfurt, between the more normative perspective argued by Richard Cox and the more regulative perspective argued by John Knox. Perhaps anachronistically speaking, Cranmer himself appears to have been more of a normativist (see Null, "Church Growth," 210-12). Aside from this what we can learn more generally about the Archbishop's understanding of the Scriptures can be discerned from his behaviors as a Cambridge don prior to his archiepiscopal

THE INADEQUATE ACCOUNTING OF CRANMER'S LITURGICAL CRITERIA

None of the above criteria, either individually or collectively, adequately accounts for all of Cranmer's editorial decisions. In fact, the more we dig into these criteriological motivations the more they beg further questions. For example, *simplification* certainly is important perhaps to save ecclesiastical resources or to allow for ease of liturgical leadership, but might there be a more fundamental reason why simplification was a priority? A united realm is certainly a noble political pursuit, but would national solidarity be a sufficient rationale for an Archbishop who was a studied and convicted theologian of the first rank? Is it simply that Henry's desire for "hegemonic legitimation" was enough for Cranmer to unify disparate liturgies and pepper the Prayer Book with more instances of the language of "service" than in the Latin original?[46] This motivation for radical unity is at least somewhat tempered by Article XXXIII of the Forty-Two Articles of 1553, which argues that while England might have one use, other realms and regions need not all keep the same traditions and ceremonies.[47] Like Luther and the other Reformers, Cranmer was aware of the need for liturgical diversity within certain bounds.

With regard to *antiquity*, modern liturgiologists have been quick to simultaneously laud Cranmer's meticulous study and employment of the church fathers and criticize his imprecision or relative ignorance with their use. Mid-century liturgical scholar E. C. Ratcliff exemplifies these voices:

---

appointment, where he had a reputation of being unbending in his demands of students' knowledge and apprehension of the Bible. Once made Archbishop, we also see quite immediately from the records of his visitation injunctions that he "demanded that the text of Holy Scripture should be interpreted according to its literal sense" (Paul Ayris, "Thomas Cranmer and the Metropolitical Visitation of Canterbury Province 1533-4," in *From Cranmer to Davidson: A Church of England Record Society Miscellany*, ed. S. Taylor [Woodbridge: Church of England Record Society, 1999], 12). As a humanist, he would have desired the "pure sense" of the text to be exposited, and he would no doubt therefore desire more plain readings, interpretation, and application of the Scriptures in and through the liturgy.

[46]See above, n36.

[47]This Article, "Of Traditions of the Church," parallels Article XXXIV of the Thirty-Nine Articles. To be clear, this article is arguing for diversity *between* regions or countries, even as the Prayer Book seeks "but one use" *within* the country of England. But the acknowledgment of even this kind of diversity tempers the absolutism that is sometimes present in some current conversations about liturgical conformity.

[Cranmer's] interests lay behind the medieval period, in Christian antiquity. To discover the usages and beliefs of antiquity, he had laboriously to read through the works of ancient ecclesiastical writers, to collect references from them, and to make of their allusions and statements what he could. A task of such dimension might well have daunted him; but he had the scholar's patience no less than the scholar's desire for exact knowledge. . . . If, moreover, in his search for the genuinely ancient, he frequently failed to perceive it, or (as often in his handling of liturgical material) cast it aside, it was because he had no early training and, later, no adequate aid to enable him to identify it.[48]

Forthcoming scholarship will, to put it mildly, put these assertions to the test,[49] but we do not necessarily need to refute them to observe some large leaps here that are made not infrequently in modern liturgical scholarship. Saturating twentieth-century liturgical thought is the assumption that because modern researchers have access to a far more complete patristic library than Cranmer, the Archbishop would have probably done things differently had he known what we now know.[50] What does not tend to enter the conversation is the positing of another viable theory for why Cranmer seemed to miss or fail to perceive the patristic witness even when he *did* have access to those sources. Could there be other criteria at play that help explain why he might cast aside the voice of the Fathers in certain instances? Could it be that he *did* perceive some ancient liturgical material as such and yet for other reasons deliberately choose to not employ them?[51]

---

[48]Ratcliff, "Liturgical Work," 202.

[49]Ashley Null continues to prepare Cranmer's notebooks, coined "Cranmer's Great Commonplaces," for publication through Oxford University Press, the first volume of which is tentatively titled *The Efficacious Word: Thomas Cranmer on Scripture*, Vol. 1, *Cranmer's Great Commonplaces*. In those notebooks is evidenced not just a haphazard study, but a mastery of patristic sources.

[50]See e.g., Hatchett, "Anglican Liturgical Tradition": "We know a lot more about this normative period of church history than Thomas Cranmer could possibly have known" (49); "While Cranmer could pick up from his sources many details about early liturgy, he could not learn about structures and the order of the elements" (50). Hatchett criticizes Cranmer's simplification of the Church Year, assuming he did so because of antiquity: "Cranmer greatly simplified the Church Year, basically adopting that of the German Church Orders. (These were based on a false assumption that days commemorating principal New Testament saints were older than Black Letter Days)" (53). Even if Cranmer did in fact assume, and assume falsely, the point is that it does not appear to enter consideration that Cranmer might have other, perhaps more fundamental criteria guiding decisions such as these.

[51]Diarmaid MacCulloch thinks that Cranmer was less committed to antiquity than many assume (*All Things*, 120-21).

Even with the criterion of *scripturality*, we too must recognize that this desire was not unique to Cranmer and the Reformers. Catholic humanists like Spanish Cardinal Francisco Quiñonez were just as interested in and motivated toward going back to the sources and making the liturgy more scriptural as their own liturgical projects testify.[52] And we also observe Cranmer in key moments making decisions to omit scriptural quotation in the liturgy, such as the removal of the Agnus Dei (Jn 1:29) and the Benedictus (Ps 118:26; Mt 21:9; Mk 11:9; Lk 19:38; Jn 12:13) from the Communion liturgy.

Ultimately, we are led to conclude that while all the above criteria were necessary for Cranmer, they were not sufficient. As a result, we hope this present work will expose two things: first, that these criteria cannot account for many of Cranmer's decisions in his liturgical redaction; and second, that even these criteria may be seen in a different light as largely springing from another more singular and fundamental criterion. In other words, we want to argue the plausibility of a theory that Cranmer's desire for liturgical catechesis, affective persuasion, missional intelligibility, participation, unification, simplification, antiquity, and scripturality was motivated by something more basic, that not only explains why he prioritizes these criteria but gives us a far more comprehensive explanation for many, if not most, liturgical changes made, even possibly answering some questions that have puzzled liturgical historians down through the ages. We will want to argue that Cranmer's fundamental criterion was, in fact, the gospel itself.

At this point, given how much time we have spent observing Cranmer's preface, one might ask, "Well then why does this gospel-criterion find no mention there?" There may be a good reason for Cranmer to have concealed this motivation in that most public document. We must remember and appreciate the political-ecclesiastical tightrope Cranmer was walking even after the death of Henry. He was not leading a unified group of bishops, clergy, and laity. In fact, as many have noted, as Reformed as the 1549 Prayer Book was, it certainly was much more of a halfway measure toward a more thoroughly Protestant, gospel-centered liturgy that would be unveiled in 1552. We therefore might do well to look at the list of criteria disclosed in the preface with the same eye that we look at the partially Protestant 1549 liturgy itself—it does

---

[52]Spinks, "Renaissance," 273.

not tell the complete story. Furthermore, as we have observed with scripturality, none of the above-listed criteria is in any way uniquely Protestant.[53] In each category, we can find contemporaneous analogues among those who remained faithful Roman Catholics. Therefore, we have some valid reasoning in pursuing the question of why in liturgical redaction Cranmer could be most fundamentally motivated by the gospel and yet not mention it in the preface to the Prayer Book, even as he mentioned other criteriological motivations.[54]

---

[53]This is to a certain degree what is argued (admittedly for different reasons than ours) in Edward Lambe Parsons and Bayard Hale Jones, *The American Prayer Book: Its Origins and Principles* (New York: Charles Scribner's Sons, 1937), 30.

[54]There is an implicit critique here of the many voices leading liturgical revision in the twentieth and twenty-first centuries which have often claimed fidelity to the work of Cranmer in their own liturgical enterprises. For instance, to cite a most recent example, the Anglican Church in North America's 2019 Prayer Book states that its liturgy "is indisputably true to Cranmer's originating vision of a form of prayers and praises that is thoroughly Biblical, catholic in the manner of the early centuries, highly participatory in delivery, peculiarly Anglican and English in its roots, culturally adaptive and missional in a most remarkable way, utterly accessible to the people, and whose repetitions are intended to form the faithful catechetically and to give them doxological voice" (The Book of Common Prayer [2019] [Huntington Beach, CA: Anglican Liturgy Press, 2019], 5; hereafter *BCP 2019*). We notice in this statement nearly all the criteria we have listed above as being that which identifies what is faithful to Cranmer's "originating vision." Given how differently the *BCP 2019* liturgy looks from Cranmer's (one need only examine the eucharistic liturgy), and given all that this book will argue, we have reason to find such claims very disputable. But assertions like these have been made for generations. One of the most influential liturgical textbooks in Anglicanism in the first half of the twentieth century, A. G. Hebert's *Liturgy and Society: The Function of the Church in the Modern World* (London: Faber and Faber, 1935), would conclude, after articulating theological emphases quite different from those of Cranmer (particularly with regard to Pauline theology), "The Prayer Book needs revision, but a revision in the same faith in which it was compiled, and a revision in the true liturgical spirit" (226). Future liturgical scholarship would take the assumptions much further. As the decades roll on, an increased boldness is notable as there is a move beyond merely believing that they are carrying the Cranmerian mantle. With the spirit of progressivism in the air, we hear talk of how the evolution of theology allows more recent generations to beat Cranmer at his own game. Urban Holmes's article, "Education for Liturgy: An Unfinished Symphony in Four Movements," in *Worship Points the Way: A Celebration of the Life and Work of Massey Hamilton Shepherd Jr.*, ed. Malcolm C. Burson (Greenwich: Seabury, 1981), 116-41, recounts the history leading to the triumph of the 1979 American revision. Holmes speaks of "the demise of classical theology" (136), "the growing theological sophistication of the Episcopal Church" (136), and "an awakening, a newly educated theological consciousness" (137). This kind of perspective would lead another prominent American liturgist, Charles Price, to conclude, "It has been said that as assurance of immortality was the acute spiritual need of the early Church, and assurance of forgiveness the acute need in sixteenth century Europe, community is the acute need of our time" (Charles P. Price, *Introducing the Proposed Book* [New York: Church Hymnal Corporation, 1976], 29). The idea is that as theology changes, the application of Cranmer's principles should change. What was not realized is that Cranmer's theology stood at the *head* of his principles. In other words, those principles were bound up in his more fundamental theological criterion of the gospel. If this is true, then many modern claims of "being true to Cranmer" must now be reexamined.

At this point, we need to entertain one more question: Even given all this, will we be able to establish that there is a clear enough correspondence between Cranmer's thought and what we have in his Prayer Books? Put another way, were Cranmer's convictions about the gospel strong enough to trump the other ecclesiastical and political forces at play which would have influenced him to make his Prayer Books more measured, compromising, and conciliar? In a way, this book attempts to build a case that answers yes to those questions. Still, even here I invite the reader to look forward to our discussion in chapter three of Cranmer's surprisingly bold interactions with Henry around the very topic of the clarity of the gospel in England's official documentation. History is very clear on this point: if there is one relationship of Cranmer's which epitomizes the need for a person in his position to compromise, it is with his king. It is therefore both surprising and telling that Cranmer, among a host of accommodations and settlements, does not waver in arguing for the good news of sinners justified by faith alone.

SETTING THE STAGE FOR WHAT WE MEAN BY GOSPEL-CENTRALITY

We come back around now to our opening inquiry. What we will see is that, for Thomas Cranmer, to be gospel-centered in the formation and enacting of worship services means far more than mentioning the cross, championing atonement, and filling the liturgy with references to the person and work of Jesus Christ. As Cranmer understood it, the nature of the gospel would require certain norms for communication between God and his people.

In part one, we will observe and summarize these norms by establishing the connection between Cranmer's theology and that of the apostle Paul, employing a few clarifying metaphors along the way—governor, grammar, and filter. We will crack the door open to this inquiry first by observing how the gospel was positioned in Cranmer's theology in the way he responded to two central debates of his day—purgatory and the Lord's Supper—noting how the good news of the finished work of Jesus Christ stood as a *governor* over where he would land in his theological decision-making (chap. 1). We then open the door more widely by establishing how this governing position actually functions. We will look at how Cranmer's understanding of the

Pauline doctrine of *sola fide* would serve as a theological *grammar* for how God would be approached, heard from, and prayed to in a worship service (chaps. 2 and 3).

In part two, we will observe the application of this theological grammar in Cranmer's formation of the 1549 and 1552 Book of Common Prayer. We will then see how *sola fide* serves as a *filter* for all liturgical form (chap. 4), language (chap. 5), ceremony (chap. 6), piety, and preaching (chap. 7). We will see that the sifting work of *sola fide* makes sharp distinctions and that this distinguishing work does in fact get to the heart of what it means to properly proclaim the gospel in liturgy. The final chapter, the conclusion, is dedicated to exploring the implications and trajectories of thought of all these insights for worship in the twenty-first century. We will more or less be answering the question, "If Cranmer were around today, in what ways would he encourage the reform of our worship that it might be more gospel-centered?"

An appreciated early reader of this book's manuscript, a Cranmer scholar, respectfully asked if this work did not suffer the fate of other treatises on the Archbishop which looked down the Cranmerian well only to find the author's own reflection. Having taken that question seriously, I still come to the conclusions of this book with confidence in what my early philosophical training taught me—a cumulative case is a powerful argument. Indeed, there is likely no lost letter of Cranmer's which confesses the chief criterion of justification *sola fide* for his theology of worship and editorial agenda. Nevertheless, my hope is that in the sometimes atomistic examination which follows, while any one neutron of evidence may appear more or less convincing, the weight of the whole matter might be found persuasive.

Some might understand the methodology of this book as presenting a kind of cipher (what we have already named as the grammar of justification by faith alone) that is then used to "decode" Cranmer's liturgical thinking and work. It is more accurate, however, to see what follows as an attempt to observe the "rules" of the grammar at play in Cranmer's liturgical work—an exposition of what is within the liturgy, rather than an imposition of an idea on the liturgy. Perhaps the reader will have to decide whether this has truly been accomplished.

Just over seventy-five years ago, in a most influential liturgical text, Dom Gregory Dix quipped that Cranmer's work was "the only effective attempt ever made to give liturgical expression to the doctrine of justification by faith alone."[55] Dix was not being complimentary. Ironically, what follows seeks to prove Dix's assertion, and not merely as complimentary, but as exemplary. What we hope is that by observing Cranmer at work, we might hold up an example of what it looks like to craft worship services "in step with the truth of the gospel" (Gal 2:14). But the goal of this is much more than to give expression to a doctrine. The goal, as noted above, is hearts on fire—changed lives.

AN IMPORTANT FINAL WORD ON LITURGICAL THEOLOGY

The clarification of Cranmer's goal just made—namely that changed lives, not mere expression of doctrine, is the aim—exposes an important feature of this book, which requires brief explanation lest its labor be misunderstood. This book is a cross-disciplinary work (biblical studies, historical theology, and liturgics) that fits well but not cleanly into the relatively recent academic field of liturgical theology.[56] Our query attempts to heed the criticism raised by this field which notes that text-heavy, word-based studies like this present work are prone to error because liturgical practice is irreducibly embodied and situational. Liturgies are first and foremost events, not texts.[57] Juan Oliver's useful summary of these insights of liturgical theology warns,

> The history of liturgical practice cannot be studied properly by examining only texts, without reference to the history of church architecture and ceremonial. When abstracted from them as the history of the development of ideas or meanings about or communicated through liturgy, we are no longer talking about the history of the liturgical *practice* but about the history of *ideas* about it.[58]

---

[55]Dom Gregory Dix, *The Shape of the Liturgy* (New York: Seabury Press, 1945), 672.

[56]Nathan Jennings measures liturgical theology as "about a half a century old," its beginning marked by the synthesis of Dom Gregory Dix and Henri de Lubac in the writing of Alexander Schmemann. See Nathan G. Jennings, *Liturgy and Theology: Economy and Reality* (Eugene, OR: Cascade, 2017), 23.

[57]See Christopher J. Ellis, *Gathering: A Theology and Spirituality of Worship in Free Church Tradition* (London: SCM Press, 2004), 30.

[58]Juan M. C. Oliver, "Worship, Forming and Deforming," in *Worship-Shaped Life: Liturgical Formation and the People of God*, ed. Ruth Meyers and Paul Gibson (Norwich: Canterbury Press, 2010), 6; emphasis original. Similarly, Stephen Sykes notes, "It is a failure of some consequence when liturgical texts are examined as though they were simply a collection of dogmatic declarations or confessional statements put into the mouths, alternately, of priest and people," and then advocates

The insights of ritual studies are indeed taken seriously in what follows even if its categories are not explicitly utilized. Indeed, textual study *is* valuable, as we shall see, but it does not tell the whole story, which is why we will examine ceremonies, practices, architecture, and other socio-cultural phenomena surrounding worship in England at the time leading up to the Reformation.[59] Thankfully, historians over the last few decades have helped us reconstruct some of the social and ritual dynamics of medieval worship practice, which allow us to better read between the (even rubrical) lines of Cranmer's liturgies. We will attempt to glean from these insights what we can, remaining cautiously aware that our knowledge of the embodied practices surrounding Cranmer's liturgical context is largely attained by examination through a spotted rearview mirror.

A similar critique of this text could be marshaled, namely that it force-fits abstract dogmatic analysis into a field of study that is highly experiential, subjective, embodied, even ascetic.[60] However, the richest understanding of justification by faith alone—especially as articulated by sixteenth-century Reformers such as Luther, Melanchthon, and Cranmer—exposes a false dichotomy between theological truth and subjective experience.[61] In fact, this book will argue for an understanding of *sola fide* as a gospel-grammar that does its best parsing *in experience*, particularly in the congregation's embodied encounter with God in a gathered worship service.

This argument will therefore challenge certain schools of thought in liturgical theology which tend to overemphasize the idea that prayer shapes

---

that we must give proper attention to the liturgy's "structure, dramatic actions, rhythms and repetitions as well." See Stephen Sykes, "'Baptisme Doth Represente unto Us Oure Profession,'" in *Thomas Cranmer: Essays in Commemoration of the 500th Anniversary of His Birth*, ed. Margot Johnson (Durham: Turnstone, 1990), 123.

[59]Though beyond the scope of this present treatment, a further feature complicating analysis is exposed in the work of Katherine Zieman, who ably demonstrates the "salient paradox of medieval Christian liturgy," namely, "that it participated simultaneously in the worlds of orality and literacy." Her elucidation of the "hybrid textual practice" of this era shows that there is more work to be done in analyzing the "embodied, communal knowledge" of late medieval England's long transitional period between oral and literary culture (Zieman, *Singing the New Song*, x).

[60]See David W. Fagerberg, *On Liturgical Asceticism* (Washington, DC: The Catholic University of America Press, 2013). Though especially Protestants need more critical reflection on liturgically appropriating the idea of theology as *askesis*. Cf., for instance, Oswald Bayer, "Theology as *Askesis*: On Struggling Faith," in *Gudstankens aktualitet: Festskrift til Peter Widmann*, ed. Marie Wiberg Pedersen, Bo Kristian Holm, and Anders-Christian Jacobsen (Copenhagen: Forlaget Anis, 2010), 35-54.

[61]On this idea, see Zahl, *Holy Spirit*, especially chap. 4.

believing (one interpretation of the maxim *lex orandi lex credendi*[62]) to the neglect of the reality that believing shapes prayer.[63] Indeed, even liturgical theology's great proponent of the distinction between primary theology and secondary theology, Aidan Kavanagh, admitted that "one thing that [the maxim] does *not*, however, say or mean is that the *lex credendi* exerts no influence upon the *lex supplicandi* [i.e., *lex orandi*], only that it does not constitute or found the *lex supplicandi*."[64] This book will admittedly go further than Kavanagh and his followers would probably be comfortable. As we will see especially in chapter two, while "constitute" and "found" may not be the best words to describe the relationship of *sola fide* to the *lex orandi lex supplicandi*, we will argue that the liturgy's *lex orandi* finds its formative power and fundamental integrity in the doctrine of justification by faith alone.[65] For,

---

[62]David Fagerberg typifies this interpretation when he summarizes the view of the "Schmemann-Kavanagh school of liturgical theology" as "the *lex orandi* of the Church establishes her *lex credendi*" (Fagerberg, *On Liturgical Asceticism,* ix). For an important history and analysis of the misunderstanding of *lex orandi lex credendi,* see the forthcoming dissertation of Steven Zank, Concordia Seminary, St. Louis.

[63]Nathan Jennings affirms the ordering of prayer over believing when he states, "One of the primary gifts of liturgical theology is the reassertion of this hermeneutical claim of a foundational ontology of action over understanding, event over meaning." Act is foundational, and "understanding [is] impotent until enacted." See Jennings, *Liturgy,* 91. I share Bryan Spinks's perspective: "Although the popular little adage *Lex orandi, lex credendi* . . . is important, the idea that doctrine only flowed from liturgy and that doctrine never impacted and changed liturgical practice is pious humbug and wishful thinking" (Bryan D. Spinks, *Do This in Remembrance of Me: The Eucharist from the Early Church to the Present Day* [London: SCM, 2013], xii). For a still useful analysis which offers a lay of the land for possible interpretations of *lex orandi lex credendi,* see Johnson, "Liturgy," 202-25.

[64]Aidan Kavanagh, "Response: Primary Theology and Liturgical Act," *Worship* 57 (1983): 324. Kavanagh first formally articulated the distinction between primary theology (*theologia prima*) and secondary theology (*theologia secunda*) in the late 1970s, which would be eventually published in his *On Liturgical Theology* (Collegeville, PA: Liturgical Press, 1984). Primary theology is that which is enacted before and with God in the liturgy, and secondary theology is what we more often think of when we use the term *theology*—reflection on the God we encounter. This distinction is akin to Kant's, between the "world-oriented task" and the "academic/school task" when it comes to learning and being human (see discussion in Oswald Bayer, *Martin Luther's Theology: A Contemporary Interpretation* [Grand Rapids, MI: Eerdmans, 2003], 18-19). One helpful summary of the primary-secondary theology distinction is found in Simon Chan, *Liturgical Theology: The Church as Worshiping Community* (Downers Grove, IL: InterVarsity Press, 2006), 48-52.

[65]Indeed, because of what we just stated above about *sola fide* being best parsed in experience, I believe there may be some consonance (or at least overlap) between liturgical theology's prioritized categories here—*lex orandi lex credendi,* primary and secondary theology (Kavanagh), act founding understanding (Jennings)—and the Protestant doctrine of justification by faith alone, especially as articulated by Luther, Melanchthon, and Cranmer. I detect part of this overlap, for instance, in Oswald Bayer's treatment of Luther's theology when he asserts, "Luther holds that the 'monastic' aspect of theology with its liturgical spirituality grounded in the divine service is constitutive, in that this provides theology with its content. On the other hand, he says that its

"whatever does not proceed from faith is sin" (Rom 14:23), including every prayer of the church both corporately and individually. We either pray and worship by faith alone, or we do not. And it is justification *sola fide* which tells us that the latter action is outside the realm of the gospel, which *is* what constitutes and founds the church. No gospel, no church.[66] In a sense, we will attempt to show that for primary theology to work, its prayers' sentences must be constructed according to the rules of the grammar that *sola fide* establishes as a norm for differentiating worship according to the true gospel of Jesus Christ, over against false gospels.

Alexander Schmemann, grandfather of modern liturgical theology, argues that the Christian liturgy's deep structural meaning—what he refers to as its "Ordo"—is found not just through participation in the liturgy, but in reflection on it:

> To find the Ordo behind the "rubrics," regulations and rules—to find the unchanging principle, the living norm or "logos" of worship as a whole, within what is accidental and temporary: this is the primary task which faces those who regard liturgical theology not as the collecting of accidental and arbitrary explanations of services, but as the systematic study of the *lex orandi* of the Church.[67]

'scholastic' academic aspect is purely regulative in that it orders, analyzes, and reflects on the content of theology and makes the necessary distinctions and connections." Bayer earlier claims, "Contemporary thinkers are scandalized when a study of Luther's understanding of theology leads to the thesis that theology and faith should not be fundamentally distinguished, let alone separated" (Oswald Bayer, *Theology the Lutheran Way* [Grand Rapids, MI: Eerdmans, 2007], 83). So it seems that Luther's "monastic" theology parallels Kavanagh's primary theology, and Luther's "scholastic" theology parallel's Kavanagh's secondary theology. But given the earlier statement of Bayer, I wonder if these distinctions, though helpful, are artificial. Perhaps there is a deeper unity between primary and monastic or secondary and scholastic theology that precludes too much ontological prioritization, contra Jennings.

[66]Perhaps this book can offer another central maxim for liturgical theology from the field's under-represented Protestant tradition: *nullum evangelium, nulla ecclesia* (or, an even more creative and chiastic phrase offered me by Samford University Latin scholar, Douglas Clapp, *abest evangelium ecclesia abest*). Though I wonder if the starting places of Eastern Orthodoxy and Roman Catholicism are too different from that of Reformation Christianity, particularly in their anthropological and soteriological assumptions. One can detect the difference in these two definitions of "liturgy." Fagerberg (Roman Catholic and Eastern Orthodox): "Liturgy is the Trinity's perichoresis kenotically extended to invite our synergistic ascent into deification" (Fagerberg, *On Liturgical Asceticism*, 9); Leithart (Reformation Protestant): "Liturgy is God speaking to and feeding His people" (Peter J. Leithart, *Theopolitan Liturgy* [West Monroe, LA: Theopolis Books, 2019], 47).

[67]Alexander Schmemann, *Introduction to Liturgical Theology* (Crestwood, NY: St. Vladimir's Seminary Press, 1966), 39.

In a way, the burden of this book is to find the "Ordo behind the rubrics, regulations, and rules" of the Book of Common Prayer as its original architect conceived it. But we are not doing so by engaging in a "systematic study of the *lex orandi* of the Church." Instead, we are attempting a systematic study of a particular theologian's systematic study of the Scriptures, which resulted in an observable conviction about what Christian liturgy's Ordo most deeply is—Jesus himself, revealed especially in his gospel.[68] Admittedly we depart, therefore, from liturgical theology's method as established by Schmemann, starting not with a sweeping investigation of liturgical practice across history and traditions. Rather, as a consciously Protestant enterprise, we will attempt methodologically to start as Cranmer did, with Scripture itself.[69] As we learned, for Cranmer this does not happen to the neglect of history and the Fathers, but simply seeks to do what the tradition at its best was always seeking to do: see and savor Christ alone, in the power of the Spirit, to the glory of God the Father.[70]

---

[68] Even if we might come to different conclusions, I find that Maxwell Johnson's articulation of the matter strikes a chord with the project of this book:

> If Schmemann is right in noting that the underlying, unchanging, and fundamental principle of the *Ordo* has been so obscured by a scholastic theology and concomitant mysteriological piety such that it has changed not only the understanding but also the "experience" of the liturgy, then the recovery of this principle might indeed provide the basis of a liturgical reform which would allow the Church's true *lex orandi* to function in a clearer fashion as "source" for both theology and piety. (Johnson, "Liturgy," 208)

[69] I therefore share Geoffrey Wainwright's concern for a boundaried, criteriological analysis of the church's *lex orandi*: "Worship . . . is a source of doctrine in so far as it is the place in which God makes himself known to humanity in a saving encounter. The human words and acts used in worship are a doctrinal locus in so far as either God makes them the vehicle of his self-communication or they are fitting responses to God's presence and action" (*Doxology* [New York: Oxford, 1980], 242-43). Because of this, I admit opening myself up to the same concluding critique Johnson offered Wainwright when he wrote that Wainwright's "focus on the superiority of the *lex credendi* over the *lex orandi* actually inhibits their complementarity in favour of a particular theological and doctrinal orientation to which the *lex orandi* must conform" ("Liturgy," 224).

[70] Though we probably have differing understandings of what the "demands of the Gospel" are, I find in the concluding sentences of Charles Price's hopeful manifesto for the 1979 Book of Common Prayer a deeply resonant statement: "The value of tradition, though great, is also not ultimate. Both must be brought under the demands of the Gospel as recorded in Scripture" (Price, *Introducing the Proposed Book*, 18-19).

PART 1

CRANMER'S GOSPEL-CENTERED THEOLOGY ESTABLISHED: PAUL'S DOCTRINE OF JUSTIFICATION BY FAITH ALONE

1

THE POSITION OF *SOLA FIDE* IN CRANMER'S THEOLOGY

BEFORE WE SET out on the path of Paul's vision of justification in Scripture, it is important to do some preliminary orienteering in this chapter in order to establish the trailhead. Having exposed the potential inadequacy of many of the prevailing arguments for what fueled the engine of Cranmer's liturgical redaction, we have proposed a theory that it is justification by faith alone which chiefly propelled the Archbishop's editorial decisions. We would do well to begin by observing examples in his nonliturgical work which illustrate just how highly Cranmer prioritized justification by faith alone in his theological thinking. It seems increasingly common in our day and age for Protestants, at least on the popular level, to place *sola fide* as an equal among many other important doctrines. This was not the case for Cranmer.

The reason we want to even briefly observe the governing position of *sola fide* in Cranmer's thinking *outside* his liturgical work is because, as we will see, his application of *sola fide* to liturgy is more structural and subterranean, which is probably why it has often gone unnamed or unidentified. Liturgy does not explain theology. It does theology.[1] We must find explanation elsewhere before we can fully appreciate how the content and structure of the Book of Common Prayer were shaped and governed by *sola fide*.

What we hope to establish here is that, as one scholar put it, "Christ-centered theology was the lens through which [Cranmer] studied everything."[2] To do so, we will focus on two central theological hot topics which dominated

---

[1] Indeed, this idea affirms liturgical theology's distinction between primary and secondary theology described in the introduction.

[2] Caroline M. Stacey, "Justification by Faith in the Two Books of Homilies (1547 and 1571)," *Anglican Theological Review* 83, no. 2 (2001): 260.

debate in sixteenth-century Europe—purgatory and the Lord's Supper. We zero in on these two doctrinal spheres because in a short amount of space they shed the broadest light on how the editorial decisions of Cranmer were governed by justification by faith alone.

GOSPEL-CENTERED ESCHATOLOGY: CRANMER ON PURGATORY

After his thorough and groundbreaking study on medieval theology and practice Eamon Duffy concluded, "There is a case for saying that *the* defining doctrine of medieval Catholicism was Purgatory."[3] This belief in the penitential, pre-heaven afterlife was not peripheral in medieval theology, nor was it a distant concern in the average medieval Christian's psyche. Purgatory was the engine block that held up the propulsion system of medieval piety, motivating countless Christians to give blood, sweat, tears, and—yes—money to Christ and his church. It is tempting for Protestants now to look back on the sixteenth century and read modernist motivations into the Reformation critique of purgatory: it is superstition built on extrabiblical sources and tradition. And while this understanding of the critique is true, it was not the center of the problem for the sixteenth-century Reformers.

To be sure, Cranmer articulated the baseline argument that purgatory was simply not found in the Scriptures. It is telling that in the first authorized English Bible—the so-called Matthew Bible of 1537, overseen by Cranmer—extensive notes were written on the classic purgatory prooftext of Ezekiel 18. In the margins of this Bible were "provocatively Protestant" annotations, which Stephen Sykes summarizes:

> God's forgiveness is final and irrevocable, says the commentary, sharply dissenting from the "sophisters" who teach the necessity of seven years' punishment in purgatory, tartly adding: "If this is not to mock with God and his Holy Word, I wot not what is mockage." The response of God to the sinner's radical repentance is an equally radical forgiveness.[4]

---

[3]Eamon Duffy, *The Stripping of the Altars: Traditional Religion in England 1400–1580* (New Haven, CT: Yale University Press, 1992), 8; emphasis original.

[4]Stephen Sykes, "Cranmer on the Open Heart," in *This Sacred History: Anglican Reflections for John Booty*, ed. Donald S. Armentrout (Cambridge: Cowley, 1990), 7.

And yet Cranmer's concern about purgatory was not merely that it was extra-biblical. His more pointed (and still thoroughly biblical) concern was that purgatory undermined justification *sola fide*. In the Archbishop's words:

> What a contumely and injury is this to Christ, to affirm that all have not full and perfect purgation by his blood, that die in his faith! Is not all our trust in the blood of Christ, that we be cleansed, purged, and washed thereby? And will you have us now to forsake our faith in Christ, and bring us to the pope's purgatory to be washed therein; thinking that Christ's blood is an imperfect lee or soap that washeth not clean?[5]

Purgatory was an untenable doctrine for Cranmer precisely because it sought purgation by a means other than Christ's blood. It diminished the finished work of Christ by insisting Christ's work was actually something *un*finished. Worse yet, this unfinished work was to be completed not by Jesus but by the believer. Cranmer would have seen this as a complete reversal of Paul—not Christ, but I; not by faith, but by works. *Sola fide*, for Cranmer, stood above eschatology as a governor, a sentinel which would guard and protect what doctrine would pass through the gates of sound teaching. Put another way, justification for Cranmer was an integrated doctrine: *sola fide* was not merely a soteriological reality; it was eschatological as well.

GOSPEL-CENTERED SACRAMENTOLOGY: CRANMER ON THE LORD'S SUPPER

While much of the landscape of Cranmer's sacramentology appears to have already been mined,[6] we find only a few of those efforts drilling past the

---

[5]Cranmer, "Answers to the Fifteen Articles of the Rebels, Devon" (1549), in *The Works of Thomas Cranmer*, vol. 2, ed. John Edmund Cox (Cambridge: The University Press, 1846), 181.

[6]Still, see the new insights emerging from Ashley Null's forthcoming work on Cranmer's Great Commonplaces, including this foretaste regarding Cyril of Alexandria and Cranmer's sacramentology: Ashley Null, "Thomas Cranmer," in *Christian Theologies of the Sacraments: A Comparative Introduction*, ed. Justin S. Holcomb and David A. Johnson (New York: New York University Press, 2017), 221-29; and Null, "Thomas Cranmer's Reputation Reconsidered," in *Reformation Reputations: The Power of the Individual in English Reformation History*, ed. D. J. Crankshaw and G. W. C. Gross (London: Palgrave Macmillan, 2021), 203-8. From research like this, Null would summarize Cranmer's mature eucharistic theology as "a supernatural, proleptic, ontological participation in the cosmic Christ" in a lecture given at All Saints Church in Belfast, released on YouTube, January 17, 2017, youtu.be/OUNiLqaHMXU. One of the better surveys and analyses of Cranmer's sacramentology is Gordon Jeanes, *Signs of God's Promise: Thomas Cranmer's Sacramental Theology and the Book of Common Prayer* (London: T&T Clark, 2008). Jeanes's introduction in particular is a

depths of politics, metaphysics, medieval philosophy, and even biblical proof-texting to its subterranean bedrock.[7] While all the above influences are certainly at play in Cranmer's thought, we might observe with some scholars a more fundamental conviction that lay at the base of his eventual sacramental landing place—Cranmer's understanding of justification—which could provide a more helpful and thorough explanation for the "why" of his mature sacramental thinking. Peter Brooks's study of Cranmer's sacramentology concludes that Cranmer built "his whole sacramental superstructure on that doctrine basic to all Reformed theology—the concept of *justificatio sola fide*." Likewise Gordon Jeanes could comfortably say at the outset of his extensive analysis that Cranmer's "sacramental theology evolved in the context of his understanding of justification." And, most notably, Ashley Null's conclusion after thorough inquiry into Cranmer's thinking is that "ultimately, Cranmer's Eucharistic teaching was determined by his doctrine of justification."[8]

What we want to observe here is that Cranmer subsumed his sacramentology under his soteriology.[9] It is telling, for instance, that in the 1547 Book of Homilies, which were intended by Cranmer to be the total homiletical content of nearly all English pulpits under his leadership and England's "doctrinal plumb line,"[10] there is no considerable focus on the sacraments.[11] Instead, there is an intense focus on the doctrine of justification by faith alone,

---

helpful overview of post-Tractarian scholarship on Cranmer's eucharistic theology, and chap. 4 offers the careful conclusion that Cranmer's mature sacramentology is indeed "Cranmerian" in that it is too nuanced to be fully aligned with Bucer, Zwingli, Calvin, Martyr, or Łaski (156).

[7] Notably Jeanes, *Signs;* Ashley Null, *Thomas Cranmer's Doctrine of Repentance: Renewing the Power to Love* (Oxford: Oxford University Press, 2000); J. I. Packer, introduction to *The Work of Thomas Cranmer,* ed. G. E. Duffield (Philadelphia: Fortress, 1965); and Peter N. Brooks, *Thomas Cranmer's Doctrine of the Eucharist* (London: MacMillan, 1965).

[8] Brooks, *Eucharist,* 94; Jeanes, *Signs,* 53; Null, *Repentance,* 26.

[9] It is probably more accurate to say that Cranmer, as a late medieval theologian, did not view soteriology and sacramentology as sharply discrete categories of theology. Nevertheless, for the sake of making certain observations, we are using the language of sacramentology "subsumed under" soteriology.

[10] Null, "Thomas Cranmer and Tudor Church Growth," in *Towards a Theology of Church Growth,* ed. David Goodhew (New York: Routledge, 2016), 205.

[11] Gordon Jeanes, noting well the brief discussion of baptism in the Homily on Salvation, probably rightly sees that the relative absence of the sacraments in the homilies is due to the then-present sensitivity of the sacramental debate—such discussions "needed cautious delay," no doubt (Jeanes, *Signs,* 98). And as Diarmaid MacCulloch notes, the Book of Homilies offered "a promise that the eucharist would be discussed in a proposed second batch of homilies" (MacCulloch, *Tudor Church Militant: Edward VI and the Protestant Reformation* [London: Penguin, 1999], 67). Nevertheless, one could argue that justification by faith alone was no less sensitive or divisive, and Cranmer

garnering the attention of three of six central doctrinal homilies: "Of the salvation of all mankind," "Of the true and lively faith," and "Of good works."[12] Perhaps all this is a nod to Cranmer's thinking: when justification is rightly preached alongside a well-ordered liturgy, the sacramental discussion is much more rightly framed. Let us observe how this might be so by exploring the way Cranmer defines a sacrament and articulates its purpose, which in turn will help us see *why* he argues against superstition, transubstantiation, and the medieval understanding of the priesthood.

Cranmer's definition of a sacrament. Ashley Null's research yields this conclusion: Cranmer defined a sacrament as "only something that the New Testament recorded as being commanded by Christ for the forgiveness of sins."[13] It is typically Protestant to note, against the Roman Catholic system of seven sacraments, that a sacrament is only something which is explicitly commanded and instituted by Christ (ruling out unction, marriage, and the like). But Cranmer's even more pointed criterion is nothing other than justification itself—that which is "commanded by Christ *for the forgiveness of sins.*"[14] This criterion is evident in Cranmer's treatment of the Lord's Supper in the parliamentary debate of 1548. Commenting there on the phrase *hoc est corpus meum,* he responds, "He that maketh a will bequeaths certain legacies, and this is our legacy: *Remission of sins,* which those only receive that are members of his body."[15] We also hear it in Cranmer's response to Henry's corrections of the Bishops' book on why marriage cannot be a sacrament. The Archbishop argues against Henry's articulation of the virtue and efficacy of the seven sacraments thus: "The causes [of grace] may not be well applied to matrimony: that it should be, as the other [sacraments] were, by the manifest institution of Christ: or, that it is of necessity to salvation: or, that thereby we

---

clearly pulled no punches there, even amidst an unstable and potentially hostile geopolitical climate (MacCulloch, *Militant,* 66-67).

[12]See Richard S. Briggs, "The Christian Hermeneutics of Cranmer's Homilies," *Journal of Anglican Studies* 15, no. 2 (June 2017): 173.

[13]Null, "Cranmer," in *Sacraments,* 211.

[14]Paul Bradshaw, *The Anglican Ordinal: Its History and Development from the Reformation to the Present Day* (London: SPCK, 1971), 14: "[Cranmer] preferred to reserve the name 'sacrament' for rites which signified the remission of sins rather than use it in a more general sense."

[15]Cranmer, "The Great Parliamentary Debate" (1548), reproduced in Colin Buchanan, ed., *Background Documents to Liturgical Revision 1547–1549* (Bramcote: Grove Books, 1983), 16; spelling and punctuation modernized, and emphasis added.

should have the forgiveness of sins, renovation of life, and justification, &c."[16] When it comes particularly to baptism and the Lord's Supper, we find Cranmer time and again at pains to establish this evangelical grounding for his sacramental convictions. In other words, the purpose of a sacrament, according to Cranmer, is to preach the gospel.[17] In fact, in discussions differentiating the two Protestant sacraments from the seven of medieval theology, Cranmer would call baptism and the Lord's Supper "sacramentes of the gospell."[18]

Cranmer's understanding of the purpose of a sacrament: the theology of promise. It is precisely at this point of sacramentology where we might first observe how similar Cranmer's articulation of the gospel is to Martin Luther's, focusing particularly on the idea central to the Wittenberg reformer's understanding of *sola fide*: faith is that which lays hold of God's promises. There may be no better summary of this theology of promise than Luther's *The Babylonian Captivity of the Church* (1520) and passages in Melanchthon's *Loci Communes* (1521). It is telling, in the former, that the center of Luther's theology of

---

[16]Cranmer, "Corrections of the *Institution of a Christian Man*, by Henry VIII, with Archbishop Cranmer's Annotations" (ca. 1538), in Cox, *Works*, vol. 2, 99-100.

[17]Not to be missed is another important treatise by Cranmer or a close associate, titled *De sacramentis* dating around 1537–1538, which not only uses this same kind of language but incorporates the explicit distinction between law and gospel: *Constat igitur sacramentum omnium consensu duabus rebus, scilicet verbo et elemento, et verbo quidem ipsius Dei, quae non est vox legis tantum praecipientis fieri ceremoniam, sed Evangelii quod pollicetur nobis in ceremonia remissionem peccatorum* (By the agreement of all, a sacrament consists of two things, that is the word and the element, and the word is indeed that of God himself, not the voice of the Law which ordains only the performance of a ceremony, but of the Gospel which in the ceremony promises to us the remission of sins). This transcription and translation are provided by Gordon Jeanes, "A Reformation Treatise on the Sacraments," *Journal of Theological Studies* 46, no. 1 (1995): 168, 182, respectively. Jeanes argues for Cranmerian authorship, whereas Null believes it to be by a close associate (Null, *Repentance*, 269-76). See the former's subsequent treatment of *De Sacramentis* in his *Signs*, 67-75.

[18]Cranmer's 1537 speech to a small convocation of bishops, recorded in Alexander Alesius, *De authoritate verbi dei liber Alexander Alesij, contra Episcopum Lundensem* (Strassburg, 1542), 23. The quoted translation comes from what Ashley Null calls the "less learned abridgement" in English, titled, *Of the auctorite of the word of God agannst the bisshop of london* (1537), sig. A9. See Null, "The Authority of Scripture in Reformation Anglicanism: Then and Now," in *Contesting Orthodoxies in the History of Christianity: Essays in Honour of Diarmaid MacCulloch*, ed. Ellie Gebarowski-Shafer, Ashley Null, and Alec Ryrie (Woodbridge: Boydell, 2021), 82n28. Though in what follows we will focus on the Lord's Supper, Gordon Jeanes has shown Cranmer's parallel development in his understanding of baptism. Particularly in chap. 2 of his *Signs*, Jeanes traces Cranmer's evolution, with special attention to his commonplace notebooks, away from baptismal regeneration, concluding that "in order to achieve *consistency in his theology of justification*, he is forced logically to break the strict link between the sacrament of baptism and the salvation which it signifies . . . the principle has been established in his mind, and it will gradually work its way through his whole theological understanding" (*Signs*, 92; emphasis added).

justification—*promissio*[19]—was articulated in a *sacramental* discussion. The reason that the sacrifice of the mass was an untenable doctrine was because justification was indeed *sola fide,* through the promise: "If the mass is a promise . . . then access to it is to be gained, not with any works, or powers, or merits of one's own, but by faith alone. For where there is the Word of the promising God, there must necessarily be the faith of the accepting man."[20] In the *Loci Communes,* Luther's compatriot defines the gospel most succinctly as "the *promise* of God's grace, blessing, and kindness through Christ."[21] Later, after tracing faith from Adam and Eve, to the Patriarchs, to Noah, through David, Melanchthon concludes: "The word that faith trusts is simply the *promise* of God's mercy and grace."[22] Likewise, we find that in Melanchthon's 1531 *Apology of the Augsburg Confession* the language of "promise" is used liberally, especially throughout Article IV (on justification) where "promise" is often interchanged with "gospel," or at least features as the chief term in defining the gospel.[23]

That Cranmer is clued in to this promise-centered soteriology is evident throughout his work in the 1530s and 1540s. In his Homily on Scripture, Cranmer says that the Bible's strength is in its "power to convert through God's promise."[24] Elsewhere in his Homily on Salvation: "Faith doth directly send us to Christ for remission of our sins, and that by faith given us of God we embrace the promise of God's mercy and of the remission of our sins."[25]

---

[19]For "promise" (*promissio*) as the center of Luther's understanding, see in particular Oswald Bayer's *Martin Luther's Theology: A Contemporary Interpretation* (Grand Rapids, MI: Eerdmans, 2003), 44-67.

[20]Luther, *The Babylonian Captivity of the Church* (1520), in *Martin Luther's Basic Theological Writings,* ed. Timothy F. Lull and William F. Russell, 3rd ed. (Minneapolis: Fortress, 2012), 212. A few months prior to *Babylonian Captivity,* Luther had penned "A Treatise on the New Testament, that is, the Holy Mass," which outlines a theology of promise from Adam to Christ in a similar fashion. See *Luther's Works* (American Edition, vol. 35 of 55 vols.), ed. Jaroslav Pelikan and Helmut T. Lehmann (St. Louis: Concordia; Philadelphia: Fortress, 1955–1986), 82-87. Hereafter, references to this series will be abbreviated as "*LW.*"

[21]Philip Melanchthon, *Commonplaces: Loci Communes 1521,* trans. Christian Preus (Saint Louis: Concordia, 2014), 94; emphasis added.

[22]Melanchthon, *Commonplaces,* 130-31; emphasis added.

[23]Philip Melanchthon, *Apology of the Augsburg Confession* (1531), in *The Book of Concord: The Confessions of the Evangelical Lutheran Church,* ed. Robert Kolb and Timothy J. Wengert (Minneapolis: Fortress, 2000), 107-294.

[24]Cranmer, "A Fruitfull Exhortation to the Reading and Knowledge of Holy Scripture," in *Certain Sermons or Homilies (1547) and A Homily Against Disobedience and Wilful Rebellion (1570): A Critical Edition,* ed. Roland B. Bond (Toronto: University of Toronto Press, 1987), 62.

[25]Cranmer, "An Homily of the Salvation of Mankind, by Only Christ Our Savior from Sin and Death Everlasting," in Bond, *Sermons,* 85.

Almost a decade earlier, in a passage that sounds very Lutheran, Cranmer responds to Henry with this definition of faith: "He that hath assured hope and confidence in Christ's mercy hath already entered into a perfect faith, and not only hath a will to enter into it. For perfect faith is nothing else but assured hope and confidence in Christ's mercy: and after it followeth, that he shall enter into perfect faith by undoubted trust in God, in his words and promise."[26]

In Cranmer's exhortation preceding the 1544 Litany, which might well function as an early manifesto of all of the Archbishop's liturgical work, we hear the language of promise liberally used:

> Our father in heaven, of his mere mercy and infinite goodness, hath bounden himself by his own free promise . . .

> But now good Christian people, that by the true use of prayer we may obtain and enjoy his gracious promise of aid, comfort, and consolation, in all our affairs and necessities . . .

> We must, upon consideration of our heavenly Father's mercy and goodness towards us, and of his everlasting truth, and free promise made unto us in his own holy word, conceive a full affiance, hope, and trust.[27]

Turning now to the sacraments, what we discover dominating the land-scape of Luther's and Melanchthon's teaching is precisely this same promise-theology. Selections from Melanchthon: "Sacraments or signs of God's mercy have been added to the promises . . . and they have a most certain testimony that God's goodwill applies to us";[28] "The signs of Baptism and participation in the Lord's Supper have been added to the promises as the autographs of Christ, so that Christians may be certain that their sins are forgiven";[29] "In the Scriptures signs are added to the promises as seals, both to remind us of the promises and to serve as sure testimonies of God's goodwill toward us, confirming that we will certainly receive what God has promised";[30] "Nothing

---

[26]Cranmer, "Corrections" (1538), in Cox, *Works*, vol. 2, 113.

[27]Cranmer, *Exhortation before the 1544 English Litany*, in J. Eric Hunt, *Cranmer's First Litany, 1544 and Merbecke's Book of Common Prayer Noted, 1550* (London: SPCK, 1939), 77; English modernized.

[28]Melanchthon, *Commonplaces*, 147.

[29]Melanchthon, *Commonplaces*, 147.

[30]Melanchthon, *Commonplaces*, 167.

can be called a sacramental sign except those signs that have been attached to God's promises";[31] "In the church the Lord's Supper was instituted that our faith might be strengthened by the remembrance of the promises of Christ."[32]

In 1526, Luther articulated that the same promises preached corporately in a sermon are re-preached individually in the Lord's Supper:

> When I preach his death, it is in a public sermon in the congregation, in which I am addressing myself to no one individually; whoever grasps it, grasps it. But when I distribute the sacrament, I designate it for the individual who is receiving it; I give him Christ's body and blood that he may have forgiveness of sins, obtained through his death, and preached in the congregation. This is something more than the congregational sermon; for although the same thing is present in the sermon as in the sacrament, here is the advantage that it is directed at definite individuals. In the sermon one does not point out or portray any particular person, but in the sacrament it is given to you and to me in particular, so that the sermon comes to be our own.[33]

This "same thing present" in sermon and sacrament is understood by Luther to be this justifying word of forgiveness—God's promise. It is precisely for this reason that Luther could not imagine leaving the Roman mass liturgically untouched for, especially in its late medieval theological and liturgical context, the mass obscured the gospel. It made the sacrament a work rather than a gift, a means of earning rather than a word of promise. Bryan Spinks observes:

> For Luther, the canon is a serious problem. It is in fact something that is incompatible with the gospel, and has in fact taken the place of the gospel. . . . Luther believed the gospel to be a declaration of the love and forgiveness of God—of what God had done for us. The canon, however, is preoccupied with what we are doing for God. It was precisely this which meant that the canon was incompatible with the doctrine of justification.[34]

---

[31]Melanchthon, *Commonplaces*, 170.

[32]Melanchthon, *Apology* IV.210, 152.

[33]Martin Luther, "The Sacrament of the Body and Blood of Christ—Against the Fanatics" (1526), in *LW* 36, 348; emphasis added. See also the passages in *Babylonian Captivity*, in Lull and Russell, *Writings*, 211-15.

[34]Bryan Spinks, *Luther's Liturgical Criteria and His Reform of the Canon of the Mass* (Bramcote: Grove Books, 1982), 30-31.

Debates about Cranmer's sacramentology have often failed to observe Luther's identical line of thinking in Cranmer's. Perhaps this is due to the fact that the debate has centered around sacramental *presence*, where the mature Cranmer, taking a Reformed position, was in disagreement with Luther.[35] This disagreement has obscured what is actually a more fundamental agreement about the sacramental *purpose*—to freely give out the promises of God to his people. Once this is recognized, we begin to see echoes of Luther and Melanchthon all over Cranmer's writing. In the Ten Articles of 1536, Cranmer describes baptism as necessarily including "firm credence and trust in the promise of God adjoined to the said sacrament."[36] In 1550, Cranmer would describe that true reception of the Lord's Supper was a "sacramental feeding in Christ's promises."[37] Again, according to Cranmer, a sacrament's purpose is that God might "assure [the believer] by the promise of his word."[38] As Caroline Stacey summarized Cranmer's sacramental theology: "The gospel promises do not point to the sacraments as special means of grace, but rather the sacraments are really visible showings of the gospel promises, as preaching is an audible showing of the same promises . . . they do not 'add grace' to the gospel."[39] Indeed, they *give* the gospel of grace.

The net effect of this insight is that the same gospel of justification by faith alone which drove the sacramental thinking of Luther dominated Cranmer's thought process as well. The purpose of the sacraments, according to Cranmer, was to preach the gospel, particularly by giving the promises of God. Suddenly, sense is made of the fact that in the 1552 Prayer Book Cranmer loaded both sacramental rites with promise-theology. Stephen Sykes notes the

---

[35] See Null, "Cranmer," in *Sacraments*, 215ff.

[36] Cranmer, The Ten Articles (1536), in Charles Lloyd, ed., *Formularies of Faith Put Forth By Authority during the Reign of Henry VIII* (Oxford: Clarendon, 1825), xx. See also Gordon Jeanes, who demonstrates the substantial linkage between Cranmer's baptismal liturgies and those of Luther: "Liturgy and Ceremonial," in *Liturgy in Dialogue*, ed. Paul Bradshaw and Bryan Spinks (London: SPCK, 1993), 22ff.

[37] Cranmer, "Defense of the True and Catholic Doctrine of the Sacrament of the Body and Blood of Our Saviour Christ" (1550); quoted in Null, "Cranmer," in *Sacraments*, 217.

[38] Cranmer, "An Answer to a Crafty and Sophistical Cavillation devised by Steven Gardiner" (1551), in Cox, *Works*, vol. 1, 52.

[39] Stacey, "Justification," 265. Sumner speaks similarly of the unity underlying preaching and sacraments when in the context of a discussion on Cranmer he states, "The Word is better understood if the sermon is its sacrament in airwaves, and the latter is the Word affixed to the elements so as to make His presence bodily immediate" (George R. Sumner, *Being Salt: A Theology of an Ordered Church* [Eugene, OR: Cascade, 2007], 37).

unprecedented rise in "promise" language throughout the baptism liturgy of 1552, concluding that "the historical reason [for this] has doubtless much to do with the promissory emphasis of Luther's sacramental theology."[40] In Holy Communion, Cranmer architected the Comfortable Words to follow Absolution—the Comfortable Words being nothing other than four bald promises of God.[41] It is clear that for Cranmer, his sacramentology is governed by the gospel, rendering an outlook succinctly described by Ashley Null as "justification and Holy Communion sola fide."[42] J. I. Packer summarizes:

> For [Cranmer], as for all the Reformers, the doctrine of justification by faith alone compelled a drastic rethinking of the sacraments. For if sacraments are really means of grace . . . and if grace means the apprehended reality of one's free forgiveness, acceptance, adoption, in and through Christ, and if grace is received by faith, and if faith is essentially trust in God's promise, then the sacraments must be thought of as rites which display and confirm the promises of the gospel, and as occasions for faith's exercise and deepening. From this it will follow that, instead of the gospel being really about the sacraments, as means for conveying specific spiritual blessings given no other way (the Medieval thesis), the sacraments are really about the gospel, in the sense that they hold forth visibly the same promises.[43]

Superstition and transubstantiation as gospel-issues. With *sola fide* established as the governor of Cranmer's sacramentology, we can now revisit other loci of Cranmer's sacramental argumentation and hear afresh this same governor featured there. Many have observed how the mature Cranmer was allergic to what he and the other Reformers described as "superstition." But were such attitudes merely the byproducts of the new humanist rationality and the early modernist outlook? For Cranmer, while this

---

[40]Stephen Sykes, "'Baptisme Doth Represente unto Us Oure Profession,'" in *Thomas Cranmer: Essays in Commemoration of the 500th Anniversary of His Birth*, ed. Margot Johnson (Durham: Turnstone, 1990), 133.

[41]And we should note well that while the Reformed liturgies which predated Cranmer had their own versions of "Comfortable Words" in eucharistic liturgies (Bucer's Strassburg liturgy of 1537, and Hermann's Cologne liturgy of 1544–1546), Cranmer's liturgy was the only one to make the Comfortable Words mandatory alongside absolution, as opposed to interchangeable with absolution. This may perhaps be a sign that Cranmer's soteriological understanding was more Lutheran than Reformed.

[42]Null, *Repentance*, 3.

[43]Packer, "Introduction," xv.

rationale was doubtless at play,[44] when it came to grappling with the meta-physics of bread and wine, his stated reasoning had far less to do with humanist disdain for medieval primitive practice and far more to do with the gospel. It is *sola fide* which motivates statements like these that seek to distinguish the elements themselves from what they signified and sealed: "Consider and behold my body crucified for you; that eat and digest in your minds. Chaw you upon my passion, be fed with my death. This is the true meat, this is the drink that moisteneth. . . . The bread and the wine which be set before your eyes are only *declarations of me*, but I myself am the eternal food."[45] Superstition, aided and abetted by the doctrine of transub-stantiation which said that the bread and wine substantially turned into the body and blood of Christ, was problematic not because it was antiquated or thought unfit for modern, rational thinking. Instead, these practices were manifestations of a more fundamental loss of scriptural truth, particularly the truth of justification by faith alone. In Cranmer's argumentation, if bread and wine are transubstantiated, people can receive Christ by means other than faith. They can receive Christ and be united to him substantially by simply physically eating the sacrament.[46] This further makes sense of why in the debates on transubstantiation in sixteenth-century England the loca-tion of Christ was ultimately an issue of the gospel. In Cranmer's under-standing, the book of Hebrews locates Christ bodily in heaven, and in heaven for a purpose—that he might live to intercede for believers as he declares his finished work before the Father (Heb 7:25). This good news of Christ's heavenly intercession is in his mind jeopardized, which is why he says, "Our faith is not to believe him to be in bread and wine, but that he is in heaven."[47] For Cranmer, transubstantiation pulls Christ away from heaven, away from the ear of the Father where intercession is to be made. Against transubstantiation, in the Archbishop's words, communion exists not to pull Christ down, but to lift us up: "Being like eagles in this life, we

---

[44]See Sykes, "Open Heart," 8.

[45]Cranmer, "Disputations at Oxford" (1554), in Cox, *Works*, vol. 1, 399; emphasis added.

[46]Cranmer, "Defence of the True and Catholic Doctrine of the Sacrament of the Body and Blood of our Saviour Christ" (1550), in Henry Jenkyns, *The Remains of Thomas Cranmer*, vol. 2 [Oxford: The University Press, 1833], 356: "[The papists] say, that Christ is received in the mouth, and entereth in with the bread and wine: we say, that he is received in the heart, and entereth in by faith."

[47]Cranmer, "Debate" (1548), in Buchanan, *Documents*, 17.

should fly up into heaven in our hearts, where that Lamb is resident at the right hand of his Father, which taketh away the sins of the world."[48] The concern about superstitious practices associated with transubstantiation (reservation, elevation, and veneration of the sacrament, processions and festivals, etc.) is therefore not a relatively insignificant metaphysical one, but a life-or-death soteriological one.[49] And this scheme creates a doctrinal order of priority. Contrary to medieval piety, the sacraments were not to be focused on for their sake. They were to be vehicles and servants of the gospel. For Cranmer, *sola fide* would govern the metaphysics of Christ's presence at the table.

Priesthood and ecclesiology as gospel-issues. We see from yet another angle that Cranmer's critique of medieval sacramental theology is governed by *sola fide* in the way he criticizes his day's theology of the priesthood. If faith alone must be in *Christ alone*, any other mediator nullifies the aloneness of faith: the object of faith (Christ) must be as alone as the faith itself for justification to be truly *by faith alone*. *Sola fide* and *solus Christus* are joined at the hip. This is why Cranmer can thunder against the priesthood thus:

> The greatest blasphemy and injury that can be against Christ, and yet universally used through the popish kingdom, is this: that the priests make their mass a sacrifice propitiatory, to remit the sins as well of themselves as of other, both quick and dead, to whom they list [i.e., desire] to apply the same. Thus, under the pretense of holiness, the papistical priests have taken upon them to be Christ's successors, and to make such an oblation and sacrifice as never creature made but Christ alone, neither he made the same any more times than once, and that was by his death upon the cross.[50]

This is furthermore why Cranmer found the doctrine of apostolic succession untenable.[51] It was not ultimately his disdain for Roman theology as such or even his loyalty to Henry's authority over that of the pope. Cranmer's gospel-governed concern was that as priests were pretending to be

---

[48]Cranmer, "Disputations" (1554), in Cox, *Works,* vol. 1, 398.

[49]For additional insights on this, see the end of chap. 6, under "*Sola Fide* and Consecration, Reception, and Blessing of the Elements."

[50]Cranmer, "Defence" (1550), in Jenkyns, *Remains,* vol. 2, 447.

[51]See Null, "Cranmer," in *Sacraments,* 215.

duplications, or "successors," of Christ as they made a sacrifice of him,[52] they take the trust and faith which should be thrown upon Christ alone and direct it to themselves. And when that happens, faith is no longer alone—the work of another, the priest, must accompany it:

> For if only the death of Christ be the oblation, sacrifice, and price, wherefore our sins be pardoned, then the act or ministration of the priest cannot have the same office. Wherefore it is an abominable blasphemy to give that office or dignity to a priest which pertaineth only to Christ; or to affirm that the Church hath need of any such sacrifice; as who should say, that Christ's sacrifice were not sufficient for the remission of our sins; or else that his sacrifice should hang upon the sacrifice of a priest. But all such priests as pretend to be Christ's successors in making a sacrifice for him, they be his most heinous and horrible adversaries. For never no person made a sacrifice of Christ, but he himself only.[53]

In conclusion, we hope to allow for a kind of argument "from the greater to the lesser." If for Cranmer *sola fide* indeed governed and directed the two most dominant subjects of theology and piety leading into the sixteenth century—purgatory and the sacraments—we have reason to believe that justification by faith alone would serve in the same post for many other spheres of theology. So it appears that *sola fide* is the governor of Cranmer's theological decisions. We turn now, beyond how *sola fide* is *positioned* in Cranmer's theology, to unpack how the doctrine actually works in Cranmer's theology.

---

[52]Cranmer, "Answer," 348: "But all such priests as pretend to be Christ's successors in making a sacrifice of him, they be his most heinous and horrible adversaries. For never no person made a sacrifice of Christ, but he himself only."

[53]Cranmer, "Defence," 452. Not surprisingly, we once again find a forerunner of this argumentation in Luther himself: "You will ask, 'If all who are in the church are priests, how do these whom we now call priests differ from lay men?' I answer: Injustice is done those words 'priest,' 'cleric,' 'spiritual,' 'ecclesiastic,' when they are transferred from all Christians to those few who are now by mischievous usage called 'ecclesiastics.' Holy Scripture makes no distinction between them, although it gives the name 'ministers,' 'servants,' 'stewards' to those who are now proudly called popes, bishops, and lords and who should according to the ministry of the Word serve others and teach them the faith of Christ and the freedom of believers. . . . That stewardship, however, has now been developed into so great a display of power and so terrible a tyranny that no heathen empire or other earthly power can be compared with it" (Martin Luther, "The Freedom of a Christian" [1520], in *Three Treatises* [Minneapolis: Fortress, 1990], 291-92).

2

THE GRAMMAR OF
SOLA FIDE DEFINED

ILLUSTRATIVELY RATHER THAN exhaustively, the previous chapter highlighted the *position* of justification by faith alone in Cranmer's theology—namely, as a governor. It was important to establish *sola fide* as central particularly in Cranmer's sacramentology because the sacraments play such a primary role in his liturgical work and the debates surrounding it. But what does it mean for *sola fide* to stand as a governor of theology generally and Cranmer's theology specifically? The key to unlocking the answer to this question is found in exploring the *method* of justification by faith alone—how it works, what it does. Understanding the way *sola fide* works will show us why it was central to Cranmer and prepare us for how it operated in the translation and redaction of liturgy according to the gospel. Here we will attempt to uncover the way Cranmer heard the Scriptures, first by attending to and tracing a significant interpretive stream of recent Pauline scholarship, and then by looking back to highlight the employment of such an interpretation in some key figures who had a particular influence on Cranmer—briefly Ambrose and Chrysostom, and more extensively in Augustine, Luther, and Melanchthon.

Given the fact that we will utilize an interpretation of Paul's theology as a paradigm throughout this book, we may ask: Why the narrow focus on Paul? What about the rest of the Scriptures? First, our particular interest in Paul lies in the observations we are about to make—namely, much of the language, many of the themes, and the strong antithetical pattern of negation and affirmation that permeates and fills the Book of Common Prayer suggest a strong and pervasive Pauline influence. Second, because Paul is both an interpreter and proclaimer of Jesus Christ and also a reader of

Israel's Scriptures, attending to Paul does not limit but rather opens up the scriptural witness.[1]

THE CENTRALITY OF JUSTIFICATION IN PAUL: *SOLA FIDE* AS A GRAMMAR

The question of the centrality of justification in modern Pauline scholarship. We begin by recognizing that justification-as-center is a highly contested notion in modern theology and Pauline scholarship.[2] If Luther's justification-centric interpretation of Paul re-bequeathed to Christianity this theological hub, then subsequent generations of scholars have dismantled it.[3] In an important essay, Jonathan Linebaugh traces this dismantling through the lineage of William Wrede, Albert Schweitzer, Krister Stendhal, and E. P. Sanders, whose collective work concludes that the centrality of justification had

---

[1] Indeed, "intertextuality" pervades the writing of Paul. One could say that his epistles *are* works of interpretation of the Hebrew Scriptures. Furthermore, the scriptural themes and controversies of Paul's day—for instance, the relationship between faith and works—run through the other books of the New Testament, such as in the epistle of James and the Gospel of John. With regard to the latter, David Ford sees the apostle John as acquainted with the writings of Paul and his "school," to the point that his gospel could be said to combine "the Synoptic narrative approach with some of the main pillars of Pauline theology" and to utilize the letter of the Ephesians as "one of the most fruitful intertexts" in John (David Ford, *The Gospel of John: A Theological Commentary* [Grand Rapids, MI: Baker, 2021], 4n3). All this is to say that the rich intertextuality between Paul, the Hebrew Scriptures, and the other New Testament writers suggests that to read Paul is, in fact, to enter through him into the entire Bible.

[2] It is beyond the scope of this work to fully rehearse the topic of justification in modern Pauline scholarship. What follows is admittedly brief and focused, relying heavily on the work of Jonathan A. Linebaugh, whose scholarship stands among the most vital and authoritative for processing this complex conversation.

[3] And Anglican liturgics would follow suit. A classic example is A. G. Hebert's *Liturgy and Society: The Function of the Church in the Modern World* (London: Faber and Faber, 1935), which was highly influential in the US and the UK over an entire generation of priests and liturgists. Though Hebert decries the wasteland of theological liberalism and articulates a commitment to Christian orthodoxy, his emphasis is much less on the gospel of Christ crucified and much more on what he calls "the Gospel of the Incarnation" (114). Hebert critiques Luther for being too individualistic in his theological approach and overly focused on "tender personal piety mixed with an anxious self-scrutiny" (163) over against a more communal vision for faith, liturgy, and society. Hebert ultimately interprets Paul, contra Luther, as supporting his premise that justification serves the more central doctrine of the church as the mystical body of Christ. Similarly we find a decade later the influential Anglo-Catholic theological work of E. L. Mascall, *Christ, the Christian, and the Church: A Study of the Incarnation and its Consequences* (originally published by Longman, Greens and Co Ltd. in 1946, but here referenced in the recent reprint by Hendrickson in 2017), redefining justification along more Roman or Thomist lines as "a real impartation of Christ's life to us and a real elevation of us to him" (88), to the end that justification would be subsumed under the incarnation and its "doctrine of the permanence of Christ's manhood" (xix), which Mascall defines as the "unifying principle" of the church (xvii) and "central principle of Christian theology" (xix).

far more to do with Luther's own personal soul-struggle (i.e., what Wrede calls, "die Seelenkämpfe Luthers") and far less to do with Paul's actual theology.[4] Justification has been displaced, says modern scholarship, not necessarily because it is theologically unimportant to Paul, but for two central reasons. First, justification has a specific context and purpose in Paul centered on Jew-Gentile relationships and the way that Gentiles can be Christ-followers without having to become doers of the Jewish law. Second, justification is merely one of many Pauline images for salvation and should not be elevated above the other important themes such as reconciliation, participation, union, redemption, election, atonement, and adoption.[5] Linebaugh effectively challenges this displacement in part by pointing out the unhelpful employment of the metaphor of justification as "center" and "middle."[6] For Paul, argues Linebaugh, it is not so much that justification is a middle hub out of which spread all other Pauline soteriological spokes. Rather, it is the gospel of Christ itself that stands at the center, with justification functioning as a kind of syntactical gatekeeper which norms the articulation of what is and what is not that gospel.[7] Linebaugh concludes that a much more useful way of describing Pauline justification is to speak of it as a "grammar."

The grammar of justification by faith alone. The notion of theology as a grammar has a rich lineage throughout Christian history and philosophy, traceable from Gregory Nazianzen to Wittgenstein.[8] The idea is similar to

---

[4]Jonathan A. Linebaugh, "The Grammar of the Gospel: Justification as a Theological Criterion in the Reformation and in Paul's Letter to the Galatians," *Scottish Journal of Theology* 71, no. 3 (2018): 288. This article also appears in Jonathan A. Linebaugh, *The Word of the Cross: Reading Paul* (Grand Rapids, MI: Eerdmans, 2022), and contains all pertinent references to Wrede, Schweitzer, Stendahl, Sanders, and others.

[5]Linebaugh, "Grammar," 289.

[6]German *Zentrum* and *Mitte* (along with the Latin *radix*), perhaps coined or at least codified by Hans Iwand, *Glaubensgerechtigkeit nach Luthers Lehre* (1941); see Linebaugh, "Grammar," 291-92.

[7]Linebaugh, "Grammar," 296n43: "The identification of justification as the 'centre' of Paul's theology is imprecise: 'the gospel of Christ' is the theological *radix*; justification relates to that gospel both critically and hermeneutically, naming not-gospels and norming the articulation of the gospel."

[8]Frederick W. Norris, "Theology as Grammar: Nazianzen and Wittgenstein," in *Arianism After Arius: Essays on the Development of the Fourth Century Trinitarian Conflicts*, ed. Michael R. Barnes and Daniel H. Williams (Edinburgh: T&T Clark, 1993), 237-49. In particular, Wittgenstein said, "Essence is expressed by grammar. . . . Grammar tells what kind of object anything is (Theology as grammar)" (§371, §373, in Ludwig Wittgenstein, *Philosophical Investigations*, trans. G. E. M. Anscombe [New York: MacMillan, 1953], 116). Two other significant voices have shaped modern conversations of theology as grammar: John Henry Newman, *An Essay on the Development of Christian Doctrine* (London: James Toovey, 1845) and *An Essay in Aid of a Grammar of Assent*

how we learn the rules of speech in linguistic grammar simply by conversing. So it is with theological grammar that we first acquire knowledge of who God is not by formal and abstract study of him, but simply by being a Christian, relating to him, and responding to his revelation. In this understanding of theology as a grammar, we operate according to the rules of this knowledge whether or not we have spent time reflecting on those rules or are even cognizant that such rules exist. Even if we do study the rules, it is often the case, at least in good study, that the rules recede from our reflective consciousness, "for it is as if the rules have become embedded in the speech textures themselves."[9] To speak of *justification* as a grammar, then, is to simply focus the scope of theological grammar—relating to God through his gospel.

At this point, we need to distinguish between justification as a doctrine, and justification as a grammar in order to recognize, first, that the two construals are not mutually exclusive, and, second, for our purposes we are focusing on the latter. George Lindbeck defines doctrines as "communally authoritative teachings regarding beliefs and practices that are considered essential to the identity or welfare of the group in question."[10] Justification by faith alone certainly fits within this definition. *Sola fide*, in this regard, can be articulated propositionally: Through Christ, God justifies sinners by his free grace, completely apart from any works or merits of their own. At the same time, however, we are attempting to recognize what Lindbeck also points out about how doctrines are often "more easily accounted for if they are taken to resemble grammatical rules rather than propositions."[11] What we will observe is that Paul not only articulates justification propositionally but makes decisions between faithful and unfaithful doctrine and practice out of the kinds of rules that justification establishes.[12] With this distinction clarified, let us unpack justification as a grammar.

(London: Burns, Oates, & Co., 1870); and George A. Lindbeck, *The Nature of Doctrine: Religion and Theology in a Postliberal Age* (Philadelphia: The Westminster Press, 1984).

[9]Paul L. Holmer, *The Grammar of Faith* (New York: Harper & Row, 1978), 18. The connection between theology as a grammar and liturgical theology's concepts of primary theology and secondary theology (discussed in the introduction) should be apparent.

[10]Lindbeck, *Doctrine*, 74.

[11]Lindbeck, *Doctrine*, 84.

[12]It should be clear, therefore, that as we discuss justification as a grammar, there will be points of continuity and discontinuity between what we are referring to and what these broader conversations around postliberalism (especially stemming from Lindbeck) mean by the term.

Perhaps coined by Luther himself,[13] the idea of justification as a grammar means that it "governs the way words run when sentences speak the Pauline gospel," functioning as an "evangelical criterion," which "says 'no' to not-gospels while norming the saying of the gospel."[14] Justification is "an evangelical canon that makes possible the judgment: this is or this is not the gospel."[15] Linebaugh critically notes that "justification often does this theological work without the specific vocabulary of justification."[16] This means that justification is structurally present in every kind of soteriological construction, running like unseen rebar throughout the other edifices of Paul's architecturally diverse salvation-theology. Agreeing with modern scholarship's insistence that Paul's development of justification is specific to his context, we recognize that justification arises in Galatians, for instance, out of the crisis that occasioned a conflict between what Paul perceives as "the gospel of Christ" and "a different gospel" (Gal 1:6-7). What we are pointing out, though, is that as Paul distinguishes between these two "gospels" for the Galatian church, justification is the *way* he determines the real gospel from its counterfeit. In this regard, though justification is functioning as a hermeneutic to parse the gospel in that specific context, its methodology becomes applicable to a limitless host of other situations. We observe this universal applicability beyond Jew-Gentile conflicts in passages like Romans 4, where Paul employs justification as a way of reading Scripture—particularly the story of Abraham and Sarah in Genesis. So justification is not merely for Paul something to apply to the sociological problem of first-century Jew-Gentile relationships, nor is it even merely a way of understanding the structure of his soteriology. It is a hermeneutic for how to read and interpret God's work in all of Scripture with application to all of life. It is a way of speaking and understanding. It is, indeed, a grammar. Linebaugh offers a useful metaphor for what this grammar does: "The excluding and including grammar of justification functions as an evangelical gold-pan, separating and filtering out all human criteria such that all that remains as gospel is the pure gold of the grace of God in Jesus Christ."[17]

---

[13]Johann Georg Hamann reports encountering Luther's words: "Theology is nothing but a grammar of the words of the Holy Spirit." See Linebaugh, "Grammar," 289n16.

[14]Linebaugh, "Grammar," 290.

[15]Linebaugh, "Grammar," 292.

[16]Linebaugh, "Grammar," 294.

[17]Linebaugh, "Grammar," 294.

How the grammar of justification works. Concretizing the above, Paul's grammar of justification sifts by making sharp distinctions of categorical exclusion. When Paul describes and defines grace, his characteristic emphasis is on what John Barclay calls grace's "incongruity"—namely that grace excludes all human standards of worth and comes as an unconditioned gift. Linebaugh picks up on this exclusionary function of grace, observing what he calls the "Pauline pattern of antithesis."[18] This theology, especially preeminent in Galatians and Romans, presents antithetical, either/or binaries: salvation is either ἐξ ἔργων νόμου ("by works of the law"), or it is διὰ πίστεως Ἰησοῦ Χριστοῦ ("through faith in Jesus Christ") (Gal 2:16; cf. Rom 3:21-22); it is either that "I live" or "Christ lives in me" (Gal 2:20). This separation is radically disjunctive: *no one* is justified by works of the law (Rom 3:20); but *all* are justified by his grace as a gift (Rom 3:24). Again, "we hold that one is justified by faith *apart* from works of the law" (Rom 3:28). And it is these antitheses, these categorically exclusive distinctions,[19] which define what is the gospel and what is ἕτερον εὐαγγέλιον ("another gospel"), which is no gospel at all (Gal 1:6-7). Out of this Pauline way of speaking come various shorthand distinctions, coined by Paul and some repackaged by the Reformers: faith and works (Rom 3:20-26); spirit and letter (2 Cor 3); old and new creature/creation (2 Cor 5:17); death and life (Rom 5:12-17); flesh and spirit (Rom 7:4-6; Gal 5:16-26); first Adam and second Adam (1 Cor 15:20-23); nothingness and creation (Gal 6:14-15); law and grace (Rom 5:20-21); the "alien work of God" and the "proper work of God."[20]

---

[18]John M. G. Barclay, *Paul and the Gift* (Grand Rapids, MI: Eerdmans, 2017), 566: "Grace is discovered in an event . . . in the gift of Christ, which constitutes for Paul *the* Gift. This gift is experienced and interpreted as an *incongruous gift*"; Jonathan A. Linebaugh, "The Uglier Ditch: First-Century Grace in the Present Tense," in *The New Perspective on Grace: Paul and the Gospel after Paul and the Gift*, ed. Edward Adams, Dorothea H. Bertschmann, Stephen J. Chester, Jonathan A. Linebaugh, and Todd D. Still (Grand Rapids, MI: Eerdmans, 2022, forthcoming).

[19]Though we will not entertain this important angle for our present discussion, this idea of radical disjunction and categorical exclusivity as inherent to the nature of justification and salvation is bound up in the *eschatological* character of Paul's soteriology. In this reading, "eschatological dogmatics" frames justification, with the cross as the hinge on which time bent over on itself. It is precisely in the radically disjunctive events of Christ's death and resurrection where the old aeon died, where the "I" died, and where the new aeon broke in. This sharp discontinuity (as sharply distinguished as death is to life) shapes the character of justification in that its business is to (a) make categorically exclusive distinctions and (b) summarize itself in the disjunctive Pauline language of "not I, but Christ," both of which we will outline in what follows. On the eschatological character of justification, see Philip G. Ziegler, *Militant Grace: The Apocalyptic Turn and the Future of Christian Theology* (Grand Rapids, MI: Baker, 2018), esp. 3-15.

[20]Latin: *opus alienum Dei* and *opus proprium Dei*. These two, in particular, are Reformation formulations of Paul.

To make these kinds of distinctions, to completely filter and sift, is to do theology "justification-ly."[21] In other words, to properly define and proclaim the gospel, not-gospels must be exposed and separated out, and the means of doing this is by making the above distinctions and making them in such a way as to be mutually exclusive, radically disjunctive.[22] And the opposite is true: to confuse and commingle these distinctions is not only to obscure the gospel. It is to lose it entirely. This is precisely why *sola fide* works as a descriptor of both justification and the gospel itself. It is in the radical distinguishing of faith apart from works that the grammar of justification is active, and when this is done, the gospel is clarified and preached, even *felt*,[23] and seen in its truth over against that which is not the gospel.

An example of the methodology of the Pauline grammar. Here we want to entertain an example from Paul, both as a means of illustrating the way this grammar works biblically and of breaking into Cranmer's own redactive method liturgically. In an insightful essay, David Lincicum contrasts how Paul, in Romans 10:6-8, reads Deuteronomy 30:12-14 with how a contemporaneous Jewish scholar, Philo of Alexandria, interpreted the same.[24] The contrast brings Paul's grammar of *sola fide* into stark relief. Philo's interpretation takes a more straightforward approach to the passage. He argues that when Deuteronomy admonishes, "the word is very near you, in your mouth and in your heart and in your hands, so that you may do it" (LXX Deut 30:14[25]), it is encouraging

---

[21]I am at least somewhat taking a cue from Stephen Westerholm who discusses the difficulty of using English equivalents of the flexibly declined δικαιο- word-group. He anglicizes and then declines *dikaios* as an adjective (*dikaiosness*) and a verb (*dikaiosify*). I'm attempting to do something similar by retaining justification language while turning it into an adverb. See Stephen Westerholm, *Perspectives Old and New on Paul: The "Lutheran" Paul and His Critics* (Grand Rapids, MI: Eerdmans, 2004), 262-63.

[22]Oswald Bayer, *Martin Luther's Theology: A Contemporary Interpretation* (Grand Rapids, MI: Eerdmans, 2003), 60: "The subject matter of theology is conceptualized as a dynamic event, which can be described only by making distinctions."

[23]That this radical distinction can be felt is a particularly important category for a study such as this, which seeks to connect doctrine to embodied liturgical practice and experience. See Simeon Zahl's notable treatment of the affective power of incongruous grace and how it is tangibly experienced in bodies and across time, where in particular he interacts with and expands on Barclay's work (Simeon Zahl, "Incongruous Grace as Patterns of Experience," *International Journal of Systematic Theology* 22, no. 1 [2020]: 60-76).

[24]David Lincicum, "Philo of Alexandria and Romans 9:30-10:21: The Commandment and the Quest for the Good Life," in *Reading Romans in Context: Paul and Second Temple Judaism*, ed. Ben C. Blackwell, John K. Goodrich, and Jason Maston (Grand Rapids, MI: Zondervan, 2015), 122-28.

[25]Quoted in Lincicum, "Philo," 124.

the attainability (and therefore pursuit) of a total and virtuous keeping of the law. Philo achieves this interpretation through a more conventional expansion, paraphrase, and explanation of the Deuteronomic text.

By contrast, Paul's interpretation of Deuteronomy comes in the form of *theological redaction* of the actual passage. Lincicum observes Paul doing three things in his redaction: (1) He renounces self-reliance; (2) he erases the "doing"; and (3) he replaces the commandment with Christ. It is worth reproducing Lincicum's side-by-side comparison here, both because of its explanatory clarity and because it will serve later as a template for observing Cranmer's own work (see fig. 2.1).[26]

DEUTERONOMY 30:12-14 (LXX)	ROMANS 10:6-8
[The command] is not in heaven that one should say,	[The command] is not in heaven that one should say, **But the righteousness that is by faith says, "Do not say in your heart,**
"Who will ascend for us into heaven and take it for us? And once we have heard, we will do it."	'Who will ascend for us into heaven and take it for us?' **(that is, to bring Christ down)** And once we have heard, we will do it. **or**
Nor is it on the other side of the sea that one should say,	Nor is it on the other side of the sea that one should say,
"Who will cross over to the other side of the sea for us and take it for us? And when he has caused us to hear it we will do it."	'Who will cross over to the other side of the sea for us and take it for us? And when he has caused us to hear it we will do it.' **descend into the deep?'" (that is, to bring Christ up from the dead). But what does it say?**
The word is very near you, in your mouth and in your heart and in your hands, in order for you to do it.	"The word is very near you; **it is** in your mouth and in your heart and in your hands, in order for you to do it," **that is the message concerning faith that we proclaim.**

Figure 2.1. Deuteronomy 30 and Romans 10

Lincicum makes us aware of three things. First, we see in Paul's redaction of the first phrase a clear renunciation of self-reliance by negating ("Do *not* say

---

[26]Lincicum, "Philo," 125-26. The table is adapted from Lincicum.

in your heart"), rather than saying something positive about, one's commitment to doing the law. Paul draws from language in Deuteronomy 8:17 and 9:4 where "do not say" precedes a stern warning not to base success on one's own righteousness. Second, Paul "erases the doing" in the second, fourth, and fifth phrases by editing out all references to how the law will be kept ("we will do it"). Third, Paul replaces the commandment with Christ in the second and fourth phrases by making Christ, not the commandment, the object of action ("bring Christ down . . . bring Christ up"). Adding to Lincicum, we can also observe in the fifth phrase Paul transposing law into gospel: the "word" was the law to be kept (Deut 30:14); now the "word" is the "message concerning faith"—that is, the gospel (Rom 10:8). In sum, "Paul has erased any hint of 'doing' the commandments, instead placing emphasis on confessing and trusting Jesus as the Messiah."[27]

What we are observing is the Pauline grammar at work. Paul is not explaining justification. In fact, *sola fide* is absent, terminologically speaking, from Romans 10:6-8. Paul already made his theological claim a few verses back: "For Christ is the end of the law for righteousness to everyone who believes" (Rom 10:4). Having made that claim, the grammar simply goes to work in Paul's editorial interpretation of Deuteronomy 30. And what does this redaction do? It separates. It distinguishes. It "erases the doing" so that faith and works avoid any commingling. This is what justification does when it functions as a grammar: it utterly separates, categorically distinguishes. It puts faith, Christ, and grace in as stark a relief as possible. To reiterate Linebaugh's words, *sola fide* filters out "all human criteria" until the "pure gold of grace" is left—alone.

Pauline shorthand for the grammar of justification: "Not I, but Christ." In another essay, Linebaugh argues that a specific Pauline passage serves as a touchstone for the grammar of *sola fide*—Galatians 2:20: "I have been crucified with Christ. It is no longer I who live, but Christ who lives in me."[28] Following justification's work as a grammar whose rules include antithetical distinction, this passage radically distinguishes the "I" in me from the "Christ"

---

[27]Lincicum, "Philo," 127.

[28]Jonathan Linebaugh, "'The Speech of the Dead': Identifying the No Longer and Now Living 'I' of Galatians 2:20," *New Testament Studies* 66, no. 1 (January 2020): 87-105. This article will appear in Jonathan A. Linebaugh, *The Word of the Cross: Reading Paul* (Grand Rapids, MI: Eerdmans, 2022).

in me. The "I" is dead. Christ now lives. While this separation brings up questions regarding the continuity and discontinuity of the "me" associated with the dead "I," versus the "me" associated with the living Christ,[29] this passage from Galatians offers a helpful hook on which to hang the identification of the grammar at work, tying together the example from Paul in the previous section above. The grammar of *sola fide* is at work when the "I" is completely removed from the equation of righteousness ("not I") and when, at the same time, Christ and his righteousness is featured, totally and exclusively ("but Christ"). In the language of audio production, for *sola fide* to be at work, it is not merely that Christ sits on top of the mix; it is that he is soloed—all other tracks are not just softer but muted entirely. In the language of theater, it is not merely that Christ is foregrounded against other actors in salvation; he is the only one on the stage.

We see this pervasive "not . . . but" structure of Paul's theology clearly, for instance, in Romans 9, where the apostle explicates one of his great soteriological themes—election—according to justification's grammar. Paul does so by employing three "οὐκ . . . ἀλλὰ" constructions to show that God's election lacks any preexisting condition outside his own grace. Whereas contemporaneous Old Testament interpreters (such as Philo) read God's election of Abraham and his offspring as conditioned by virtue, worth, or status intrinsic to those people, in an unprecedented move Paul surprisingly asserts that God's election occurs apart from those things.[30] God's election of Isaac is "not" based on Abrahamic genealogy, "but" God's promise (9:8). God's election of Jacob is "not" based on Jacob's moral worth, "but" God's calling (9:11-12). It is "not" based on Jacob and Esau's social status (primogeniture), "but" on God's mercy (9:12, 16).[31] Again, quite apart from the *language* of *sola fide*, here we see a clear example of the *structure* of justification by faith alone norming how Paul articulates the gospel as he explores the theme of the

---

[29]Linebaugh answers these questions well in the essay.

[30]Douglas Moo, *The Epistle to the Romans*, NICNT (Grand Rapids, MI: Eerdmans, 1996), 583n60: "Paul's exclusion of 'works' from God's election is probably directed against a certain segment of early Jewish theology." Moo goes on to cite Philo's contrasting interpretation in *Allegorical Interpretation of the Laws*, 3.88.

[31]These insights are drawn from Barclay, *Gift*, 520-61. See also Orrey McFarland, "Philo of Alexandria and Romans 9:1-29: Grace, Mercy, and Reason," in *Reading Romans in Context: Paul and Second Temple Judaism*, ed. Ben C. Blackwell, John K. Goodrich, and Jason Maston (Grand Rapids, MI: Zondervan, 2015), 115-21.

unfailing word (9:6) that calls and sustains Israel from generation to generation. And Paul's way of going about this is through the repeated "not . . . but" categorical contrast.

The "not I, but Christ" of Galatians 2:20, therefore, serves not only as one of the many disjunctive antitheses in the Pauline corpus. It also serves as a tidy shorthand uniquely suited for the work of identifying how justification works in theological redaction of texts (as with Paul in Rom 10) and liturgies (as we will observe with Cranmer in the Book of Common Prayer). "Not I, but Christ" neatly illustrates the kind of subtraction and addition taking place when texts are edited according to *sola fide*. In Paul's theology, the human remains in the story of salvation as God's beloved creature—the finite, fallen person under sin that God loves, redeems, adopts, and calls righteous. When Paul says, "not I," therefore, he is not urging a negation of human personhood or dignity. Rather, "not I" is an exclusion of the person as an actor of righteousness, as an agent in their justification before God. To negate and exclude *this* "I" is a way to display the depths of God's love, according to the grammar of justification—God loves even *that* "I," *that* one who has nothing to offer. It is for this reason, for the sake of displaying and magnifying the love of God in Christ, that one is led to excise any reference to "I," except where the "I" is confessing inadequacy, need, inability, offense, sin, transgression, and so on. And where righteousness and law-keeping before God are concerned, Christ and only Christ is mentioned. The "I" is either negated or excised; Christ is showcased and exalted. And the former and the latter are never confused or commingled. Given the unique suitability of "not I, but Christ" as a way into observing the operation of *sola fide* particularly in texts, it will serve as a primary paradigm in the next chapters to observe the gospel as it is clarified and distinguished by Cranmer in the Book of Common Prayer. But before we get there, we might first briefly trace the "pedagogical lineage" of the grammar's transmission from Paul to Cranmer.

HIGHLIGHTING THE GRAMMAR FROM PAUL THROUGH THE REFORMATION

Part of the reason it is important to trace key figures in the transmission of the Pauline grammar is that Cranmer's own employment of the grammar takes on the characteristics of those predecessors. And the more we understand how those forerunners articulated theology through the grammar of *sola fide* (albeit with more or less clarity depending on the person), the more we will see how thoroughly Cranmer's filter was operating. What we want to argue is that these key historical figures, who interpreted Paul similarly to what we have outlined above, collectively employed a theological way of speaking worth identifying. We make this identification not so much that we might marshal a kind of genealogical argument regarding Cranmer's uses of similar terms and constructs (i.e., we do not want to go so far as to say that Cranmer's use of certain terms was copied from these other thinkers or that his usage of those terms proves some sort of direct theological ancestry), but that we might more modestly and cautiously observe a correspondence and overlap in language in order to support a cumulative case for Cranmer's commitment to *sola fide*. In other words, for these Reformation predecessors (including Augustine), we do not want to give the impression that we are summarizing their complete soteriology or even their entire understanding of justification, much less that their conceptions of the latter aligned with Cranmer and the Reformers on all points (for they did not). We are simply trying to observe some language that exposes the grammar of *sola fide* that Reformers like Cranmer appear to have picked up on and utilized in their more distinctive reading of Paul. With those disclaimers, let us trace the lineage and note a few terms and concepts that emerge when the Pauline grammar is at work.

Ambrose. Early in the church's history, we find peppered through the teaching of key leaders the interpretation of Paul according to the lines drawn above. Ambrose, archbishop of Milan (c. 340–397), may very well have plowed certain ground that would become the initial pathways for more thorough paving by Augustine only a few years later.[32] In Ambrose, we hear these distinctions: "the law was able to close the mouth of all, but it was not able to change their mind"; and "the law condemns the action; it

---

[32]Indeed, Ambrose is bountifully appealed to as Augustine interprets Paul in conjunction with refuting the theology of Pelagius, which is of keen interest to us precisely because it is in Augustine's anti-Pelagian writings where we see the Pauline grammar most obviously at work. See esp. Augustine, "A Treatise on the Grace of Christ, and on Original Sin," I.47-55, in Philip Schaff, ed., *Nicene and Post-Nicene Fathers, First Series, Volume V—St. Augustine: Anti-Pelagian Writings* (New York: The Christian Literature Company, 1887), 233-36.

does not take away its malice."[33] Ambrose here explains the sifting work of the Word of God. Elsewhere we find Ambrose setting forth the worthlessness of our works "in Adam" in order to utterly set apart justification: "I fell in Adam, in Adam was I expelled from Paradise, in Adam I died; and [God] does not recall me unless He has found me in Adam,—so as that, as I am obnoxious to the guilt of sin in him, and subject to death, I may be also justified in Christ."[34] And even more pointedly: "This is the ordinance of God, that he which believeth in Christ should be saved *without* works, by faith *only, freely* receiving remission of his sins."[35] In Ambrose's understanding of Paul here, when a person comes to faith, justification categorically excludes our works.

John Chrysostom. This same line of interpretation of Scripture is present in one of Christianity's first great expository preachers, John Chrysostom (c. 349–407).[36] In effect, Chrysostom would articulate a very Pauline way of looking at all of Scripture, and it is noteworthy that Cranmer himself would pull out this particular jewel from the golden-mouthed preacher's works: "He that is hard-hearted and an obstinate sinner shall there [in the Scriptures] find eternal torments, prepared of God's justice to make him afraid and

---

[33] Ambrose, *Flight from the World (De fuga saeculi)*, 3, 15 and 7, 39: CSEL 32/2, 175 and 194. Quoted by Augustine, "Answer to the Two Letters of the Pelagians," IV.30, in *Answer to the Pelagians, II*, ed. John E. Rotelle, trans. Roland J. Teske (New York: New City Press, 1998), 212.

[34] Ambrose, *Concerning the Resurrection*, ii.6, quoted in Augustine, "On Original Sin," II.47, in *Answer to the Pelagians*, 254.

[35] This is Cranmer's own quotation of Ambrose in his Homily on Salvation from Roland B. Bond, ed., *Certain Sermons or Homilies (1547) and A Homily Against Disobedience and Wilful Rebellion (1570): A Critical Edition* (Toronto: University of Toronto Press, 1987), 82; emphasis added.

[36] While Ambrose and Chrysostom serve here as illustrative exemplars, more work could be done in outlining how the grammar worked throughout and beyond the patristic period, and it certainly would be fruitful for our purposes, given the findings of Ashley Null in Cranmer's notebooks. Evidently, Cranmer gathered extensive quotations of the Fathers around certain soteriological loci such as "*sola fides*," "*ex sola fide iustificamur*," and "*contra merita humana*." The breadth of the Fathers (and beyond) included Ambrose, Chrysostom, Origen, Jerome, Bede, Gregory, Bernard, Thomas Netter, Irenaeus, Cyprian, Athanasius, Prosper, and Cassiodorus. The evidence is clear: Cranmer had a keen interest in how *sola fide* was engaged by the early and late church fathers. See Null, *Thomas Cranmer's Doctrine of Repentance: Renewing the Power to Love* (Oxford: Oxford University Press, 2000); J. I. Packer, introduction to *The Work of Thomas Cranmer*, ed. G. E. Duffield (Philadelphia: Fortress, 1965); 264. Null's more recent research ("Thomas Cranmer's Reputation Reconsidered," in *Reformation Reputations: The Power of the Individual in English Reformation History*, ed. D. J. Crankshaw and G. W. C. Gross [London: Palgrave Macmillan, 2021], 201-3, 215-16) shows even more patristic sources with lengthier texts analyzed than previously realized, including Cranmer's substantial study of Chrysostom.

mollify him. He that is oppressed with misery in this world shall there find relief in the promises of eternal life, to his great consolation and comfort."[37] Note here in Chrysostom's writing a sharp distinction between two *experiences* of God's Word: "torment" and "fear" for the hard-hearted; "consolation" and "comfort" in God's "promises" for those in misery. One can observe even from these two sentences that Chrysostom read Scripture through the Pauline lens outlined above. One might even read in these lines a proto-Reformation distinction between law and gospel.[38]

Augustine. Certainly, it is in Augustine's writings against Pelagius where we find the sharpest distinctions regarding salvation being made, and it would be the rereading of these treatises by the sixteenth-century Reformers which would spark a rediscovery of the gospel. One example: against Pelagius, Augustine interpreted the very words of Jesus (in Jn 15:5) in a way that employs Paul's grammar of exclusivity: "The Lord did not say, 'Without me you can with difficulty do something,' but said, *Without me you can do nothing.* And in order to answer these people in advance, in that same gospel statement he did not say, 'Without me you can complete nothing,' but *Without me you can do nothing.*"[39] In Augustine's view, justification does not merely demote works; it excludes them. We note well here that for Augustine as with Ambrose, this categorical exclusion of works pertains to initial justification, and that for these Fathers works indeed factor into cooperation with grace on the other side of one's first confession of faith. The Reformers, including Cranmer, would differ here. Nevertheless, it is through these insights of Augustine that the Reformers arrived at their understanding of what Paul was saying, and so we turn to some terminology of the Bishop of Hippo that Cranmer would pick up and employ.

---

[37] Quoted in Cranmer, "Scripture," in Bond, *Sermons,* 62. Cranmer goes on in this homily to return, again and again, to that particular favorite term, "comfort."

[38] If one is rightly reading the directionality, one might be able to say that as Cranmer articulated a very Luther-like approach to hermeneutics (i.e., the law-gospel distinction) in his Homily on Scripture, the Archbishop sought patristic corroboration in the likes of Chrysostom rather than mere allegiance to one of Cranmer's contemporaries. In other words, Cranmer defended his Lutheran interpretation of Paul by mining the Fathers (as Luther himself did). However, we acknowledge important differences between Cranmer and the Fathers around these theological matters, for example: Chrysostom denies unconditional election—a contrast with Cranmer and the Reformers.

[39] Augustine, "Answer to the Two Letters of the Pelagians," II.18, in *Pelagians,* II, 155; emphasis original.

"Assisting grace" in Augustine. Augustine repeatedly uses the language of assisting grace. To the modern ear, *assistance* implies coming alongside the agency of something else to, as it were, give it a boost. Based on Augustine's employment of the term, however, the exact opposite is implied, especially as it pertains to the initial justification of the believer. For instance, in *On the Spirit and the Letter,* in which we find some of the bishop's strongest distinctions drawn between faith and works, he says, "For whatever did even what the law commanded, without the assistance of the Spirit of grace, acted through fear of punishment, not from love of righteousness."[40] In other words, works done apart from faith (the only pathway for the love of righteousness) are not even partially meritorious or acceptable to God. After another long section sifting faith from works, Augustine summarizes the life of faith as the life which is "assisted by the grace of God."[41] For Augustine, then, assistance is not to be understood as God coming alongside a decently righteous person to elevate their merited or partially-merited efforts to an acceptable plane. Assisting grace is Augustine's shorthand, rather, for the kind of work God does in the absence of meritorious good works: "Our very will without which we cannot do any good thing, is assisted and elevated by the importation of the Spirit of grace, without which help mere teaching is 'the letter that kills.'"[42]

In another work, Augustine discusses how the human condition is such that it becomes "difficult to be obedient unto righteousness; and unless this defect were overcome by assisting grace, *no one* would turn to holiness; nor unless it were healed by efficient grace would anyone enjoy the peace of righteousness."[43] That Augustine's theology of assisting grace precludes any notion of a partnership with the inherent righteousness of the believer is abundantly clear in the fact that he uses the phrase to contrast his soteriology with that of Pelagius: "Perhaps, however, [Pelagius] thinks the name of Christ

---

[40] Augustine, *On the Spirit and the Letter,* chap. 13 (Lexington: Beloved Publishing, 2014), 12. I should note that in this particular discussion this translation and those of Schaff are at times more useful than the more critical New City Press editions, because those editions repeatedly translate Augustine here as "help."

[41] Augustine, *On the Spirit and the Letter,* 16.

[42] Augustine, *On the Spirit and the Letter,* 20.

[43] Augustine, "A Treatise on the Merits and Forgiveness of Sins, and on the Baptism of Infants," II.33, in Schaff, *Writings,* 57; emphasis added. Again, the more critical New City Press edition translates the word here as "help."

to be necessary on this account, that by his gospel we may learn how we ought to live; but not that we may also be assisted by his grace, in order withal to lead good lives."[44] Even in his latest writings, Augustine was found affirming the distinction between law and grace with this understanding of God's assistance: "A man is assisted by grace, in order that [God's] will may not be uselessly commanded."[45] Augustine's understanding is that the law does not provide what it commands. Only grace can do that. Without grace, the law's command is "useless."

Yet elsewhere, Augustine describes this assisting grace as the very grace that resurrects the one who is dead in their trespasses and sins (Eph 2:1). Far from being a grace that comes alongside a decent person to help them become better, God's assistance is a "grace [that] by coming to his assistance makes him alive."[46] In distinguishing between righteousness that comes by the law and righteousness that comes by grace through faith, Augustine uses God's assistance to explain how the latter is distinct from the former.[47]

Assisting grace is not only something that converts; it also sustains the believer, propelling the believer toward good works. After conversion, "we then have his assistance to lead good lives."[48] Every good work is "always assisted by God's grace."[49] This kind of assistance is equated with the power and presence of the Holy Spirit to prevent future sin,[50] helping us to resist evil.[51] Nevertheless, Augustine is clear that the believer will not know sinless perfection until the final day:

> They, however, are in a great majority, who, while not doubting that to the last
> day of their life it will be needful to them to resort to the prayer which they can

---

[44] Augustine, "A Treatise on Nature and Grace, Against Pelagius," I.46, in Schaff, *Writings*, 137.

[45] Augustine, "A Treatise on Grace and Free Will," I.9, in Schaff, *Writings*, 447. Though we will not make mention of it beyond this note, we see here a doctrine worth tracing from Augustine, through Luther, to Cranmer, as it bolsters the argument in favor of the grammar of *sola fide*—namely, the bondage of the will. It would be worth further study to explore more thoroughly this doctrine through the liturgy of Cranmer.

[46] Augustine, "Two Letters," III.2, in Schaff, *Writings*, 403.

[47] Augustine, "Two Letters," III.20, in Schaff, *Writings*, 412.

[48] Augustine, "Faith and Works," in *On Christian Belief*, trans. Ray Kearney (New York: New City Press, 2005), 254.

[49] Augustine, "Two Letters," I.36, in Schaff, *Writings*, 388.

[50] Augustine, "Nature and Grace," I.13, in Schaff, *Writings*, 125: "Not again to be committed, by God's assisting grace."

[51] Augustine, "Nature and Grace," I.79, in Schaff, *Writings*, 149.

so truthfully utter, "Forgive us our trespasses, as we forgive those who trespass against us," still trust that in Christ and his promises they possess a true, certain, and unfailing hope. There is, however, no method whereby any persons arrive at absolute perfection, or whereby any man makes the slightest progress to true and godly righteousness, but the assisting grace of our crucified Saviour Christ, and the gift of His Spirit; and whosoever shall deny this cannot rightly, I almost think, be reckoned in the number of any kind of Christians at all.[52]

In light of all this, it is clear that "assisting grace" is a pervasive phrase in Augustine with a distinct theological meaning. It is, indeed, a phrase which speaks according to the grammar of *sola fide*.

Martin Luther and Philip Melanchthon. Though contemporaries of Cranmer, Luther and Melanchthon serve as key figures in the reception of Paul and his grammar of *sola fide*.[53] These German Reformers were in fact the most prolific expositors of this particular aspect of Pauline theology. Without question, their reception of Paul (particularly through Augustine[54]) was a key critical influence on Cranmer's conversion to Protestantism in general and on his understanding of the Pauline grammar of the gospel in particular. Luther and Melanchthon would take the Augustinian distinctions—faith and works, law and grace, spirit and letter—and codify them in such a way as to bring the Pauline grammar into intense focus. The German Reformers landed particularly on a singular dialectic of the grammar of *sola fide*—the distinction between law and gospel—which would be a prominent pairing among all the Reformers of the sixteenth century and beyond.

---

[52]Augustine, "Nature and Grace," I.70, in Schaff, *Writings*, 146.

[53]We have leaped over significant spans of time and thought from Augustine to the Reformation—most notably Aquinas—when it comes to justification and other aspects of soteriology. In the interest of brevity and clarity of thought (the Reformers would take significant issue with late medieval scholasticism's soteriology in particular, and would often appeal to Augustine to do so), we move on to the sixteenth century. We should also note with respect to Melanchthon that for our purposes, we are interested in what later scholarship would identify as the "early Melanchthon," especially as understood from his *Loci Communes* (1521) and his *Apology of the Augsburg Confession* (1531). In this period of Melanchthon's thought, his soteriology was more closely aligned with that of Luther, which is why we treat them together in this section.

[54]On the reception of Augustine by Luther and Melanchthon, see especially the treatment of those Reformers' "affective Augustinianism" in Simeon Zahl, "The Bondage of the Affections: Willing, Feeling, and Desiring in Luther's Theology, 1513-25," in *The Spirit, the Affections, and the Christian Tradition*, ed. Dale M. Coulter and Amos Yong (Notre Dame: University of Notre Dame Press, 2016), 181-206; and Zahl, "Bondage of the Affections," 183-231.

The distinction appears in Luther's early writing and is tantamount to his "Protestant breakthrough."[55] For instance, in his 1517 *Disputation Against Scholastic Theology*, we read, "What the law wants, the will never wants, unless it pretends to want it out of fear or love." And again, a few lines down, "Every deed of the law without the grace of God appears good outwardly, but inwardly it is sin."[56] We observe the Pauline grammar of justification at work in the totality of the claims. The will "never" wants what the law wants, and "every" deed done apart from God's grace "is sin." A year later, in his *Heidelberg Disputation*, the lines are drawn even more clearly. "The law of God . . . cannot advance persons on their way to righteousness, but rather hinders them." "The law brings the wrath of God, kills, reviles, accuses, judges, and condemns everything that is not in Christ."[57] Again, we observe the categorical nature of the grammar at play: righteousness is something which the law "cannot" provide; "everything" not in Christ is utterly condemned, accused, judged, and ultimately killed by the law. We arrive at Luther's famous phrase: "The law says, 'Do this,' and it is never done. Grace says, 'Believe in this,' and everything is already done."[58]

Three years later, Melanchthon would take this distinguishing language and process it through Augustine's theology of the affections for a more existential rendering of the law-gospel distinction. Throughout his 1521 *Loci Communes* and later in his 1531 *Apology of the Augsburg Confession*, Melanchthon returns to the experiential language of the law, whose job it is to "terrify" and "confound," and the gospel, whose job it is to "comfort" and "console."[59] That Melanchthon sees this distinction as grammatical is manifested in how he explains the *hermeneutical* payoff of the distinction for interpreting the Bible:

> There are two parts of Scripture: Law and Gospel. The Law displays sin, the Gospel grace. The Law shows the disease, the Gospel the cure. To use the words

---

[55]Luther: "After I discovered the difference, that the law is one thing and the gospel is another, then I broke through." Quoted in Bayer, *Luther's Theology*, 58.

[56]Martin Luther, *Disputation Against Scholastic Theology*, theses 72 and 79, in Timothy F. Lull and William F. Russell, eds., *Martin Luther's Basic Theological Writings*, 3rd ed. (Minneapolis: Fortress, 2012), 6.

[57]Luther, *Heidelberg Disputation*, theses 1 and 23, in Lull and Russell, *Writings*, 15.

[58]Luther, *Heidelberg Disputation*, thesis 26, in Lull and Russell, *Writings*, 16.

[59]See esp. Simeon Zahl, "On the Affective Salience of Doctrines," *Modern Theology* 31, no. 3 (July 2015): 438-44. And notice here the echoes of Chrysostom, quoted above.

of Paul, the Law is the minister of death, the Gospel the minister of life and peace (2 Cor 3:7-10). "The power of sin is the law" (1 Cor 15:56), whereas, "The Gospel is the power of salvation for everyone who believes" (Rom 1:16). But Scripture has not handed down Law and Gospel in such a way that you should think that the Gospel is only what Matthew, Mark, Luke, and John wrote, or that the books of Moses are nothing but Law. Rather, the message of the Gospel is spread throughout all the books of the Old and New Testament.[60]

In the interpretation of Paul by Luther and Melanchthon, the distinction between law and gospel becomes the key to separating the gospel from not-gospels. Returning to the language used above, the law's job is to "erase the doing," utterly crucifying "all human criteria" that would seek to let a righteous deed stand on its own two feet. The law calls a supposedly righteous deed what it actually is—unrighteous, not worthy. It pushes works completely out of the realm of what pleases the Lord, leaving only faith. Faith, then, is freed to lay hold of that other word—the word of pure grace, the gospel.

Promise in Luther and Melanchthon. As hinted at in the previous chapter, central to the Reformation articulation of the Pauline grammar is the theology of promise, and its greatest champions were Luther and Melanchthon. Luther appears here to have run with Augustine's interpretation of Paul, for in Augustine we find this strong statement nestled in a passage where the bishop makes some of his sharpest distinctions between law and gospel: "God promises what he himself performs: he does not himself promise, and another perform; which would no longer be promising, but prophesying."[61] This theology of promise is anchored and amplified in one of Luther's most seminal texts, "On the Freedom of a Christian." There he distinguishes between faith and works and between law and gospel. In the latter distinction, he equates the gospel, the assurance of salvation, with the promise of God:

> How can it be that faith alone can make one righteous and can provide such superabundant riches apart from all works, when it is obvious that so many laws, commands, works, estates, and instructions are prescribed for us in Scripture? One ought to note here with diligence and to consider with all seriousness that faith alone, apart from all works, makes one righteous, free,

---

[60]Melanchthon, *Commonplaces*, 91.
[61]Augustine, *Spirit*, 39 (chap. 40).

and joyful, . . . and one must know that the entire Holy Scripture is to be divided into two words: the commandments or the law of God and the assurances or the *promises*. . . . When the human being learns about and has discovered his own powerlessness on the basis of the commandments, that there will be only fear about how he is to do enough of what is asked in the commandment. . . . Following upon this comes the other Word, the divine assurance and *promise*, which says: If you want to fulfill all the commandments, if you want to be free of your evil desires and sins, as the commandments pressure and demand, look here, believe in Christ, through whom I *promise* you all grace, righteousness, peace, and freedom. . . . This is what the *promises* of God provide, what the commandments demand.[62]

Central to the Reformation reading of Paul is pure, divine promise—unprompted, unconditioned. Indeed, this is the mutual exclusivity of the grammar of *sola fide* at work. The promise is God's eschatologically-loaded forgiving word, and faith hangs on that promise. For Luther, the idea of promise by definition excludes any notion that the recipient of the promise has prompted or motivated the gift.[63] Melanchthon would go on to say the same thing, as well, equating the promises with the gospel itself (and justification).[64] In the Reformation, then, promise is another terminological shorthand for the grammar of justification *sola fide*.

Comfort in Luther and Melanchthon. Another important word in the vocabulary of the Reformation was comfort. And while this word does not so much do the work of the Pauline grammar of justification, it appears as the fruit and necessary byproduct of the grammar's distinction-making work. In other words, when the grammar is operating, the *effect* is comfort. The idea of faith as a means of comfort is certainly not merely the property of Reformation Christianity. And yet, comfort as a chief emphasis is undoubtedly a Reformation priority largely previously unknown. According to

---

[62]Quoted in Bayer, *Luther's Theology*, 59-60; emphasis added; *n.b.* the affective language. Not only does justification make us righteous, it makes us "free, and joyful."

[63]For promise (*promissio*) as central in Luther, see especially Bayer, *Luther's Theology*, 44-67.

[64]See, for instance, Melanchthon's interpretation of Genesis: "This is the first promise, the first Gospel. By it Adam was consoled, and by it he conceived a sure hope of his salvation. Therefore, he was also justified. And then the promise was made to Abraham that his seed and all the nations would be blessed. Surely this promise could not be understood except concerning Christ. . . . These promises are clearly nothing other than the Gospel itself" (Melanchthon, *Commonplaces*, 93).

Eamon Duffy, "Horror and fear are the emotions most commonly associated with late medieval perceptions of death and the life everlasting, and preachers, dramatists, and moralists did not hesitate to employ terror—of death, of judgment, of the pains of hell or purgatory—to stir their audiences to penitence and good works."[65] The Reformation emphasis on the gospel as a means of comfort and assurance about death and the life to come could not be more opposite. It makes sense, therefore, that we find comfort a central theme in Luther. In fact, one of Luther's earliest Protestant disputations carries this title: *Disputation for Seeking the Truth and Comforting the Fearful Conscience* (1518).[66] Likewise, we find comfort all over the works of Melanchthon.[67] And as we noted above, it is only when the grammar is at work—when non-gospels (such as the law) can be distinguished from the gospel—that true comfort can result. Law not distinguished from gospel, or works not separated from faith, by necessity carries with it the hook, "you could always do more; you could always try harder." And there is no comfort in such a word. Law mixed with gospel collapses into pure law—which loses the gospel entirely. Faith mixed with works collapses into works-righteousness—which by definition loses faith entirely. One only finds comfort *in* the separation. In other words, the experience of comfort is a definite sign of the grammar of *sola fide* at work. When we observe comfort in Cranmer, therefore, we should see it as a telltale sign of the operation of justification by faith alone.

From the first century to the Reformation, we have attempted to trace a kind of theological pattern of speech whose commonality is less observable by shared vocabulary (though we've noted some terminological overlap) and more observable by a theological syntax we are calling a gospel-grammar. This commonality of thought emerges from the fact that all the above theologians were readers of Paul and shared at least a basic understanding that

---

[65]Eamon Duffy, *The Stripping of the Altars: Traditional Religion in England 1400–1580* (New Haven, CT: Yale University Press, 1992), 313-14.

[66]Latin: "*Pro veritate inquirenda et timoratis conscientiis consolandis conclusiones*," Martin Luther, *D. Martin Luthers Werke. Kritische Gesamtausgabe* (Weimar: Herman Böhlaus Nachfolger, 1883–2009), I.631, 33-34.

[67]See, for example, the employment of the term in the *Apology of the Augsburg Confession* throughout Article IV on justification; cf. Robert Kolb and Timothy J. Wengert, eds., *The Book of Concord: The Confessions of the Evangelical Lutheran Church* (Minneapolis: Fortress, 2000), 121, 127, 130, 139, 141, 149, 167, 168, 169, 172, 173.

justification by faith alone was a key concept for Paul when it came to the gospel of Jesus Christ and its proclamation. Justification *sola fide* is what helps distinguish the gospel from non-gospels and therefore is the gospel's great grammatical key. It is now time to turn to Cranmer to observe how all these same concepts are at play.

3

THE GRAMMAR OF
SOLA FIDE IN CRANMER

IN THE PREVIOUS chapter, we attempted to vindicate a Reformation reading of Paul—namely, that justification by faith alone is central to the apostle as a kind of grammar whose rules structure and boundary his theological interpretation of the Scriptures. We then traced that reading's "reception history" with special attention to Augustine, Luther, and Melanchthon. What we will argue in this chapter is that Cranmer found Paul's interpretation of the Bible decidedly persuasive. For the Archbishop, this reading of Scripture's most central message would unlock not only how to understand and receive the Word, but how to shape and guide the worship of the church.[1]

THE GRAMMAR OF *SOLA FIDE* IN CRANMER'S THEOLOGY AND LITURGY

The grammar in Cranmer's theological writing. Once the evidence is presented, despite nearly five centuries of wildly disparate biographical sketches

---

[1]Below, we are arguing for a very "Lutheran" Cranmer. This discussion focuses its arguments on the framework established, but there exist far more thorough treatments of the "Lutheran" Cranmer worth noting. Chiefly, Gil Kracke's dissertation ("Häuptartikel") most exhaustively outlines Cranmer's soteriology as Lutheran, and he has built on the work of Ashley Null, *Thomas Cranmer's Doctrine of Repentance: Renewing the Power to Love* (Oxford: Oxford University Press, 2000). If Cranmer indeed was soteriologically Lutheran, we are forced to reevaluate much of Anglicanism's current self-understanding as a via media between Rome and the Reformation. While by evolution this is now true of modern Anglicanism (for the Laudian, Tractarian, and Anglo-Catholic movements have decidedly had their impact), it at least cannot be claimed that such a notion was in the minds and hearts of Cranmer and the founders of the Church of England in the sixteenth century. Rather, at its founding, the Church of England might best be understood historically as a via media not between Protestantism and Roman Catholicism but between the Lutheran reformation (soteriology) and the Reformed reformation (sacramentology).

and theological interpretations of Thomas Cranmer,[2] it is hard to come away with any other reading of the Archbishop besides one that is fiercely Pauline in his understanding of the Scriptures, and particularly so as Paul is received through the interpretative lineage of Augustine and Luther.[3] The claim we are making is that the English reformer internalized the grammar of *sola fide* to such an extent that its "rules have become embedded in the speech textures"[4] of his mature theological and liturgical work. The difficulty in evaluating the evidence, however, is that unlike the other Protestant Reformers, as Linebaugh notes,

> Cranmer did not write a commentary. He wrote prayer books and sermons, kept extensive notebooks organizing the discoveries unearthed in the books in his famously vast library, offered marginal comments during the formative stages of what would be public documents, penned a preface to the Bible, maintained prolific correspondences with political players at court and religious Reformers on the Continent, . . . and engaged in (transcribed) debates related to the Lord's Supper and other topics du jour. This means that locating texts or passages that can be called readings of Paul is not as easy as pulling a commentary on Galatians or Romans off the shelf.[5]

Linebaugh goes on to observe the tense political climate under the vicissitudes of King Henry's theological-political whims, which often drove Cranmer's evangelical theology underground. It is not an overstatement to say that under Henry, to champion certain articulations of Protestant theology was to flirt

---

[2]See especially the history traced by Diarmaid MacCulloch, "Thomas Cranmer's Biographers," in *All Things Made New: The Reformation and Its Legacy* (Oxford: Oxford University Press, 2016), 256-78.

[3]There is perhaps no better proof of this claim than Gerlach Flicke's 1545 portrait of Cranmer (originally intended to be set in side-by-side contrast with his predecessor, William Warham), where the reformer is depicted with the Pauline epistles in hand and Augustine's *De fide et operibus* laid on the desk in front of him. See especially Ashley Null's expositions of this painting in *Repentance*, 84-85, 96-97, 102-3, 109-10; "Thomas Cranmer and Tudor Evangelicalism," in *The Emergence of Evangelicalism: Exploring Historical Continuities*, ed. Kenneth J. Stewart and Michael A. G. Haykin (Downers Grove, IL: InterVarsity Press, 2008), 236-38; "Thomas Cranmer's Reading of Paul's Letters," in *Reformation Readings of Paul*, ed. Michael Allen and Jonathan A. Linebaugh (Downers Grove, IL: InterVarsity Press, 2015), 211-13; and Null, "Thomas Cranmer's Reputation Reconsidered," in *Reformation Reputations: The Power of the Individual in English Reformation History*, ed. D. J. Crankshaw and G. W. C. Gross (London: Palgrave Macmillan, 2021), 189-94.

[4]See chap. 2, n9.

[5]Jonathan Linebaugh, "The Texts of Paul and the Theology of Cranmer," in *Reformation Readings of Paul: Explorations in History and Exegesis*, ed. Michael Allen and Jonathan A. Linebaugh (Downers Grove, IL: InterVarsity Press, 2015), 237.

with death. Notwithstanding these things, scholars are generally agreed that Cranmer's three 1547 homilies on salvation, faith, and good works "come closest to a sustained interpretation of Paul."[6] And if we allow Cranmer at this place to speak for himself, we notice the Pauline grammar clear as day, making distinctions of total exclusion:

> The grace of God doth not exclude the justice of God in our justification, but only *excludes the justice of man,* that is to say, the justice of our works as to be merits of deserving our justification. And therefore Saint Paul declareth here *nothing* upon the behalf of man concerning his justification, but *only* a true and lively faith. . . .
>
> If justice come of works, then it cometh not of grace; and if it come of grace, then it commeth not of works. . . .
>
> This proposition—that we be justified by faith *only,* freely, and *without* works— is spoken for to take away clearly *all* merit of our works . . . thereby *wholly* to ascribe the merit and deserving of our justification unto Christ *only.* . . .
>
> Justification is not the office of man, but of God. . . . Justification is the office of God *only,* and is not a thing which we render unto him, but which we receive of him, not which we give to him, but which we take of him by his free mercy and by the *only* merits of his most dearly beloved Son, our *only* redeemer, savior and justifier, Jesus Christ. . . .
>
> *Only* faith doth justify us.[7]

Observe here the terminology of categorical separation—"excludes," "nothing," "only," "without," "all," "wholly." In fact, "only" appears to be a critical word for Cranmer's understanding of the grammar of justification.[8] Beside the homilies, the next most poignant place to find Cranmer's understanding of the gospel is in his annotations on Henry's corrections to the Bishops' book, officially titled *Institution of a Christian Man* (1537),[9] where he

---

[6]Linebaugh, "Texts," 238. See also Packer, introduction to *The Work of Thomas Cranmer,* ed. G. E. Duffield (Philadelphia: Fortress, 1965), xxiii, and Ashley Null, "Salvation and Sanctification in the Book of Homilies," *The Reformed Theological Review* 62, no. 1 (April 2003): 14-28.

[7]Cranmer, "Of the Salvation of All Mankind," in *Certain Sermons or Homilies (1547) and A Homily Against Disobedience and Wilful Rebellion (1570): A Critical Edition,* ed. Roland B. Bond (Toronto: University of Toronto Press, 1987), 81-85; emphasis added.

[8]It is telling of the Reformation grammar that the single most important word to summarize its theological emphasis is *sola.*

[9]Indeed, scholarly consensus generally agrees that these 1537 annotations are the earliest record of Cranmer's mature understanding of justification; cf. e.g., Null, *Repentance,* 121; Gordon Jeanes,

boldly challenges Henry's theology chiefly by arguing for the necessity and right placement of that one word, "only." When presented with the Bishops' book for review, Henry sought to correct this sentence: "The penitent must conceive certain hope and faith that God will forgive him his sins, and repute him justified, and of the number of his elect children, not for the worthiness of any merit or work done by the penitent, but for the *only* merits of the blood and passion of our Saviour Jesus Christ." Henry's correction included changing the last two phrases: "Not *only* for the worthiness of any merit or work done by the penitent, but *chiefly* for the only merits of the blood and passion of our Saviour Jesus Christ." Cranmer responded to Henry's correction thus:

> "Only, chiefly." These two words may not be put in this place in any wise for they signify that our election and justification cometh partly of our merits, though chiefly it cometh of the goodness of God. But certain it is, that our election cometh only and wholly of the benefit and grace of God, for the merits of Christ's passion, and for no part of our merits and good works as St Paul disputeth and proveth at length in the epistle to the Romans and Galatians, and divers other places, saying, *Si ex operibus, non ex gratia; si ex gratia, non ex operibus.*[10]

Works and faith are distinguished and ordered. Here we see the grammar at work, saying no to the not-gospel of a salvation commingling works and faith, and yes to a gospel "wholly of the benefit and grace of God."

Even more explicit than this is Cranmer's exposition of spiritual hunger and thirst in his 1550 *Defence of the True and Catholic Doctrine of the Sacrament of the Body and Blood of Our Saviour Christ.*[11] As he begins to lay out his most complete understanding of the Lord's Supper, he frames spiritual hunger in terms of law and gospel:

> This earnest and great desire is called in Scripture the hunger and thirst of the soul. . . . And this hunger the silly, poor, sinful soul is driven unto by means of the law, which showeth unto her the horribleness of sin, the terror

---

Signs of God's Promise: Thomas Cranmer's Sacramental Theology and the Book of Common Prayer (London: T&T Clark, 2008), 63.

[10]John Edmund Cox, ed., *The Works of Thomas Cranmer,* vol. 2 (Cambridge: The University Press, 1846), 95.

[11]Cranmer brilliantly ties together Ps 42; Mt 5:6; Lk 1:53; Jn 4; Jn 6; Mt 11:28; Jn 7; and Gal 2:20.

of God's indignation, and the horror of death and everlasting damnation. And when she seeth nothing but damnation for her offences by justice and accusation of the law, and this damnation is ever before her eyes; then, in this great distress, the soul being pressed with heaviness and sorrow seeketh for some comfort, and desireth some remedy for her miserable and sorrowful estate. . . . The meat, drink, food, and refreshing of the soul, is our Saviour Christ; as he said himself: "Come unto me all you that travail and be laden, and I will refresh you." . . . For there is no other kind of meat that is comfortable to the soul, but only the death of Christ's blessed body. . . . And as the body liveth by meat and drink, and thereby increaseth and growth from a young babe unto a perfect man, . . . so the soul liveth by Christ himself, by pure faith. . . . And this St. Paul confessed of himself saying, "That I have life, I have it by faith in the Son of God. And now it is not I that live, but Christ liveth in me."[12]

Here we see all the themes we have been observing gathered in one place: the explicit distinction between law and gospel, the separation out of a "pure faith," the affective fruit of the grammar in "terror" and "comfort," and even a concluding summary punctuated with Galatians 2:20.[13]

The grammar in Cranmer's liturgy as generally observed by scholars. Certain scholars, whether or not they are familiar with terminology and nuances of our articulation of the grammar of the gospel, have observed the grammar at work in Cranmer's liturgies. For instance, without explicit

---

[12]Cox, *Works*, vol. 1, 38-40. Notice here the connection between a very Pauline-Augustinian-Lutheran soteriology and a scriptural passage which would become Cranmer's unique contribution to the Reformation liturgies' newly minted "Comfortable Words." Though the usage of Comfortable Words in the Communion liturgy predates Cranmer, the Archbishop appears to be one of the first to employ Mt 11:28, but see comments below on Zwingli's earlier use in chap. 4, under "'Not I, But Christ Structurally: Holy Communion (1552)," in the section titled, "On the positioning and use of the Comfortable Words and Absolution."

[13]All this calls into question the conclusion of Basil Hall who criticized Peter Brooks's assessment of Cranmer's theology by arguing that Brooks confused the locus "faith" with the locus of "justification by faith." In Hall's words, "Cranmer wrote that our justification could be confirmed and enlarged through the renewal of the knowledge of forgiveness of sins at the Eucharist, as did Luther, but not that justification *sola fide* was the means to this nor was it the basic principle of the sacrament" (Basil Hall, "Cranmer, the Eucharist and the Foreign Divines in the Reign of Edward VI," in *Thomas Cranmer: Churchman and Scholar*, ed. Paul Ayris and David Selwyn [Woodbridge: The Boydle Press, 1993], 257). If what we have argued and will argue is true, then the distinction Hall makes between "faith" and "justification by faith" (not only in Cranmer, but in Luther, Melanchthon, Augustine, and Paul) does not hold. Against Hall, we are arguing that justification *sola fide* actually *is* "the basic principle of the sacrament."

reference to either Augustine or the Reformers, Stephen Sykes summarizes Cranmer's liturgies as gathered around the central motif of the "ascent of the heart."[14] He describes the aim of Cranmer thus: "So we uncover an ambivalence: an ecclesiastical demand for repentance from the bottom of the heart; and a theological and psychological perception that the knowledge of what lies in the depths is possible only to God."[15] What Sykes is observing in this "ambivalence" is that Cranmer's liturgy is always speaking two words to worshipers: a word that makes impossible demands; and a word that places the possibility of meeting those demands solely in the hands of God. In Reformation language, Sykes is observing in the *effects* of the liturgy the distinction between law and gospel, the separation of works and faith—in fact, the grammar of *sola fide*. Sykes recognizes that at the center of this work in the heart lies the doctrine of repentance. He points out that in the liturgy, Cranmer chooses his scriptural quotations and allusions ultimately "to illustrate and teach the evangelical doctrine of the completeness of divine forgiveness."[16]

J. I. Packer similarly observes the grammar at work in his summary of Cranmer's liturgical agenda. He argues that the Archbishop "rooted the doctrine [of justification] in two basic realities. The first is man's sinfulness and impotence to do God's will, which brings him into a state of failure, guilt, and condemnation. . . . The second reality is God's mercy to sinners, the measure of which is his gift of his son to be crucified for them."[17] Much like Sykes, Packer is observing the work of God's two words—law and gospel—in the Cranmerian liturgy, even naming those specific categories.[18]

---

[14]Stephen Sykes, "Cranmer on the Open Heart," in *This Sacred History: Anglican Reflections for John Booty*, ed. Donald S. Armentrout (Cambridge: Cowley, 1990), 1-20.

[15]Sykes, "Open Heart," 7.

[16]Sykes, "Open Heart," 7.

[17]Packer, "Introduction," xxiv.

[18]Ibid., xxvi. Though Packer's preferred paradigm is to speak of cycles of "sin-grace-faith." See also J. I. Packer, *The Gospel in the Prayer Book* (Downers Grove, IL: InterVarsity Press, 2021), 4-11: Samuel Leuenberger analyzes Cranmer according to Packer's themes, as well in *Archbishop Cranmer's Immortal Bequest: The Book of Common Prayer of the Church of England: An Evangelistic Liturgy* (Eugene, OR: Wipf & Stock, 1990), 105-19. These cycles, as we will observe later, are quite compatible with a law-gospel framework, and Leuenberger does specifically mention law and gospel in relation to Peter Martyr's (Reformed) influence (see 24-25). But very little attention or connection is drawn to Augustine or Luther (much more to Calvin and Peter Martyr), and none is given to Melanchthon.

Sylvia A. Sweeney[19] and Gavin Dunbar[20] observe and expand upon Packer's insights, revealing just how pervasive this pattern is in Cranmer's liturgical work.

The work of Ashley Null is by far the most extensive, both in breadth of sources studied and in depth of theology processed. Null argues, convincingly and systematically, for what we have been stating above: Cranmer's soteriology was that of Paul in the tradition of Augustine under heavy influence of contemporaneous Lutheran thought.[21] Though Null does not speak in terms of the (Pauline, Augustinian, and Lutheran) grammar of *sola fide*, what he culls from Cranmer is without a doubt the selfsame outlook. Particularly impressive is the amount of content and intricate organization of thought discovered in Cranmer's personal notebooks, which Null calls "Cranmer's Great Commonplaces." There we discover that not only was Cranmer a serious exegete of Scripture, he was also a dedicated student of the church fathers, East and West.[22]

---

[19]Sylvia A. Sweeney, *An Ecofeminist Perspective on Ash Wednesday and Lent* (New York, NY: Peter Lang, 2010), 107-121, observes the sin-grace-faith structure permeating Cranmer's reformed Ash Wednesday liturgy, which by 1552 he calls "A Commination Against Sinners" (Ketley, *Liturgies,* 323-327).

[20]Gavin Dunbar, "Like Eagles in this Life: A Theological Reflection on 'The Order for the Administration of the Lord's Supper or Holy Communion' in the Prayer Books of 1559 and 1662," in *The Book of Common Prayer: Past, Present and Future,* ed. Prudence Dailey (New York, NY: Continuum, 2011), 86-89. Dunbar uses the language of "repentance, faith, and works" (87), referencing a 2006 sermon of Rowan Williams which notes how this triad cycles in a "spiral movement" (88). Special thanks to Samuel L. Bray, whose article, "Ashes in a Time of Plague," *The North American Anglican,* January 6, 2021, accessed July 9, 2022, https://northamanglican.com/ashes-in-a-time-of-plague/, pointed me to the work of Sweeney and Dunbar.

[21]Null, *Repentance.*

[22]See esp. the appendix in Null, *Repentance,* 254-78. Null's conclusion, refuting K. J. Walsh whose article ("Cranmer and the Fathers"), which argued for a Cranmer who rather carelessly proof-texted patristic sources to bolster his Protestant positions, appears to have held sway for around two decades: "The suggestion [by Walsh] that Cranmer's scholarly method relied on patristic gobbets for proof-texting rather than undertaking systematic study of the fathers must be revised" (Null, *Repentance,* 268). Null's more recent study of the notebooks of Cranmer's secretary, Pierre Alexandre, who was tasked with creating massive, indexed epitomes of the works of the major early church theologians, reveals that Cranmer's study of the Fathers was even more comprehensive than we realized. Those manuscripts are Bibliothèque nationale de France Latin MSS 3396, 624, and 1647. Null describes the contents of these manuscripts in his lecture, "Cranmer in Context: The Patristic Sources for his Theology under Henry VIII," given at Nashotah House Theological Seminary on October 2, 2019. The lecture is found here: www.youtube.com /watch?v=Eta5hHZSNQs&t=828s.

KEY CONCEPTS FOR THE GRAMMAR
OF SOLA FIDE IN CRANMER

"Assisting grace" in Cranmer. It is clear that Cranmer, like Luther, Mel-anchthon, and Calvin, heavily favored Augustine among the church fathers: the Archbishop's writings are liberally littered with references to the Bishop of Hippo; his notebooks are filled with lengthy extracts of Augustine's works; and his commissioned portrait by Gerlach Flicke[23] testifies to the centrality of Augustine in his thought. Cranmer's usage of the phrase "assisting grace" very much echoes Augustine, especially when we note the surrounding context: like Augustine, assisting grace is used as a shorthand in conversations surrounding justification by faith alone as a distinction-making grammar. In his Homily on Scripture, the tone is set in the begin-ning about what Cranmer perceives the thrust of the Bible to be: it is "necessary for our justification" and a "perpetual instrument of salvation."[24] Shortly after, the Scriptures are said to "have power to convert through God's promise and they be effectual through God's *assistance*." This assis-tance, for Cranmer, factors specifically in the work of God's Word in Holy Communion. At the table, we are edified by the effectual word, says Cran-mer, "wherein the ministry of the church travaileth to bring man to perfec-tion in Christ, which Christ himself doth *assist*, and absolutely perform in his church, his mystical body."[25]

Liturgically, Ashley Null points out that the idea of assistance is particularly strong in Cranmer when it comes to living the Christian life, as if to say, even good works done *after* conversion can only be done by Christ's "assistance," that is, in Christ and by the power of the Holy Spirit.[26] Though this

---

[23]See chap. 3, n3.

[24]Cranmer, "A Fruitful Exhortation to the Reading and Knowledge of Holy Scripture," in Bond, *Sermons,* 62; English modernized. Diarmaid MacCulloch notes that, though we do not know for certain, Cranmer's composition of this homily is probable. See MacCulloch, *Thomas Cranmer: A Life* (New Haven, CT: Yale University Press, 1996), 372.

[25]Cranmer, "An Answer to a Crafty and Sophistical Cavillation devised by Stephen Gardiner," in Cox, *Works,* vol. 1, 83.

[26]This is where the soteriology of Cranmer and the Reformers departs from Augustine. For the Reformers, even good works done after initial justification are still the work of God through faith, because in their understanding of Paul, initial and final justification are wrapped up in the same event—the entire justification secured at the cross of Christ. For Augustine, assisting grace works with the believer after initial justification such that one's future final justification, which as yet remains to be rendered, will be secured.

pneumatological theme does not specifically use the term "assist," Null notes this as a "special grace" of "supernatural assistance" which "runs as a red thread through Cranmer's collects."[27] The striking usage of the assistance of grace, however, is chiefly found in one pivotal liturgical moment: the post-Communion prayer. There, having received the bread and wine, the believer prays, "We now most humbly beseech thee, O heavenly father, so to *assist us with thy grace* that we may continue in that holy fellowship, and do all such good works, as thou hast prepared for us to walk in: through Jesus Christ our Lord."[28] At this doxological zenith, we find even here the grammar of *sola fide* distinguishing faith from works: post-conversion works are works done "through Jesus Christ." Heralded by the Augustinian construction of assisting grace, we hear quite clearly the grammar at work via the radical disjunctive, "Not I, but Christ."

That Cranmer's understanding of assisting grace here in the Communion liturgy is totalizing and disjunctive is evident especially when one juxtaposes this post-Communion statement of "assistance" alongside his most stark statement in the Confession of Morning Prayer: "There is *no health* in us" (a quotation of Ps 38:3). For Cranmer, grace does not assist an already healthy or partially healthy individual. Grace assists the *ungodly*—the person with *no* health.[29]

---

[27]Null, "Thomas Cranmer and the Anglican Way of Reading Scripture," *Anglican and Episcopal History* 75, no. 4 (2006): 510-11. In an email to the author on December 28, 2021, Null summarized Cranmer's medieval context which elucidates how "pneumatologically-loaded" the grace-centered collects are, even as they do not mention the Spirit by name: "From a Protestant view, Grace is an attribute of God's character. From a traditionalist, liturgical point-of-view, grace is the function of the Holy Spirit at work in the individual. . . . In scholastic theology, there are two kinds of graces, Uncreated Grace, i.e., the Holy Spirit, and Created graces, e.g., sanctifying grace, which is the power of God at work in an individual." (Logically the scholastics could not accept that the infinite, i.e., the Holy Spirit, could be confined in the finite, i.e., a human being, so a theory of a form of the Holy Spirit that could be within a human being was developed, i.e., sanctifying grace.) So if you read grace as the power of the Holy Spirit at work in human beings, you find the Holy Spirit throughout Cranmer's Collects. This will be an important insight given what we will argue below, esp. in chap. 3, n48.

[28]Joseph Ketley, ed., *The Two Liturgies, A.D. 1549, and A.D. 1552* (Cambridge: Parker Society, 1844), 280.

[29]For an excellent treatment of pneumatology, Christian experience, transformation, and how justifying grace operates in them with a "strongly disjunctive character"—a discussion which I believe fleshes out, in modern theological conversation, Cranmer's own Augustinian perspective here—see Simeon Zahl, "The Bondage of the Affections: Willing, Feeling, and Desiring in Luther's Theology, 1513-25," in *The Spirit, the Affections, and the Christian Tradition*, ed. Dale M. Coulter and Amos Yong (Notre Dame, IN: University of Notre Dame Press, 2016), 183-231.

Promise in Cranmer. We now turn to the strains of promise-language permeating Cranmer's theological and liturgical work. The centrality of promise very much mirrors Luther and Melanchthon. In the Homily on Salvation, Cranmer speaks of the promises of God in the context of the faith-works distinction: "Because faith doth directly send us to Christ for remission of our sins, and that by faith given us of God, we embrace the promise of God's mercy and of the remission of our sins, which thing none other of our virtues or works properly doth, therefore Scripture useth to say that faith without works doth justify."[30]

The Homily on Faith spends its first half distinguishing between faith and works and then moves on to quote Augustine and Chrysostom, after which Cranmer illustrates the doctrine using the language of how Abraham trusted and laid hold of the "promise" of God.[31] In a letter to Henry in 1536, Cranmer refers to the gospel as "promise."[32] Ashley Null aptly summarizes the evangelical promise-theology of Cranmer in this way: "Cranmer anchored hope for forgiveness in the *promise* of God's Word, rather than the depth of human penitence. In Scripture God said he would justify penitent sinners who put their trust in him to forgive their sins for Christ's sake. Those who *pondered the benefits of this promise* developed 'a firm trust and feeling of God's mercy.'"[33]

Null's findings in Cranmer's Great Commonplaces corroborate that this promise-theology stood at the center of the Archbishop's reflections on Paul, Augustine, and the faith-works distinction. Evidently the third section of the Cranmer's notes contain heavy "extracts from the anti-Pelagian works of Augustine," including a grouping of quotations of the church fathers in support of Protestant Reformed interpretation of Augustine's soteriology, all gathered around the theme of "praising God and praying to him for those things which he has *promised*."[34]

It is most telling, however, to observe where the language of promise appears in Cranmer's liturgies, especially when we recognize that such language was not present in the prior liturgies which made up the source material

---

[30]Cranmer, "Salvation," 85; English modernized.
[31]Cranmer, "A Short Declaration of the True, Lively, and Christian Faith," in Bond, *Sermons,* 94.
[32]Cox, *Works,* vol. 2, 324.
[33]Null, *Repentance,* 125; emphasis added.
[34]Null, *Repentance,* 262, 264-65; emphasis added.

for the Book of Common Prayer. The language of promise makes its liturgical debut at the high point of the gospel—the confession and words of pardon in both the Holy Communion and Morning Prayer liturgies. We observe in the words of pardon in Holy Communion that Cranmer did not merely translate the Sarum Mass text into English. He added both the language of promise and its content (see fig. 3.1).[35]

SARUM (HOLY COMMUNION)	1549 BOOK OF COMMON PRAYER
Almighty God	Almighty God,
	our heavenly father, who of his great mercy hath promised forgiveness of sins to all them, which with hearty repentance and true faith, turn unto him:
have mercy upon you, pardon and deliver you from all your sins.	have mercy upon you, pardon and deliver you from all your sins,
	confirm and strengthen you in all goodness, and bring you to everlasting life: through Jesus Christ our Lord. Amen.

Figure 3.1. The Holy Communion words of pardon compared

Similarly, nestled into Cranmer's original composition of Morning Prayer's Confession (1552) is an anchoring appeal to the promises of God, said by the "whole congregation":

> Almighty and most merciful Father, we have erred and strayed from thy ways, like lost sheep. We have followed too much the devices and desires of our own hearts. We have offended against thy holy laws. We have left undone those things which we ought to have done, and we have done those things which we ought not to have done, and there is no health in us: but thou, O Lord, have

---

[35]See the comments on the connection between the Holy Communion Absolution and "promise" in Stephen Sykes, "Baptisme Doth Represente unto Us Oure Profession," in *Thomas Cranmer: Essays in Commemoration of the 500th Anniversary of His Birth*, ed. Margot Johnson (Durham: Turnstone, 1990), 140. This comparison, including the translation of the Latin, is made in Andrew Atherstone, "The Lord's Supper and the Gospel of Salvation: Grace Alone and Faith Alone in the Book of Common Prayer," in *Feed My Sheep: The Anglican Ministry of Word and Sacrament*, ed. Lee Gatiss (Watford: Lost Coin Books, 2016): 93.

mercy upon us miserable offenders. Spare thou them, O God, which confess their faults. Restore thou them that be penitent, *according to thy promises declared* unto mankind, in Christ Jesus our Lord.[36]

In Cranmer's principal liturgies, promise takes center stage with (and as) the gospel, heretofore unparalleled in preceding Christian rites. It is also noteworthy that, right out of the gate of Cranmer's liturgical production, in his first piece of official English liturgy—the 1544 Litany—the opening exhortation announces a God who "hath bounden himself by his own free promise, and certified us by the same, by his own Son, our only Saviour and Lord Christ Jesus."[37]

Comfort in Cranmer. Even more prominent than the language of promise is the language of comfort in Cranmer's writings.[38] The term saturates Cranmer's short Homily on Scripture as a predominant purpose of the Word of God. The Bible "giveth wisdom to the humble and lowly hearts; it comforteth, maketh glad, cheereth, and cherisheth our consciences."[39] The homily makes clear that comfort is not simply a work of the Bible in general but of the gospel in particular.

Liturgically, that comfort is an important theological concept for Cranmer is revealed in the prevalence of the language of "comfort and console" in the 1544 Litany. There, in the short exhortation before the Litany proper, those words are used three times.[40] Similarly, Cranmer's freshly composed Collect for the second Sunday in Advent (1549) encourages that as we "read, mark, learn, and inwardly digest" the Scriptures, we receive the "comfort of thy holy Word."[41] Yet when the choice is presented, Cranmer appears at times to have

---

[36]Ketley, *Liturgies,* 218, 219; emphasis added.

[37]J. Eric Hunt, *Cranmer's First Litany, 1544 and Merbecke's Book of Common Prayer Noted, 1550* (London: SPCK, 1939), 68.

[38]This will be the final terminological and conceptual connection drawn in tracing the Pauline grammar from the apostle, through the Fathers and Reformers, to Cranmer. Space does not here permit some other possible avenues of research, but in my studies I found the concepts of will-heart and service-freedom to be two additional points of connection between Cranmer and his predecessors. On the former, I found significant Ashley Null's article, "Thomas Cranmer's Theology of the Heart," *Anvil* 23, no. 2 (2006): 207-17. On the latter, insights can be culled from David Evett, "Luther, Cranmer, Service, and Shakespeare," in *Centered on the Word: Literature, Scripture, and the Tudor-Stuart Middle Way,* ed. Daniel W. Doerksen and Christopher W. Hodgkins (Newark: University of Delaware, 2004), 87-109.

[39]Cranmer, "Scripture," in Bond, *Sermons,* 62.

[40]"Comfort" by itself is used once. "Comfort and consolation," as a pair, is used twice.

[41]Ketley, *Liturgies,* 42.

deliberately chosen "comfort" even over synonyms like "consolation." We see this, for instance, when we set side-by-side the preceding source-prayers for Cranmer's Collect for Whitsunday (fig. 1.1). There we note that both preceding primers of 1530 and 1545 contain the word "consolation," and Cranmer, in full knowledge of those translations, opts for the language of "rejoice in his holy *comfort.*"

Sacramentally, Cranmer is clear that the purpose of Holy Communion is comfort. In fact, in February 1537, Cranmer delivered a speech to the Assembly of Bishops as they prepared to discuss the sacraments. He set the tone by reminding them of the more "weighty controversies," which in his mind centered not on the sacraments themselves, but on justification. His articulation there is one of the most powerful summaries of his understanding of the comforting power of Paul's distinction-making theology:

> There be weighty controversies now moved and put forth, not of ceremonies and light things, but of the true understanding of the *right difference of the law and the gospel,* of the manner and way how sins be forgiven, of *comforting doubtful and wavering consciences* by what means they may be certified that they please God, seeing they feel *the strength of the law accusing them of sin,* of the true use of the sacraments, whether the outward work of them doth justify man, or whether we receive our *justification through faith.*[42]

Following suit with this clear statement, Cranmer's liturgies speak explicitly and extensively of Holy Communion's objective of comfort. It is hard to appreciate just how emphatic this objective is for Cranmer until we recognize that the medieval liturgy on which Cranmer's were based—the Sarum rite—only uses "*consolationem*" one time throughout the entire service.[43] By

---

[42] Alesius, *Auctorite,* sig. A8; *De authoritate,* 21-22. The speech is also recorded in Cox, *Works,* vol. 2, 79. For a good summary of this event, see Null, "The Authority of Scripture in Reformation Anglicanism: Then and Now," in *Contesting Orthodoxies in the History of Christianity: Essays in Honour of Diarmaid MacCulloch,* ed. Ellie Gebarowski-Shafer, Ashley Null, and Alec Ryrie (Woodbridge: Boydell, 2021), 82-83; for context and dating, see also Null, *Repentance,* 133 (esp. n52); and MacCulloch, *Cranmer,* 188ff.

[43] It is used at the moment of Absolution: "*Absolutionem et remissionem omnium peccatorum vestrorum, spatium verae poenitentiae et emendationem vitae, gratiam et consolationem sancti Spiritus, tribuat vobis omnipotens et misericors Dominus*" (Absolution and remission of all your sins, space for true repentance, amendment of life, grace, and the *consolation* of the Holy Spirit, the Almighty and merciful God grant to you). From William Maskell, *The Ancient Liturgy of the Church of England,* 3rd ed. (Oxford: Clarendon, 1882), 18.

contrast, Cranmer's 1549 liturgy uses the word "comfort" nine times, and "consolation" once. For instance, punctuating the first exhortation of the 1549 eucharistic liturgy is that Communion exists to preach the gospel to us "to our endless comfort and consolation."[44] The second exhortation reiterates this by calling communion "the most comfortable Sacrament of the body and blood of Christ."[45]

More centrally, even modern Anglicans still recognize this pillar of the Cranmerian liturgy—the Comfortable Words. The source material for the Comfortable Words is noteworthy as it appears that Cranmer made a decision at this liturgical moment to use explicitly the language of comfort. While it has been shown that the usage of similar groupings of Scripture sentences in the eucharistic liturgies is a Reformation innovation, not all Reformation liturgies before Cranmer introduced those sentences in the same way. Some liturgies introduced the Comfortable Words with the language, "*audite evangelium*" ("hear the gospel"). Other liturgies were more specific: "*höret den Evangelischen Trost*" ("hear the gospel *comfort*").[46] Our case for a Lutheran-Melanchthonian grammar of *sola fide* is only bolstered when we add to all these observations that "conscience" appears with similar frequency.[47]

---

[44]Ketley, *Liturgies*, 80.

[45]Ketley, *Liturgies*, 216.

[46]This observation of John Dowden was rearticulated and clarified in Geoffrey Cuming, *The Godly Order: Texts and Studies Relating to the Book of Common Prayer* (London: SPCK, 1983), 80. NB that Cranmer's source liturgies were both Latin and German. For more on the background of the Comfortable Words, see below chap. 4, under "'Not I, But Christ Structurally: Holy Communion (1552)," in the section titled, "On the positioning and use of the Comfortable Words and Absolution."

[47]Perhaps speculative, it is interesting that Cranmer's novel addition to the marriage service includes a listing of the benefits of marriage, one of which was comfort. It is as though Cranmer was saying, among other things, that marriage becomes for us a picture of the gospel itself. In his liturgical work, Cranmer often appears to liberally expand on received liturgies where there might be a chance to expound the gospel. Cranmer's addition here also makes sense of his own appropriation of Erasmus's positive view of the affective benefits of marriage toward godliness against the more negative perspective (in tandem with clerical celibacy) that had dominated medieval thought for at least a thousand years prior. On this, see relevant passages in Ashley Null, *The Word of God and its Efficacy in Thomas Cranmer: New Insights into his Sources and Mature Thought* (Oxford: Oxford University Press, forthcoming). Worth noting at the end of this section is the theological connection between comfort and pneumatology. Not a few modern liturgiologists have criticized Cranmer and the other Reformation liturgies for being devoid of the Holy Spirit (and therefore functionally binitarian). For instance, in a paper delivered to the Evangelical Theological Society in 2014, Frank Lyons charged, "Where does the Spirit go? He is mentioned only infrequently and as such is very much in the background. . . . The lack of reference to the Spirit is because the Reformers are wont to remove any attention from Jesus and his effective sacrifice, and they value a direct encounter

In conclusion, we have sought to establish this critical idea: justification *sola fide* is not best understood as one of many Pauline soteriological images, nor is it even best described as the center of Paul's thought. Instead, justification functions criteriologically as a gatekeeper for what passes as gospel against competing non-gospels. In making proper distinctions of an exclusive and categorical nature, *sola fide* functions as a theological grammar, governing how theology is constructed according to the gospel. And we noted that Paul's paradigm of "not I, but Christ" will be a uniquely suitable shorthand for investigating the grammar in Cranmer's liturgy. We traced briefly how this interpretation of the Pauline grammar of *sola fide* appeared in the Fathers—especially Augustine—and was then received and reiterated by Luther and Melanchthon at the time of the Reformation. This all gave us a lens through which to more clearly observe Cranmer's own central commitment to this same theological distinctive as he did theology according to the grammatical rules of *sola fide* generally in his writing. We are moving toward this conclusion: if we are to receive well Cranmer's work *in* his day, to be

---

with God without magical or mystical properties that can be misunderstood" ("Critiquing Cranmer: *Ordo* and Ecclesial Identity," *Evangelical Theological Society* 66 [November 2014]: 5). Similarly, Paul Bradshaw heralds the "rediscovery of the Holy Spirit" in modern liturgical work ("The Rediscovery of the Holy Spirit in Modern Eucharistic Theology and Practice," in *The Spirit in Worship—Worship in the Spirit,* ed. Teresa Berger and Bryan D. Spinks [Collegeville, MN: Pueblo, 2009], 79-98). Additionally, in speaking of the Spirit in Cranmer's sacramental theology, Gordon Jeanes laments that "the Spirit is so totally subsumed to [Cranmer's] Christocentric emphasis" (*Signs*, 156). And yet, Cranmer seems to have understood biblically that comfort was a particular function of the Holy Spirit (cf. Acts 9:31). In Cranmer's day, the common English translation of John 15:26's παράκλητος was "comforter" (1537 Matthew Bible). Cranmer's Confirmation rite acknowledges the "Holy Ghost the Comforter." Cuming observes this when he says that "the substitution of 'comfort' for 'consolation' provides both a stronger word and a link with 'the Holy Ghost,' the 'Comforter'" (Geoffrey Cuming, "Thomas Cranmer: Translator and Writer," in *Language and the Worship of the Church,* ed. David Jasper and R. C. D. Jasper [New York: St. Martin's Press, 1990], 111). All these observations and more lead us more readily to the conclusion offered by Packer, namely that one of Cranmer's top concerns in the liturgy "was to do justice to the ministry of the Holy Spirit, as the one who mediates experimental knowledge of the presence, power, and grace of Jesus Christ to the people of God. The *Institution*, the Prayer Book, and Cranmer's weighty and glowing expositions of Christ's spiritual presence at the sacrament . . . all testify to this concern" ("Introduction," xxxiv). In light of this, I appreciate *BCP 2019* for its slight but (in light of this discussion) significant shift in the language of the vows made by parents and Godparents at baptism. Whereas the *BCP 1979* responds, "I will, with God's help" (*BCP 1979*, 302, 304-305), *BCP 2019* more clearly alludes to (if not names, though the word isn't capitalized) the Holy Spirit: "I am, the Lord being my *helper*" (*BCP 2019*, 163, 165). Apparently, this shift toward greater pneumatological clarity was accidental, as I directly asked the Rt. Rev. Robert Duncan (who oversaw the formulation and publishing of *BCP 2019*) about the change in a class on the Prayer Book through Trinity School for Ministry (June 7-8, 2021).

gospel-centered in worship and liturgy in *our* day is to do in particular this kind of parsing, sifting, and separating. We want the following chapters to observe this five-hundred-year-old work in detail perhaps in order to gain a more timeless model for critiquing worship and liturgy through the grammar of *sola fide*.

Early in the previous chapter, we noted Linebaugh's statement of how justification serves as an "evangelical gold-pan" whose filter's mesh is finely woven to sift the gospel from non-gospels. As we turn to part two, what we hope to observe is that, among the sixteenth-century Reformers, Thomas Cranmer may very well be the era's liturgical master panhandler.

PART 2

CRANMER'S GOSPEL-CENTERED THEOLOGY APPLIED: ANALYSIS OF WORSHIP ACCORDING TO THE BOOK OF COMMON PRAYER

4

"NOT I, BUT CHRIST"
STRUCTURALLY

SOLA FIDE IN CRANMER'S LITURGICAL FORM

WE BEGIN PART TWO utilizing an admittedly broad brush as we paint two portraits of Cranmer's successive Edwardian liturgies: the 1549 Book of Common Prayer applied *sola fide* to the content of the liturgy,[1] while the 1552 Prayer Book applied *sola fide* more thoroughly to the liturgy's structure.[2] This observation alone speaks into contemporary conversations about "gospel-centered worship," where the lion's share of the dialogue tends to be about the content of our worship services—song lyrics, prayers, and preaching all centered on Jesus Christ and his finished work. Less often do we hear talk of how the structure of a worship service is or is not "in line with the truth of the gospel" (Gal 2:14). Yet when it came to fidelity to the gospel, the structure of the liturgy seems to have been just as important as the content in Cranmer's construction of the Book of Common Prayer. What we will observe is that the grammatical rules of *sola fide* may have been what necessitated for Cranmer a restructuring of the liturgy's order. In other words, the gospel had something to say to (and in) worship's sequence of events.

---

[1]Ashley Null, "Thomas Cranmer's Theology of the Heart," *Anvil* 23, no. 2 (2006): 210: "The 1549 Prayer Book insisted on English as the language of the liturgy, institutionalized the systematic reading of Scripture, *removed all references to personal merit* and emphasized a eucharistic sacrifice of praise and thanksgiving"; emphasis added.

[2]Null, "Thomas Cranmer," in *Christian Theologies of the Sacraments: A Comparative Introduction*, ed. Justin S. Holcomb and David A. Johnson (New York: New York University Press, 2017), 227: "The 1549 Book of Common Prayer removed all references to personal merit and emphasized a eucharistic sacrifice of praise and thanksgiving only. The 1552 Prayer Book, however, broke up the traditional order of the prayers in the Canon of the Mass so that the thanksgiving of the people was now their response to the grace received with the elements, not its grounds."

What we are attempting to argue is that the structure of a worship service—i.e., the ordering of events in how a worshiper approaches God—either proclaims the gospel or mutes (and therefore loses) the gospel, and that justification by faith alone norms whether that gospel-proclamation has been a success or a failure. Whether or not Cranmer would have articulated what was just said in that way, we will now observe that this appears to be his method for liturgical redaction to such a degree that J. I. Packer could call the 1552 Prayer Book "the gospel of justification in liturgical *form*."[3]

"NOT I, BUT CHRIST" STRUCTURALLY: MORNING PRAYER (1552)

The Morning and Evening Prayer services were Cranmer's liturgical answer to the Sarum Breviary.[4] That rite of Salisbury was his baseline and reference point. Condensing the eight Daily Offices of Sarum into two,[5] what we observe in Cranmer's work is not merely redaction-as-shortening. Instead, the Archbishop takes the opportunity to restructure. Observe the morning Hours set side-by-side with Cranmer's rite (see fig. 4.1).

SARUM BREVIARY, 1085[6]	MORNING PRAYER, 1552
(Matins—before daybreak)	
The Lord's Prayer Hail Mary	Opening Sentence* Exhortation*

---

[3]Packer, introduction to *The Work of Thomas Cranmer*, ed. G. E. Duffield (Philadelphia: Fortress, 1965), xxvi; emphasis added.

[4]We take for granted what is unfortunately still contested in some conversations, namely, that the 1552 Prayer Book best represents Cranmer's mature Protestant theology, and that the 1549 Prayer Book was a pastorally-motivated mid-point between the medieval Roman liturgies and the more thoroughgoing Reformation liturgy of 1552.

[5]"Sarum" refers to the medieval liturgical rites originating out of Salisbury, whose use was perhaps more widespread in England than any other region's liturgies (e.g., York, Hereford). A "breviary" is a book containing services for each day (i.e., Daily Office). Matins, Lauds, and Prime were condensed into Morning Prayer, and Vespers and Prime were condensed into Evening Prayer, while Terce, Sext, and None (the shorter midday offices) were left out altogether. See Anthony Gelston, "Cranmer and the Daily Services," in *Thomas Cranmer: Essays in Commemoration of the 500th Anniversary of His Birth*, ed. Margot Johnson (Durham: Turnstone, 1990), 61.

[6]This order is reproduced from Charles Neil and J. M. Willoughby, *The Tutorial Prayer Book: For the Teacher, the Student, and the General Reader* (London: The Harrison Trust, 1913), 90-91. It is taken from the first, second, and third editions of the Sarum Breviary, printed in 1516, 1531, and 1541, respectively.

SARUM BREVIARY, 1085	MORNING PRAYER, 1552
O Lord, open thou our lips . . . O God, make speed . . . Gloria	**Confession**
Alleluia, or Praise be	**Absolution**
Invitatory	The Lord's Prayer
Response	O Lord, open thou our lips . . . O God,
Venite	make speed . . . Gloria
Hymn	Venite
Psalms + Gloriae	
Benedictions	Psalms + Gloriae
Lessons	
Homily	Lesson
Responsories	Te Deum or Benedicite
Te Deum (on Sunday)	Lesson
	Benedictus or Jubilate
(Lauds—at daybreak)	Apostles' Creed
	The Lord be with you . . .
O God, make speed . . . Gloria	Lesser Litany
Alleluia, or Praise be	The Lord's Prayer
Psalms	Suffrages
Jubilate (on Sunday) + Gloriae	Collect of the Day
Canticle	Collect for Peace
Benedicite (on Sunday)	Collect for Grace
Short Chapter	
Hymn	
Benedictus	
Suffrages	
Collect for the Day	
Collect for Peace	
(Prime—at c. 6 a.m.)	
The Lord's Prayer	
O God, make speed . . . Gloria	
Alleluia, or Praise be	
Hymn	
Psalms + Gloria	
Athanasian Creed	
Short Chapter	
The Lord be with you	
Lesser Litany	
The Lord's Prayer	
Apostles' Creed	
Suffrages	
Confession	
Absolution	
Collect for Grace	
Prayers for the Intercession of Virgin and	
Saints	* = new additions to the liturgy
Benediction	**bold = significant structural shift**

Figure 4.1. Sarum Breviary and 1552 Morning Prayer

Structurally, there are two significant changes. First, Morning Prayer begins not with the Lord's Prayer, but with an opening Scripture sentence. By itself, this is not structurally significant, except when we note what sentences were chosen by Cranmer. Each sentence is either a call to repentance (Ezek 18:21-22; Ps 51:17; Joel 2:13; Mt 3:2), a confession of total depravity and utter helplessness (Ps 51:3; Dan 9:9-10; Ps 143:2; 1 Jn 1:8), or a desperate plea for mercy in the face of sin (Ps 51:9; Jer 10:24; Lk 15:18-19).[7] If the grammar of *sola fide* distinguishes false good works and self-righteousness from faith and the righteousness of Christ, perhaps we are witnessing the sifting, right at the top of the liturgy.[8] Cranmer makes this work explicit in the exhortation to follow, which says that we should "acknowledge" our "sin and wickedness, and that we should not dissemble nor cloke them before the face of Almighty God our heavenly Father."[9] Exposing sin and separating it out (negating the "I") is the sifting work of *sola fide* in operation, that faith and Christ might shine alone in the gold-pan.[10]

Second, and more surprising to those who would have been familiar with the flow of the Daily Office, Confession and Absolution are moved from the end of the series of morning prayers (Prime) to its beginning. Whereas medieval theology might stress the need to confess the day's sins committed later in the day, we could interpret Cranmer's approach as a statement that we woke up sinners. Behind such a move would be the

---

[7]It is worth noting that one of the earliest commentators on the Book of Common Prayer, Thomas Comber, in his 1670s *A Companion to the Temple; or, A Help to Devotion in the Use of the Common Prayer*, identified five groupings of the sentences, each addressed to different kinds of hearers: "support to the fearful" (Ps 51:9; 143:2; Jer 10:24); "comfort to the doubtful" (Ps 51:17; Dan 9:9-10; Luke 15:18-19); "instruction to the ignorant" (1 John 1:8-19; Ezek 18:27); "admonition to the negligent" (Ps 51:3; Matt 3:3); "caution to the formal" (Joel 2:13). This is outlined in Bray, "Sentences."

[8]Sykes well observes: "All these scriptural verses are chosen to illustrate and teach the evangelical doctrine of the completeness of divine forgiveness" (Stephen Sykes, "Cranmer on the Open Heart," in *This Sacred History: Anglican Reflections for John Booty*, ed. Donald S. Armentrout [Cambridge: Cowley, 1990], 7).

[9]Joseph Ketley, ed., *The Two Liturgies, A.D. 1549, and A.D. 1552* (Cambridge: Parker Society, 1844), 218.

[10]It is noteworthy that the Exhortation is opened with the congregation addressed as "Dearly beloved." In these first two words, sinners are addressed as insiders, God's children. Even the call to confession is done in a context of grace. This move appears to be original to the Reformation. Osiander's 1533 Brandenburg-Nürnberg liturgy for the Lord's Supper begins with a similar address, "Beloved in God," which Cuming notes was lifted from Wolfgang Volprecht's Mass of 1524 (*A History of Anglican Liturgy* [London: MacMillan, 1969], 328n1). Cranmer has followed suit with his Morning Prayer liturgy and elsewhere.

Reformation debate over what was called "concupiscence"—a word utilized heavily by Augustine to describe those internal disordered desires, "the puddly concupiscence of the flesh (*limosa concupiscentia carnis*),"[11] from which all sins spring. The sixteenth-century debate was whether the concupiscence, which led to sinful acts, was sin itself. In other words, was sin merely restricted to deeds, or was it also the condition of the heart? The Continental Reformers argued the latter,[12] as did the English Reformers, spelled out clearly in Article VIII of the Forty-Two Articles of Religion: "Concupiscence, and lust hath of it self the nature of sinne."[13] Morning Prayer's opening Confession and Absolution was a significant move therefore, potentially offering liturgical shape to the Reformation's understanding that concupiscence itself required repentance.

If the above reasoning holds, what we are observing is an implicit critique of the Sarum rite—namely, that it confused faith and works and commingled law and gospel. Sarum Matins begins not with an acknowledgment of sin but with human works: the Lord's Prayer, the Hail Mary, and other psalms and statements of praise. The grammar of *sola fide* demands that works like these flow out of (rather than prepare for) repentance. Structurally in Sarum, faith is not set apart from works. What is needed, Cranmer possibly observed, is the structural application of the distinction between law and gospel, in order that the people of God might not be led to believe that God is approached by the merits of one's own piety. Justification by faith alone calls this kind of approach a not-gospel. That the gospel might be made clear, there must be a *structural*

---

[11]The English translation is from Augustine, *Confessions,* trans. Albert C. Outler (Nashville: Thomas Nelson, 1999), 25. The Latin is from Augustine, *Confessions I: Introduction and Text,* ed. James J. O'Donnell (Oxford: Clarendon, 1992), 16.

[12]As early as 1517, in his *Disputation Against Scholastic Theology,* Luther was arguing that concupiscence "is evil and a fornication of the spirit" (thesis 22). Melanchthon likewise includes all sinful desire under *concupiscere* (*Commonplaces,* 71, see esp. n22), and his *Apology* denies the medieval notion that concupiscence is merely a "weakness" or "inclination" to sin (à la Peter Lombard, Thomas Aquinas; see references in Robert Kolb and Timothy J. Wengert, eds., *The Book of Concord: The Confessions of the Evangelical Lutheran Church* [Minneapolis: Fortress, 2000], 113n13). Calvin likewise says that because our flesh "has been defiled and crammed with this concupiscence," the result is that "by this great corruption we stand justly condemned and convicted before God" (*Institutes of the Christian Religion,* I.1.8, ed. John T. McNeill, trans. Ford Lewis Battles [Philadelphia: Westminster, 1960], 251-52. Hereafter "*Institutes.*")

[13]Charles Hardwick, *A History of the Articles of Religion* (Cambridge: Deighton, Bell, & Co., 1859), 288. In 1571, this would become Article IX in the Thirty-Nine Articles (Hardwick, *History of the Articles,* 289).

movement from the "not I" clarified by the law to the "but Christ" revealed by the gospel. In Morning Prayer, this is accomplished in two cycles (see fig. 4.2).

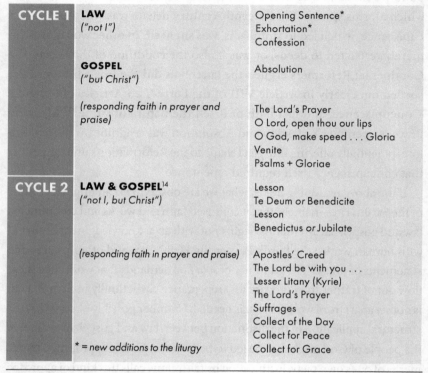

CYCLE 1	LAW ("not I")	Opening Sentence* Exhortation* Confession
	GOSPEL ("but Christ")	Absolution
	(responding faith in prayer and praise)	The Lord's Prayer O Lord, open thou our lips O God, make speed . . . Gloria Venite Psalms + Gloriae
CYCLE 2	LAW & GOSPEL[14] ("not I, but Christ")	Lesson Te Deum or Benedicite Lesson Benedictus or Jubilate
	(responding faith in prayer and praise)	Apostles' Creed The Lord be with you . . . Lesser Litany (Kyrie) The Lord's Prayer Suffrages Collect of the Day Collect for Peace
	* = new additions to the liturgy	Collect for Grace

Figure 4.2. The law-gospel structure of Morning Prayer (1552)

We see here in Confession, Absolution, and what follows that once God declares forgiveness by grace through faith in Jesus Christ, immediate access to the Father is granted. The believer is brought straight into the throne room. Meritorious requirements for entry are not assumed (Sarum's structure), but

---

[14]This categorization here is admittedly more ambiguous. Still, what we observe is that Cranmer grouped the Scripture together and separated out the acts of response—the "I believe" of the Creed and the following prayers. The Word stands alone. Given that the Reformation hermeneutic was that "there are two parts of Scripture . . . Law and Gospel" (Melanchthon, *Commonplaces*, 91), it seems plausible that Cranmer would have understood that as the Word was read, it would be doing its work in this fashion. The grammar of *sola fide* trusts the Word to be heard the way the hearer needs to hear it—terror for some, or the comfort it leads to for others. Even if this is an overinterpretive reach into Cranmer's thinking, what *is* clear is the separation of the work of the Word (Scripture reading) from its effects (works of prayer and praise).

instead, "faith comes by hearing" (Rom 10:17), the pronouncement of the Absolution (cycle 1), and the reading of the Scriptures (cycle 2).[15]

"NOT I, BUT CHRIST" STRUCTURALLY: HOLY COMMUNION (1552)

If we were to attempt a side-by-side comparison of the Sarum rite with Cranmer's 1552 Holy Communion liturgy[16] (as we did with the Breviary and Morning Prayer), we would find the two so dissimilar in content and arrangement that parallel placement would do little for analysis such as we are making here. In fact, the dissimilarity has led to much speculation and, in some cases, accusation of either carelessness or ineptitude on Cranmer's part. For instance, influential turn-of-the-century liturgical scholar Walter Frere believed Cranmer's liturgy to be "out of joint," and while Frere points to how Cranmer moved certain prayers to completely different moments in the liturgy, he does not (at least in that essay) stop to ask if there may be a motive behind such extreme shifts.[17] Samuel Leuenberger begins to identify Cranmer's possible structural motivations when he calls the Communion service "a confrontation of the law and gospel."[18] Leuenberger does not go on to unpack how law and gospel play out structurally in the liturgy, but he does end up offering a parallel paradigm of what he calls cycles of "sin-grace-faith." Packer, following Leuenberger, identifies

---

[15]Oswald Bayer observes Luther, in the reformer's sermons and more formally in the 1520 catechism, similarly parsing the distinction between law and gospel in his treatments of the Decalogue (law) and the Creed and Lord's Prayer (gospel). As Bayer notes, "Prayer belongs to the gospel, not the law, because it is a gift, not a work." One sees the echoes of Luther's distinctions in Cranmer's structure. See Bayer, *Theology the Lutheran Way* (Grand Rapids, MI: Eerdmans, 2007), 71.

[16]Such a comparison exists in Charles Neil and J. M. Willoughby, *The Tutorial Prayer Book: For the Teacher, the Student, and the General Reader* (London: The Harrison Trust, 1913), 256-59 (a more detailed synopsis of Sarum and the 1549 rite), and 281 (an abridged synopsis of Sarum, 1549, 1552, and 1662). A full-text comparison (in English) of Sarum and 1549 is set forth in E. E. Estcourt, *The Dogmatic Teaching of the Book of Common Prayer on the Subject of the Holy Eucharist* (London: Longmans, Green, Reader, and Dyer, 1868), 17-39.

[17]Walter Howard Frere, *Some Principles of Liturgical Reform: A Contribution Towards the Revision of the Book of Common Prayer* (London: John Murray, 1911), 191-93. We hear inklings of this critique, too, in James F. White's comments about Cranmer's "drastic restructuring" of the liturgy when "the canon was cut in two." He seems to offer at least subtle praise of the American tradition when he says that those "prayer books utilized a much richer Scottish eucharistic prayer." He does not pause, however, to ask the question of why Cranmer restructured or abandoned the "richer" eucharistic prayer. See James F. White, *Introduction to Christian Worship*, 3rd ed. (Nashville: Abingdon, 2000), 246.

[18]Samuel Leuenberger, *Archbishop Cranmer's Immortal Bequest: The Book of Common Prayer of the Church of England: An Evangelistic Liturgy* (Eugene, OR: Wipf & Stock, 1990), 24.

three cycles,[19] and I believe we can expand those cycles out to four when we include the pairing of Sermon and Offertory as a separate cycle. Here we have Leuenberger's and Packer's framework transcribed and transposed into the key of *sola fide*, identifying in particular the distinction between law and gospel at play.[20] With Packer we observe that "Cranmer's use of this cycle as the basic structural principle for his eucharistic liturgy reflects his conviction that justification by faith, in and through Christ, is what the sacrament is about—the message that it proclaims, and the promise that it seals"[21] (see fig. 4.3).

CYCLE 1	**LAW** ("not I")	Collect for Purity Ten Commandments + Kyrie The Collects
	GOSPEL ("but Christ")	Epistle Reading Gospel Reading
	(responding faith)	Nicene Creed
CYCLE 2	**LAW & GOSPEL** ("not I, but Christ")	Sermon (optional) Homily (prescribed)[22]
	(responding faith in self-offering)	Offertory Sentence Offertory (taking up a collection for the poor) Prayers for the Whole State of Christ's Church Militant
CYCLE 3	**LAW** ("not I")	Exhortations for Communion Invitation Confession
	GOSPEL ("but Christ")	Absolution Comfortable Words
	(responding faith)	Sursum Corda

---

[19]Packer, "Introduction," xxvi.

[20]These insights from Leuenberger recast in a law-gospel framework were introduced to me by Ashley Null in a doctoral course at Knox Theological Seminary, "DM826: The Theology of Cranmer and the Book of Common Prayer," January 12-16, 2015. They are presented here with only slight modification.

[21]Packer, "Introduction," xxvi.

[22]The sermon and homily were discrete options in 1552. The homily would have been the prescribed text from the 1547 Book of Homilies to be read by the priest. As we will expand on in chap. 7, not every priest in Cranmer's day was capable of preparing and delivering a sermon, which is most likely why the rubric reads "After the Creed, if there be no sermon, shall follow one of the homilies already set forth," and then, "After such sermon, homily, or exhortation . . ." (Ketley, *Liturgies*, 268).

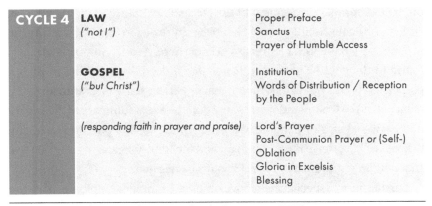

CYCLE 4	**LAW** ("not I")	Proper Preface Sanctus Prayer of Humble Access
	GOSPEL ("but Christ")	Institution Words of Distribution / Reception by the People
	(responding faith in prayer and praise)	Lord's Prayer Post-Communion Prayer or (Self-) Oblation Gloria in Excelsis Blessing

Figure 4.3. The law-gospel structure of Holy Communion (1552)

Cycle 1: The Collect for Purity Through the Creed. The Communion service begins with the same kind of gravity as Morning Prayer. The Collect for Purity functions as its own kind of Confession of Sin, with the Pauline grammar identifiable by its totalizing and categorical modifiers: "Almighty God, unto whom *all* hearts be open, and *all* desires known, and from whom *no* secrets are hid: cleanse the thoughts of our hearts, by the inspiration of thy Holy Spirit: that we may *perfectly* love thee, and *worthily* magnify thy holy name: through Christ our Lord."[23]

And then immediately, without any precedent in the Sarum rite, Cranmer apparently puts forth a confrontation with the law of God in the form of the Decalogue.[24] While other preexisting Reformation rites contain the Ten Commandments, the usage of the Decalogue at the beginning of the liturgy also appears to be unprecedented and therefore a unique innovation of Cranmer.[25] Liturgical historian John Dowden expressed confusion as to why Cranmer would make such a move, preferring some of the German Reformed

---

[23]Ketley, *Liturgies*, 77; emphasis added.

[24]As Oberman points out, the Decalogue does appear in pre-Reformation liturgies, but nearly always in the form of the private devotional prayers of the priest as opposed to the public rite. He notes well that there were in fact pre-Reformation liturgies, such as Surgant's *Manuale Curatorum* (1502), which paved the way for making the Decalogue and other such priestly prayers public. See Heiko Oberman, "Preaching and the Word in the Reformation," *Theology Today* 18, no. 1 (1961): 20.

[25]Null indicates that Martin Bucer's 1537 Strassburg rite for Communion included at the front of the service "three possible confessions from which to choose, the last being based on the Ten Commandments," but that appears to be about as close as we get to a parallel. See Ashley Null, *Divine Allurement: Cranmer's Comfortable Words* (London: The Latimer Trust, 2014), 228.

orders to Cranmer's placement of the Decalogue.[26] Since then, the trail has largely gone cold, as little interest has been expressed in figuring out why the Archbishop would do something so original here. A satisfying explanation is found in the Pauline grammar. If *sola fide* indeed distinguishes law from gospel and faith from works, then it makes perfect sense of Cranmer's placement of the Ten Commandments—that quintessential summary of the *totality* of the law—alongside penitential phrases which confess one's total inability to keep it: "Lord, have mercy upon us, and incline our hearts to keep this law." That faith might stand alone, the "I" must be negated.

Furthermore, especially when we observe Cranmer's employment of the Decalogue in comparison to other preceding and contemporaneous Reformation church orders, we find the grammatical rules of *sola fide* operating in Cranmer with a great deal more thoroughness. Martin Bucer's Strassburg liturgy of 1524 placed the Ten Commandments as an option to be sung in between Scripture lessons, nowhere near Confession and Absolution. More interestingly, Vallerand Poullain's 1551 liturgy for the Glastonbury Stranger Church (which likely would have been fresh on Cranmer's mind during his work on the 1552 liturgy) follows the lead of Calvin's Strassburg liturgy of the early 1540s:[27] it divides the Decalogue, with the first table being spoken before Confession, and the second table after Absolution.[28] It seems that the Archbishop deliberately chose *not* to construct his liturgy in this more Reformed[29]

---

[26]John Dowden, *Further Studies in the Prayer Book* (London: Meuthen & Co., 1908), 171.

[27]Calvin brought back his Strassburg liturgy, originally printed in 1540, to Geneva in 1541. This liturgy, derived from Bucer (according to Calvin's farewell address on his deathbed), was put together by Calvin to lead his French-speaking congregation in Strassburg. There are no extant copies of this 1541 liturgy, but we do have an edition from 1545, indicating that even after Calvin left, the Strassburg congregation continued using Calvin's rite. Poullain himself followed Calvin as pastor to Strassburg's French-speaking congregation (see Jonathan Gibson and Mark Earngey, *Reformation Worship: Liturgies from the Past for the Present* [Greensboro: New Growth Press, 2018], 304). It is notable that Calvin himself apparently added the use of the Decalogue into the liturgy (it does not appear in Bucer), including splitting the first and second table, with the second clearly following all prayers of Confession. See Bard Thompson, *Liturgies of the Western Church* (Philadelphia: Fortress, 1961), 188-89, 198, and also Gibson and Earngey, *Worship,* 309-10.

[28]Perhaps unaware of Reformed perspectives on the law and law-keeping (see the next note), Dowden considered Poullain's division of the Decalogue "grotesque" (*Further Studies,* 171).

[29]While the distinction between law and gospel finds much common ground between the Lutheran and Reformed traditions, it is the Reformed tradition which has been historically more willing to speak of how the law functions for the regenerate Christian after grace and forgiveness. At that point, it is grace-enabled "delight in God's gift of the law without being condemned by it." It becomes a "living under the blessings of divine favor" (see Kelly M. Kapic, "The Law-Gospel Distinction in

way, opting for a more starkly (and grammatically) Lutheran approach of not commingling law and gospel, but distinguishing them structurally.[30] So it seems that for Cranmer, the law would not only precede Confession and Absolution. It would be the first word out of the liturgical gate. Then and only then would the hearer be ready to receive the words of comfort that could be found in the Scripture readings to follow.[31] And only after that, structurally, is the worshiper ready to utter the words of faith, "I believe," in the Creed.

Reformed Theology and Ministry," in *God's Two Words: Law and Gospel in the Lutheran and Reformed Traditions*, ed. Jonathan A. Linebaugh [Grand Rapids, MI: Eerdmans, 2018], 136-37). The Reformed tradition stresses how the preface to the Ten Commandments indicates the law's function *after* grace: because the believer has been redeemed out of slavery, the law is heard not as condemnation but something positive—the fruit and calling of the redeemed life (cf. e.g., the Westminster Larger Catechism question and answer 101). In this sense, Poullain's reservation of the second table of the Decalogue for *after* Absolution is a very Reformed move. A good brief summary of the nuances of difference between the Reformed and Lutheran traditions on the law can be found in Jonathan A. Linebaugh, introduction to *God's Two Words: Law and Gospel in the Lutheran and Reformed Traditions*, ed. Jonathan A. Linebaugh (Grand Rapids, MI: Eerdmans, 2018), 1-11.

[30] Jan Łaski's Reformed *Forma ac ratio* (1555), which had an influence on Cranmer, keeps the Decalogue all together (albeit after the sermon), after which immediately follows an admonishment of the minister "to acknowledge those sins, to bring an accusation against themselves on that basis, and to implore Divine Mercy" through a confession of sin which prays, "we are convicted of seeking all these things and of being liable to all these troubles by the testimony of this divine law" (see Gibson and Earngey, *Worship*, 464-65). We should note here the fifth homily of 1547, probably by Cranmer, on "Good Works, Annexed unto Faith." In it the Archbishop identifies the Ten Commandments as the fruit of the justified, faith-filled life: "The works of the moral commandments of God be the very true works of faith, which lead to the blessed life to come" (Bond, *Sermons*, 106). But even while Cranmer identifies law-keeping as the fruit of faith, it appears that in his liturgy, in contrast to Poullain, he still recognizes that the *function* of the law—both liturgically and in life—is properly to kill, to terrorize, and to prepare the heart for the (fruit-bearing) gospel. This is furthermore where Cranmer stands in contrast to two of his influential colleagues, Bullinger and Hooper, and the burgeoning Zurich "covenant theology." This emerging perspective taught that the Decalogue was "an expression of the covenant relationship between God and man. Decalogue and covenant have a pronounced soteriological meaning. The covenant relationship implies that the partner in the covenant holds himself bound by the conditions of the covenant." In this scheme, "the absolute requirement for remaining now in the relationship is the keeping of the Ten Commandments, or, to say it in other words, sanctification in one's daily life" (Leuenberger, *Bequest*, 51). W. M. S. West summarizes Hooper's understanding: "The way into the covenant is that of repentance and faith and the way to remain within it is to live the Christian life" (quoted in Leuenberger, *Bequest*, 51).

[31] Admittedly, whether one hears gospel here depends, first, on what readings are utilized from the lectionary and, second, on what the hearer hears in those readings. This second idea gets at the subjective nature of hearing and receiving the objective Word we explored above, in fig. 4.2. The ambiguity of this subjectivity is most likely why Packer would see my first two cycles as one cycle together—the sermon itself would bear the burden of preaching the gospel. This is therefore the weakest point in the argument for the flow of continuity of law→gospel→faith. Still, because the Creed functions so strongly as a faith-response, it seems more clear to me that if the grammar truly is at work, Cranmer would understand the readings as functioning as gospel-words.

Grammatically, each part of speech (law, gospel, faith) falls into its appropriate part of the "liturgical sentence" constructed by justification by faith alone.

Cycle 2: The sermon, offertory, and prayers. As we will see in chapter seven, it is hard to come to any other conclusion about Cranmer's homiletical philosophy than that the sermon was an event which unleashed the Word of God to do its work of diagnosing and delivering sinners. Indeed, Cranmer would have understood preaching to be a place where *sola fide* would be operating, governing, guiding, and distinguishing. The activity of law and gospel would naturally produce a faith-filled response *after* the Word does its work. The Offertory that follows, then, appears to be seen more by Cranmer as a response to the sermon and less as a preparation or lead-in to Holy Communion. Perhaps this view is only possible as the presentation of bread and wine was disassociated with the liturgical moment of the Offertory, for in Cranmer's time that was the ritual's established meaning—presenting the bread and wine as "offerings" or "oblations" for special use at the table.[32] Yet in Cranmer's liturgy, bread and wine go unmentioned until the rubrics of administration and therefore appear to play no role in the reconfigured Offertory of 1552.[33] Perhaps Cranmer felt the same as the future Archbishop of Canterbury, Michael Ramsey, who expressed concern at twentieth-century attempts to reintroduce this older Offertory practice by saying it exhibited a kind of Pelagianism.[34] The concern appears to have been for the commixture of our offering with the perfect offering of Christ, obscuring the fullness, perfection, and sufficiency of the latter.[35]

---

[32]Colin Buchanan traces the development of the "Offertory," noting that up to the fourth century, "In no instance is the 'bringing in' given any greater significance than that, though it was usual to describe the gifts as 'oblations' or 'offerings,' and even to say that they were 'presented' or 'offered' to the president—though this was an untechnical use of the same word in slightly different contexts. The eucharistic action itself had not begun" (*The End of the Offertory—An Anglican Study* [Bramcote: Grove Books, 1978], 12). Once Cranmer's 1552 Prayer Book arrived, "The title 'offertory' is not used here, but is still introducing 'Collects to be said after the Offertory, when there is no Communion' at the end of the service. . . . Thus there is a difference of presentation, in that the wardens gather the money, and take it to the 'poormen's box' which is now standing isolated at the East end, as the high altar itself has gone. The people have no need to go from the nave to the chancel, and the ante-communion continues after the offertory, so the people stay where they are in order to give" (21).

[33]Buchanan, *Offertory*, 22.

[34]This quote from Michael Ramsey is found in Bryan D. Spinks, "Mis-Shapen: Gregory Dix and the Four-Action Shape of the Liturgy," *Lutheran Quarterly* 4, no. 2 (1990): 166.

[35]Granted, Roman Catholic theologians would point out that a proper theology of sacrifice does not entail that we offer something of our own but rather that we liturgically and mystically share and

If it is true that Cranmer sought to unmoor the Offertory from its potential Pelagianism by removing any ceremonial offering of bread and wine, the Offertory's function within the structure of the liturgy changes. It becomes clearer then, when we view Cranmer's overall Communion liturgy through the historic two-fold structure of the "Liturgy of the Word" and the "Liturgy of the Upper Room,"[36] that the grammar of *sola fide* places the Offertory (the responding fruit of self-offering) at the *end* of the Liturgy of the Word (the Ante-Communion liturgy), not the *beginning* of the Liturgy of the Upper Room (the Communion liturgy proper). If it were viewed as the latter, it would structurally confuse the distinction of faith and works, because the Offertory in that schema could be experienced as a "paying in" before receiving the grace of the table.[37] And this construal seems corroborated in some of the simple changes we will now observe.

Though this sequence of Sermon, Offertory, Prayers, and Communion liturgy proper was present in the Sarum rite, Cranmer introduced a few important structural and conceptual tweaks which lead us to believe that he was aware of how *sola fide* could be confused or lost in this liturgical moment. Most tellingly, in a break with Roman tradition, the Offertory is reimagined not as a place where the bread and wine are presented and offered with ceremonial crossings, kissings, censings, and washings,[38] but as a place

---

participate in the sufficient offering of Christ's own sacrifice. In this sense, Cranmer was indeed responding to something different from Ramsey (who was concerned with erroneous interpretations initiated by Dom Gregory Dix and perpetuated by others in his wake [see Spinks, "Misshapen," 166-67]). Nevertheless, given what we are arguing, it does appear that Cranmer had a concern for a kind of Pelagianism present both in the Offertory rituals of his day and in the theology of sacrifice that gave it context.

[36] This two-part division of the liturgy is evidenced as early as the second century, detectible in Justin's *First Apology*, chap. 65 (c. 150 AD); see Spinks, *Do This in Remembrance of Me: The Eucharist from the Early Church to the Present Day* (London: SCM, 2013), 31. The particular nomenclature used here appears to have been coined by William D. Maxwell, *An Outline of Christian Worship: Its Developments and Forms* (London: Oxford, 1936), 13n1, though I have not done extensive research into the origin of this language. As Maxwell indicates, dipartite designation in the East has traditionally been *Proanaphora* and *Anaphora*, while in the West *Missa catechumenorum* and *Missa fidelium*.

[37] Calvin seems to have shared this perspective. In his 1545 Preface to his own rite, he links the prayers after the sermon (which in the historic liturgy would follow the post-sermon Offertory as it does in Cranmer) to the sermon itself, indicating it as a response and outflow of the sermon's gospel proclamation: "Quickened and stirred by the reading and preaching of the Gospel and the confession of our faith, . . . it follows that we must pray for the salvation of all men, for the life of Christ should be greatly enkindled within us" (quoted in Maxwell, *Worship*, 116).

[38] Neil and Willoughby, *Tutorial*, 257.

where people take up a financial collection for the poor and for the ministry of the parish.[39] In 1547, the newly crowned Edward VI issued a series of injunctions, including instructions about the installation and use of the poor-men's box.[40] It is clear from those injunctions that the practice of giving alms was particularly intended to replace the kind of devotional giving associated with currying favor with God—paying for pardons, the well-being of the deceased, and the like.[41] The poor-men's box "was an official reminder that people's charity was to be directed not to masses or graven images, but to needy people made in God's image."[42] The rubrics around the Offertory, unlike Sarum, make no mention of bread and wine. Instead: "After such sermon, homily, or exhortation, the Curate shall . . . earnestly exhort [the people] to remember the poor, saying one or more of these Sentences following."[43] And what are the sentences Cranmer adds here? They are short

---

[39]Indeed, in medieval corporate worship, "oblations" were given to the priest by some of the devout, and four times a year on "offering days" a "Mass-penny" was obligatory, but, as John Dowden observes: "The prominent place given in our Service to a collection of money for the poor in the Service for the Holy Communion was a novelty in England. . . . That the ordinary rule should be that a collection for the poor was to form the normal order on every Sunday and holy day was quite a new thing" (*Further Studies*, 174-75). While Dowden observes that Cranmer may have taken a cue from the German *Kirchenordnungen*, he does not proffer any explanation (as we are attempting) as to *why* Cranmer may have introduced this novelty.

[40]Cox, *Works*, vol. 2, 503:

> [The parish] shall provide . . . a strong chest, with a hole in the upper part thereof, to be provided at the cost and charge of the parish . . . , which chest you shall set and fasten near unto the high altar, to the intent the parishioners should put into it their oblation and alms for their poor neighbours. And the parson, vicar, or curate, shall diligently from time to time, and specially when men take their testaments, call upon, exhort, and move their neighbours, to confer and give, as they may well spare, to the said chest, declaring unto them, whereas heretofore they have been diligent to bestow much substance otherwise than God commanded, upon pardons, pilgrimages, trentals, docking of images, offering of candles, giving to friars, and upon other like blind devotions, they ought at this time to be much more ready to help the poor and needy, knowing that to relieve the poor is a true worshipping of God.

Note in this injunction the similarity to 2 Kings 12:9-10, which describes some of the reforms of King Joash of Judah: "Then Jehoiada the priest took a chest and bored a hole in its lid. He placed it beside the altar." Perhaps, given Cranmer's commitment to reform according to biblical practice, this too was a move of his "scripturality."

[41]Cf. comments by Diarmaid MacCulloch, *Tudor Church Militant: Edward VI and the Protestant Reformation* (London: Penguin, 1999), 125. For some of the complexities (and, in my opinion, atrocities) of these late medieval "clerical economics," see esp. Zieman's explanation of what she calls "contractual" liturgy in *Singing the New Song: Literacy and Liturgy in Late Medieval England* (Philadelphia: University of Pennsylvania Press, 2008), 73-113.

[42]MacCulloch, *Militant*, 160.

[43]Ketley, *Liturgies*, 269.

Scripture passages that encourage people unto "good works" (Mt 5:16), storing up "treasure in heaven" (Mt 6:19-20), contributing to the ministry of the gospel (1 Cor 9:13-14), and indeed giving to the poor (Lk 19:8; Ps 41:1). None of the sentences has any sacramental reference or overtone. The Offertory collection ritual is completed with this rubric: "Then shall the church wardens, or some other by them appointed, gather the devotion of the people, and put the same into the poor men's box."[44] The grammar of *sola fide* structurally distinguishes faith and works by sequestering works to *after* the word of law and gospel in the Sermon. And the first "good works" to flow forth are the Offertory and then the Prayer "for the whole state of Christ's Church militant here in earth."[45]

That Cranmer probably viewed the Offertory as the ending response to the Sermon and Liturgy of the Word (and not as the beginning of the Communion liturgy proper) is also shown in the fact that the Archbishop places the Exhortations, which are the first liturgical mention of the Lord's Supper, *after* the sequence of the Offertory and intercessory prayers. Structurally, it appears that the Archbishop is drawing a clean boundary-line with the Offertory and prayers, so as to avoid any confusion that grace is somehow purchased or earned.

Cycle 3: Exhortations through the Sursum Corda. There is a shift in pastoral tone moving out of the prayers and into the Exhortations. This shift is an indicator of a new cycle of law and gospel, whose pattern again resembles the opening of Morning Prayer. The Exhortations offer grave warnings to not refuse to come to the table, to not make "feigned excuses" that might "offend" and "provoke God's indignation against you."[46] They urge self-examination, climaxing in the Invitation, which is a clear call to repentance. The sinner, feeling the weight of the law, is thus driven to Confession, after which the Absolution[47] declares that God does "pardon" (dealing with guilt) and "deliver

---

[44]Ketley, *Liturgies*, 84.

[45]Ketley, *Liturgies*, 84.

[46]Ketley, *Liturgies*, 383.

[47]Matthew S. C. Olver understandably questions the wisdom of labeling this liturgical moment "absolution," at least in reference to the Roman rite, given that absolution in Roman theology more specifically pertains to the sacrament of Reconciliation. From about the eleventh century, the mass contained a *kind* of confession—the *Confiteor*—said by the priest, followed by prayers requesting forgiveness (see Matthew S. C. Olver, "Confessions of a Penitential Orderer," *Covenant* [May 10, 2022], https://covenant.livingchurch.org/2022/05/10/confessions-of-a-penitential -orderer/). Nevertheless, the Reformers appear to have understood this public moment of

you" (dealing with spiritual bondage). In line with the grammar of *sola fide*, too, is the clarity that this forgiveness is "from *all* your sins"—complete, total- izing, categorical grace. This "all" would stand in contrast to the medieval understanding that full payment for sin was a combination of Christ's work and our sincere penance.[48] After the continued absolution heard in the Com- fortable Words, we see, for the first time, the fruit of faith emerge in the form of the Sursum Corda. The Old Adam, having been killed ("not I") by the law in Confession and made alive ("but Christ") by the gospel in Absolution and the Comfortable Words, now speaks as the new creature, able to rise and respond to the call, "Lift up your hearts." In a way, the Sursum Corda is a "second Offertory," except this time the faithful response is not a giving of money, but the giving of our very hearts: "We lift them up unto the Lord." It very much feels like the liturgical equivalent of the great hinge point in Paul's epistle to the Romans: after eleven chapters of outlining and proclaiming the gospel through the distinguishing grammar of justification, believers are exhorted to present themselves as a θυσίαν ζῶσαν—a sacrifice that is in fact not dead, but living (Rom 12:1). The only response of such a being is the "work" of faith—praise which cries, "Let us give thanks unto our Lord God."[49]

On the positioning and use of the Comfortable Words and Absolution.
The Comfortable Words are a Reformation innovation, appearing in *Kirche- nordnungen* (church orders) composed on the Continent in the 1520s, '30s, and '40s.[50] Well attested in his own liturgical work is Cranmer's use of the 1543 Cologne *Kirchenordnung* of Archbishop Hermann von Wied.[51] In that liturgy, Hermann included five Scripture sentences:[52] John 3:16;

---

declaration of forgiveness as an instance of (effectual but non-sacramental) absolution (see, for instance, Bucer's rubrics in n54 below). Though Olver's point is well taken, given the Reformation perspective, we have chosen especially for comparison's sake to refer to the declaration in Sarum as an absolution.

[48]To be clear, the Absolution of Sarum likewise offered forgiveness of "*omnium peccatorum*," but the absence of a structure governed by the grammar of *sola fide*, combined with an entire context of medieval piety emphasizing personal penance, would have muted the clarity of the totalizing "all." In fact, the "all" is voided in such a scenario, because what the liturgy gives verbally with the left hand it takes away structurally with the right.

[49]Ketley, *Liturgies*, 277.

[50]See references in chap. 1, n41 and chap. 4, n56.

[51]An English translation of the Cologne liturgy is available in Geoffrey Cuming, *A History of Anglican Liturgy* (London: MacMillan, 1969), 334-57.

[52]I am intentionally avoiding calling Hermann's sentences "Comfortable Words" because it appears that his liturgy sometimes did and sometimes did not include "comfort" in the announced heading.

1 Timothy 1:15; John 3:35-36; Acts 10:43; and 1 John 2:1-2. In 1552 Cranmer removed two of the verses (Jn 3:35-36; Acts 10:43) and added his own original, Matthew 11:28, on the front.[53] Hermann's liturgy, following suit with Bucer's liturgies which preceded it, allows the Scripture sentences to be used as alternatives to the Absolution.[54] In a new move, Cranmer relocates the Comfortable Words *after* the Absolution and makes neither the Absolution nor any of the Comfortable Words optional. Ashley Null believes that this was because Cranmer was giving the Comfortable Words a new function. Rather than being alternative or merely additional words of absolution, they functioned as a liturgical hinge, where Confession and Absolution turned to flow into the Communion liturgy proper.[55] If this is true, Cranmer is portraying God as wooing sinners to him saying, "You're forgiven, now come to my table."[56] This idea is corroborated by the fact that Cranmer was likely aware of Zwingli's 1523 liturgy, *Attack on the Canon of the Mass*, which employs Matthew 11:28 as a lone sentence, just after the words of institution,

The 1543 German version of Hermann's liturgy (*Einfältiges Bedenken*) does announce, "*Höret den Evangelischen Trost*" (hear the gospel's comfort), but the 1545 Latin version (*Simplex ac pia Deliberatio*) announces, "*Audite Evangelium*" (hear the gospel). See Cuming, *History*, 343; Cuming, *The Godly Order: Texts and Studies Relating to the Book of Common Prayer* (London: SPCK, 1983), 80; and Null, "Comfortable Words," 228.

[53] Ashley Null has pointed out that it was Katherine Parr, the last of Henry's queens, who had recorded Mt 11:28 as being instrumental in her conversion experience, and that Cranmer's knowledge of Parr's testimony is likely. I first heard Dr. Null make these observations in the doctoral course mentioned above (chap. 4, n20), but he also discusses Parr's testimony in: "Comfortable Words: Thomas Cranmer's Gospel Falconry," in *Comfortable Words: Essays in Honor of Paul F. M. Zahl*, ed. John D. Koch, Jr. and Todd H. W. Brewer (Eugene, OR: Pickwick, 2013), 220-21, 232; and "Thomas Cranmer and Tudor Church Growth," in *Towards a Theology of Church Growth*, ed. David Goodhew (New York: Routledge, 2016), 197-98.

[54] Bucer's 1537 liturgy flows in this way: A rubric that begins this section reads, "*ein absolution oder trotspruch*" (an absolution or comfortable word), followed by 1 Tim 1:15, then an Absolution, then a rubric ("*Etwann nimmet er andere sprüch, die uns der verzeihung der sünden und bezalung Christi für unsere sünd getrosten*"), and then four alternative verses are listed (Jn 3:16, 35-36; Acts 10:43; and 1 Jn 2:1). See Friedrich Hubert, *Die Straßburger Liturgischen Ordnungen Im Zeitalter Der Reformation* (Göttingen: Vandenhoeck & Ruprecht, 1900), 94-95. For more on the sources of the Comfortable Words, see Null, "Comfortable Words," 227-28. See also Cuming, *Godly Order*, 80-81.

[55] From a personal conversation with Dr. Null on November 10, 2017, in Birmingham, Alabama.

[56] "In his revisions for the 1552 Book of Common Prayer, he decided to insert the Comfortable Words immediately before the *Sursum corda*. Thus, he put his twin means of moving human affections heavenward—scriptural rumination and cultural contextualization" (Null, "Church Growth," 215). For an extended treatment of the "wooing" power of the Comfortable Words, see Ashley Null, *Divine Allurement: Cranmer's Comfortable Words* (London: The Latimer Trust, 2014).

and just before the words of administration.[57] It could be that Cranmer's desire was to combine Zwingli's emphasis on "Come to me" as a table invitation with Hermann's connection of the Comfortable Words to Absolution. For our present discussion of the grammar of *sola fide*, this all tells us that the Comfortable Words most likely are intended to function as something more than an extension of Absolution. They are a springboard into the final law-gospel cycle of the Communion liturgy.

Cycle 4: *The proper preface to the blessing.* When it comes to fidelity to the grammatical structure of justification by faith alone, no other liturgical passage or service in the Prayer Book has undergone such a tedious editorial process. The moves made by Cranmer have baffled and sometimes horrified succeeding generations of liturgists.[58] And yet it is the grammar of *sola fide* which accounts for why, when compared to the historic liturgy with which he was working, Cranmer's seems so "out of joint." At this point, it *is* worth setting Sarum and 1552 side-by-side (see fig. 4.4).

SARUM MASS[59]	HOLY COMMUNION, 1552
Sursum Corda (with salutation)	Sursum Corda (without salutation)
Proper Preface	Proper Preface
Sanctus	Sanctus
Benedictus	~~Benedictus~~
	Prayer of Humble Access

[57]See R. C. D. Jasper and G. J. Cuming, *Prayers of the Eucharist: Early and Reformed* (Collegeville, MN: Liturgical Press, 1987), 186. As Ashley Null points out, "Two years later, Zwingli deleted the biblical text from the new German communion service, but retained the verse on the cover of the book" ("Comfortable Words," 227).

[58]Particularly in the last two centuries, largely because of the emergence and establishment of the ideals of the Oxford/Tractarian Movement (nineteenth century) and then again because of the ecumenically-oriented Liturgical Movement (twentieth century), Cranmer's Communion structure came under intense criticism, particularly by Protestant scholars, precisely because of its deviation from the architecture of the historic Canon of the Mass and its abandonment of the historic prayers of older Christian rites. This criticism was especially effectual in the United States, yielding successive step after step away from Cranmer's intention, particularly discernible in the 1928 and 1979 Prayer Book revisions. That said, the die was cast with the formulation of the first American Prayer Book back in 1789. Charles P. Price (*The Prayer Book in the Church* [Cincinnati: Forward Movement Publications, 1997], 11-12) notes the political nature of the move to include in the 1789 American Prayer Book what Cranmer had excised—namely, the *anamnesis* and *epiclesis*. Evidently, when Samuel Seabury, a minister in Connecticut, sought consecration as a bishop in the Scottish Episcopal Church, one of the stipulations of his ascendancy was that he would ensure the inclusion of those prayers in the American book as the Episcopal Church was forming.

[59]I am grateful to an anonymous reviewer of this book who significantly helped me in properly laying out this section of the Sarum Mass.

SARUM MASS	HOLY COMMUNION, 1552
(Canon of the Mass)	
First request for acceptance of the offering "here"	~~First request for acceptance of the offering~~
First oblation	~~First oblation~~
	Prayer remembering the sufficient oblation of Christ's once-for-all offering "there"
Intercession for church, and for those present who offer the sacrifice with second oblation	~~Intercession for church, and for those present who offer the sacrifice with second oblation~~
First commemoration of saints and intercession for those present	~~First commemoration of saints and intercession for those present~~
Second request for acceptance of offering Intercession for peace and salvation	~~Second request for acceptance of offering Intercession for peace and salvation~~
Third request for acceptance of offering so that the gifts become body/blood	**Request for hearing of prayer so that we be made partakers of body/blood**
Institution Narrative (with expanded language)	Institution Narrative (Scripture text only)
Anamnesis	~~Anamnesis~~
Third oblation	~~Third oblation~~
Fourth request for acceptance of offering	~~Fourth request for acceptance of offering~~
Fifth [implicit] request for acceptance (through angel)	~~Fifth [implicit] request for acceptance~~
Intercession for departed	~~Intercession for departed~~
Second commemoration of apostles/martyrs	~~Second commemoration of apostles/martyrs~~
Intercession for those present	~~Intercession for those present~~
Doxology	~~Doxology~~
Lord's Prayer	
Embolism	~~Embolism~~
Fraction	~~Fraction~~
Peace/Pax	~~Peace/Pax~~
Agnus Dei	~~Agnus Dei~~
Commixture	~~Commixture~~
Prayer that concerns peace	~~Prayer that concerns peace~~
Priest's reception/communion	**People's reception/communion**
Private thanksgiving and ablutions	~~Private thanksgiving and ablutions~~
	Lord's Prayer*
	Self-Oblation
	(or)
Post-Communion Prayer	**Post-Communion Prayer**
	Gloria in Excelsis*
	Blessing

SARUM MASS	HOLY COMMUNION, 1552
Dismissal	**bold = new additions or significant alterations to language** * = significant structural shift

Figure 4.4. The Sarum Mass and Holy Communion (1552)

From a structural perspective, every move Cranmer makes, either to excise a prayer altogether, to amend it, or to move it to a different location, appears to have been subjected to the grammatical rules of *sola fide*. The first thing we notice besides the removal of the Benedictus[60] is the addition of a newly composed prayer, the Prayer of Humble Access, just after the Sanctus. The prayer functions as yet another moment of confession. It seems that Cranmer understood the Sanctus as a raw encounter with the holiness of the living God (an encounter with the law). As in Isaiah 6—the passage most likely on Cranmer's mind—the response to such an encounter is not, per Sarum, our own offering of "gifts," "presents," or "unspotted sacrifices" (the first request for acceptance), much less our own "sacrifice of praise" (the second oblation).[61] Rather, with Isaiah, the focus of the Prayer of Humble Access is on our unworthiness and confession of sin.[62] And notice the emphasis on faith and the stark distinguishing between the mercy and grace of God and the unrighteousness of the sinner. This prayer in particular constructs its sentences in order to highlight the distinctions made by *sola fide*:

Our unrighteousness	We do not presume to come to this thy table (O merciful Lord) trusting in our own righteousness,
God's mercy	but in thy manifold and great mercies:
Our unworthiness	we be not worthy so much as to gather up the crumbs under thy table:
God's mercy	but thou art the same Lord, whose property is always to have mercy . . .

---

[60]For more on this change, see chap. 6, under "*Sola Fide* and Consecration, Reception, and Blessing of the Elements."

[61]Sarum: *dona, munera, sacrificia illibata*, and *sacrificium laudis*.

[62]Granted, in the Sarum Mass there are four references to being "unworthy" (*indignus*), but due to the mixture of merit and self-offering throughout the liturgy, such expressions of unworthiness are not as sharp and unequivocal as in Cranmer.

Our sinfulness	that our sinful bodies
God's perfection	may be made clean by his body,
Our sinfulness	and our souls
God's perfection	washed through his most precious blood . . .[63]

We see here a moment where *sola fide* is separating and distinguishing, preparing the way for the clarity of what is the gospel ("but Christ") from that which is not the gospel ("not I"). Contrast this with the language of the second oblation in Sarum:

> Remember, O Lord, thy servants . . . N. and N. and all present, whose faith and devotion to thee is known: for whom we offer unto thee, or who themselves offer to thee *this sacrifice of praise for themselves, and all theirs for the redemption of their souls, for the hope of their salvation and safety and render their own thanks to thee,* the eternal God, the living and the true.[64]

The grammar of justification identifies this confusion of faith and works as a not-gospel. In the face of the holiness of God, Sarum does not urge unequivocal repentance, but mixes in the commendable "devotion" which is "known" by and "offered" unto God. Instead of looking *only* to the sacrifice of Christ, the liturgy encourages offering the sacrifice of oneself and others before coming to receive the grace of the table. This confusion of faith and works is a not-gospel precisely because, structurally speaking, the grace of the table is no longer a *gift* (χάρις), but something earned. This self-offering, along with the veneration of the host in these prayers, ends up being the combined offering—"We therefore beseech thee, O Lord, that being appeased thou wouldst accept this oblation of our servitude" (second request for acceptance of offering)[65]—which yields a combined presentation of "both I, and Christ" instead of the radical disjunctive "not I, but Christ."

---

[63]Ketley, *Liturgies,* 7. The parallelism of "bodies" and "souls" implies that the adjective "sinful," which modifies "bodies," also modifies "souls."

[64]English translation taken from R. P. Blakeney, *The Book of Common Prayer in Its History and Interpretation,* 2nd ed. (London: Miller, 1866), 398; emphasis added.

[65]Blakeney, *Book,* 399. There is controversy in Roman Catholicism surrounding the translation of *placatus* as "appeased." An alternate translation of the same year as Blakeney's renders the phrase, "*graciously* to accept this oblation of our service" (Charles Walker, *The Liturgy of the Church of Sarum* [London: Hayes, 1866], 65). The concern is over misrepresentation of Roman Catholic theology in the former translation. Roman Catholic scholar David Power has shown, however, that "graciously accept" is ultimately a mistranslation as a result of the unfortunate, even "elementary," confusion of *placare* for *placere,* and that "being appeased" is integral as a

Structurally for Cranmer, once faith and works have been distinguished, and once the law has been spoken or sung in the Sanctus and confessed in the Prayer of Humble Access, the grace of the gospel is the only thing left to receive. And so Cranmer provides only a brief prayer whose language of offering is reminiscent of Sarum but turns the oblation on its head. We pray, not offering "our" oblation, but remembering Christ's oblation. And such an offering is not offered "here" (*haec*), but "there," on the cross. And after this brief prayer, the worshiper is brought straight to the words of institution, and without pause or even an "Amen"[66] the people come to receive the bread and the wine, along with the gracious words of reception, again highlighting faith alone: "Take and eat this, in remembrance that Christ died for thee, and feed on him in thy heart *by faith*."[67] Once again, this is contrasted with Sarum, which, after institution does not move straight to reception, but doubles back to more prayers and presentations until the Commixture which offers "a salutary preparation for the meriting and embracing of eternal life," and the following prayer that concerns peace, which prays "that I may merit to receive through this the remission of all my sins."[68] Then and only then does reception happen (for the priest). The contrast is stark. For Cranmer, once Christ offers himself by his Word in the institution ("take, eat . . . drink ye all of this"), there is nothing left to

---

part of the appropriate sphere of meaning of *placare* in both the Vulgate and the Roman Liturgy. Power therefore concludes, "The Latin tendency in medieval and pre-Reformation times was to reduce the offering of the Mass to this aspect of satisfaction or appeasement, but dissatisfaction with this should not lead to an annulment of this idea when it is kept alongside others" (David Power, "Theology of the Latin Text and Rite," in *A Commentary on the Order of the Mass of the Roman Missal: A New English Translation, Developed Under the Auspices of the Catholic Academy of Liturgy*, ed. Edward Foley, John F. Baldovin, Mary Collins, and Joanne M. Pierce [Collegeville, MN: Pueblo, 2011], 276n47, 277). If Power is correct, then not only is "being appeased" an acceptable translation of *placatus*, but given its medieval setting in Sarum, it is the more accurate translation.

[66]The absence of the "Amen" is significant. Institution, Reception, and the Post-Communion Prayer (after which there *is* an "Amen") are one fluid act of prayerful encounter with Christ through the Word of God.

[67]Ketley, *Liturgies*, 279; emphasis added.

[68]From justus.anglican.org/resources/bcp/Sarum/English.htm, accessed September 7, 2019. Note here, too, an instance where Cranmer's liturgical criterion of scripturality is trumped by his commitment to the clarity of the gospel. Cranmer eliminates Scripture quotation—the Agnus Dei from Jn 1:29—because, while it may be straight biblical verbiage, its liturgical use (to encourage believers to adore the elements *as* Christ himself) is contrary to the scriptural gospel. For more on what we mean by this, see chap. 6 below on Cranmer's application of *sola fide* to liturgical ceremonies.

do—no prayers, no offerings, no supplications. The only thing left to do is simply receive.[69]

Sola fide insists that any self-offering, any sacrifice of praise, follows, rather than precedes, the work of the Word in law and gospel. So that there might not be any confusion of what prompts and initiates the grace of the table, for Cranmer any prayers which "present" ourselves happen only after God's grace has been presented to us in Christ. Unlike Sarum, and in contrast to Cranmer's half-way liturgy of 1549, the post-Communion Prayer and its other option, the Prayer of Self-Oblation, reserve the following language for *after* reception: "Accept this our sacrifice of praise and thanksgiving . . . we offer and present unto thee, O Lord, our selves, our souls, and bodies, to be a reasonable, holy, and lively Sacrifice unto thee"; and "assist us with thy grace, that we may. . . do all such good works, as thou has prepared for us to walk in."[70] In other words, these prayers of responsive faith only follow when the gospel has been clearly preached and received at the table, and its clarity for Cranmer would be dependent on the grammatical rules of *sola fide*. Far from "out of joint," here we have a liturgy whose broken structural bones have been set right again in order to re-form in the shape of the gospel.

On a final note, we observe what many have called an odd move by Cranmer in taking the Gloria from the beginning of the entire Communion service to here, after the post-Communion Prayer. However, according to the grammatical rules of *sola fide*, the Gloria is exactly where it should be. Praise and thanksgiving are only possible in response to, rather than prior to, the work of God through his Word. When God has given us his very Son, all that remains to do is simply to thank and praise him.[71] This, too, mirrors the arc of Paul's epistle to the Romans, which ends its exposition of law and gospel with an effusive doxology (Rom 11:33-36).

Is all this analysis of the possible reasoning behind Cranmer's significant redaction of the Canon of the Mass speculative? Is there anything in his

---

[69]We will return to this idea in further detail in chap. 6.

[70]Ketley, *Liturgies*, 94.

[71]I received this insight from Dr. Null in the aforementioned personal conversation (see chap. 4, n55). But Leuenberger gets close when he says, "This great hymn at the close of the service is intended just by its placement to indicate in connexion with all of the liturgy that the most noble activity and indeed the acme of faith consists of laud and praise" (Leuenberger, *Bequest*, 111).

thinking and writing, besides the edits themselves, that helps us to see the exposition above as a plausible articulation of both his interpretation of the Canon and his potential reasoning for his 1552 alternative? To answer these questions, we need to turn to Cranmer's writings on sacrifice as it is situated in the context of broader Reformation thinking on the subject.

The theology of sacrifice in Cranmer and the Reformation. At the time of the Reformation, the biblical concept of sacrifice became a particular hotspot where *sola fide* would operate to make proper distinctions. The distinctions made in these discussions directly inform the structure of sacramental liturgies. They explain both why the Reformers could not tolerate the mass as a sacrifice or re-sacrifice (or even re-presentation of the once-for-all sacrifice) of Christ, and why sacrifice language in the liturgy needed to be reserved for specific moments in the structure of the Communion rite. We first hear Luther insisting on proper distinctions of *who* is sacrificed. Bryan Spinks summarizes:

> [For Luther,] any good work or offering to God which was connected with petition for forgiveness was untenable, because this would imply that Christ's single sacrifice was not altogether complete for the redemption of men. . . . There was a sacrifice at the Eucharist—of prayer, praise, and thanksgiving; but we do not offer Christ as a sacrifice, because he offers us.[72]

Theologically, according to Luther, there were only two sacrifices identifiable for the Christian—the sacrifice of Christ on the cross (Heb 10:10), and the sacrifice of praise we responsively offer (Heb 13:15).[73] Vilmos Vajta, in his exposition of Luther's liturgical theology, emphasizes that Luther found it important to distinguish between *beneficium* and *sacrificium*—the God who gives blessing, and the God who requires sacrifice.[74] Spinks follows Vajta's assessment of Luther:

> Luther charged the Roman church with having made the mass a human *sacrificium* directed towards God, whereas the Gospel sacrament is a divine *beneficium* directed towards humanity, and our offering of praise and life can only

[72]Spinks, *Luther's Liturgical Criteria and His Reform of the Canon of the Mass* (Bramcote: Grove Books, 1982), 29.

[73]See references in Spinks, *Criteria*, 29.

[74]Vilmos Vajta, *Luther On Worship: An Interpretation* (Minneapolis: Fortress, 1958), 27-63.

be a response to God's gift. It is this contrast which explains Luther's violent criticisms of the canon of the mass, and he set about removing features of the human *sacrificium* and turning the sacrament more clearly into a divine *beneficium*. For Luther all worship is a *beneficium* of God.[75]

Cranmer, following the lead of his influential colleague, Peter Martyr, shared this perspective. We observe how the language of the post-Communion Prayer may be indebted to Peter Martyr, as he articulated his understanding of the "Word-centered union of sacrament and sacrifice" and its resulting centrality of the Lord's Supper as a Holy *Communion*.[76] What we see in Martyr's sacramental theology is the kind of distinctions that *sola fide* makes. According to Martyr's liturgical theology, what is offered by God in the sacrament is himself, Christ, reconciliation, grace, and remission of sin; what is offered by us in sacrifice is thanksgiving, alms, prayers, singing, preaching, obedience to God's Word, and love of neighbor.[77] These distinctions sound strikingly similar to Cranmer's theology of sacrifice articulated in his 1550 *Defence*. There, he distinguishes between Christ's sacrificial offering as "propitiatory and merciful" and our offering as a response of praise and thanksgiving. In Cranmer's words, "The first kind of sacrifice Christ offered to God for us; the second kind we ourselves offer to God by Christ."[78] A year later, Cranmer would again reiterate in another sacramental tome: "[Christ's] sacrifice was the redemption of the world, ours is not so: his was death, ours is but a remembrance thereof: his was the taking away the sins of the world; ours is a praising and thanking for the same: and therefore his was satisfactory, ours is gratulatory."[79]

It is this stark division of sacrificial labor (identical to Luther's construal) which would compel Cranmer to erect the same theological partitions in his 1552 liturgy. It explains why any self-oblation or "sacrifice of praise" would

---

[75]Spinks, *Criteria*, 15. See also the brief discussion in Andrew Atherstone, "Reforming Worship: Lessons from Luther and Cranmer," *Churchman* 132, no. 2 (Summer 2018): 106.

[76]Donald Fuller, "Sacrifice and Sacrament: Another Eucharistic Contribution from Peter Martyr Vermigli," in *Peter Martyr Vermigli and the European Reformations: Semper Reformanda*, ed. Frank A. James III (Leiden: Brill, 2004), 236.

[77]Adapted from a chart in Fuller, "Sacrifice," 234.

[78]Cranmer, "Defence," 449.

[79]Cranmer, "An Answer to a Crafty and Sophistical Cavillation Devised by Stephen Gardiner" (1551) in Cox, *Works*, vol 1., 359.

fall *after* reception, not before it, as we noted above. Structurally then, this is why, as Andrew Atherstone put it, "Cranmer was careful not to use the language of 'sacrifice' or 'offering' until after communion. The Prayer of Self-Oblation is deliberately placed after we receive from God, not before."[80] In sum, the theology of sacrifice at the time of the Reformation became a particularly poignant place where the distinctions made by *sola fide* would clarify and name the gospel against not-gospels, and this in turn demanded a restructuring of the liturgy.[81]

"NOT I, BUT CHRIST" STRUCTURALLY: BAPTISM (1552)

Space does not allow for a full treatment of how Cranmer appears to have applied the same structural "gospel-logic" to the baptism rite as he had to Morning Prayer and Holy Communion. We will simply highlight the observation of Stephen Sykes in his analysis of the structure of the 1552 baptism liturgy. He notes that the "basic pattern" present in Morning and Evening Prayer is replicated in baptism. According to Sykes, the liturgy's structure

> comprises two main elements, those of Word and Sacrament, prefaced and followed by brief transitional statements and prayers. Between the reading of the Gospel (from Mark 10), and the actual Baptism of the child, are a set of promises made by the godparents in the name of the child, which constitute a kind of hinge in the service on which entry into the grace of Baptism turns. These promises are the human response to God's promises declared in the

---

[80] Atherstone, "The Lord's Supper and the Gospel of Salvation: Grace Alone and Faith Alone in the Book of Common Prayer," in *Feed My Sheep: The Anglican Ministry of Word and Sacrament,* ed. Lee Gatiss (Watford: Lost Coin Books, 2016), 83. It is at least a little misleading for Nathan Jennings to contrast Luther's total rejection of sacrificial language around the communion service with "the Anglican tradition within Protestantism" which, according to him, "never rejected the language of sacrifice with regard to the divine service" (*Liturgy and Theology: Economy and Reality* [Eugene, OR: Cascade, 2017], 72n64). Based on what we have here observed, at least *these* members of the Anglican tradition did in fact reject such language, evidenced by its inclusion only after the completion of the rite. While subsequent Anglicans (such as Jeremy Taylor) would indeed *not* reject sacrificial language around the Eucharist, there is still a strong witness in the tradition that follows in Cranmer's footsteps.

[81] Despite the clarity of teaching on sacrifice offered by Cranmer and the English Reformers here outlined, Anglicanism's post-Reformation history has fostered ambiguity. For a brief treatment of this history, see Colin Buchanan, *An Evangelical Among the Anglican Liturgists* (London: SPCK, 2009), 152-57. We should point out that many modern Anglican treatments of eucharistic sacrifice are more nuanced than the more flattened presentations offered here of what Cranmer is responding to in his day. Cf. e.g., Colin Dunlop, *Anglican Public Worship* (London: SCM, 1953), 77-87, and Jennings, *Liturgy,* 48-73.

Gospel. The whole service therefore has the form of a covenant between God and the child, initiated from God's side.[82]

Again we see, as we have observed with other exegetes of Cranmer's liturgies, that though Sykes does not use the language of justification, or law, or gospel, the structure of the baptism service is inevitably parsed according to the grammar of *sola fide*. Our works are clearly set apart from God's, and clearly the action is "initiated from God's side." God's promises must be spoken *first*; then and only then do parents and godparents make promises that are "the human response to God's promises declared in the gospel." This movement constitutes a cycle of law, gospel, and responding faith, similar to what we saw above. After that movement, the administration of baptism begins another cycle, where the ritual of baptism itself is a proclamation of law and gospel (burial and resurrection), with the responding faith demonstrative in the Lord's Prayer, and prayer of thanksgiving.

We have walked through two of Cranmer's most significant liturgies (Morning Prayer, Holy Communion), and briefly overviewed a third prominent rite (baptism), having discerned a common structural motif. This repeated theme leads us to the conclusion that for Cranmer, the shape of liturgy must conform to the shape of the gospel. Structural exposition such as this may not seem like an intuitive starting place. Oftentimes, liturgical analysis begins with the *words* of the liturgy, which is precisely where we will turn in the next chapter. Part of the reason we began our exploration of Cranmer's liturgies with structure, however, is that we wanted to first foreground the skeletal structure on which those words are hung. The choices made by Cranmer about which terms and phrases should be translated, transposed, eliminated, or added become all the more vivid for our purposes of discerning his evangelical agenda.

---

[82]Stephen Sykes, "'Baptisme Doth Represente unto Us Oure Profession,'" in *Thomas Cranmer: Essays in Commemoration of the 500th Anniversary of His Birth*, ed. Margot Johnson (Durham: Turnstone, 1990), 129-30.

5

"NOT I, BUT CHRIST" THEOLOGICALLY

SOLA FIDE IN CRANMER'S LITURGICAL TERMINOLOGY

WE SAW HOW the grammar of *sola fide* would function for Cranmer like a pair of scissors, taking existing liturgies, cutting them into sections, and rearranging those pieces or throwing away whole sections altogether. This is how justification works on the level of liturgical structure, filtering out not-gospels that the true gospel might shine forth. When it comes to liturgical content, therefore, we could say that *sola fide* functions more like a scalpel, making precision edits, right down to the word, sometimes down to a few letters. Many have observed that Cranmer's "liturgical surgery" revealed a virtuosic creativity less of the *ex nihilo* type and far more of the kind which took the preexisting works of others, cut them up, and stitched them together anew in a surprisingly functional, fluid, and moving manner. And as we move on from structure (the last chapter) and into content (the next three chapters), we recall our discussion in the introduction borne from the insights of liturgical theology—namely, that liturgical *content* is far more than liturgical texts. It also includes physicality (liturgical action, spaces, and tools) and dispositions (liturgical piety). Therefore, as we move from structure into the analysis of liturgical content, we will observe the work of the grammar of *sola fide* as Cranmer redacts liturgical content with "not I, but Christ" in four arenas: (1) theologically and terminologically in this present chapter; (2) ceremonially in chapter six; and (3) devotionally and (4) homiletically in chapter seven.

The Archbishop's method of redaction of the liturgy's words is perhaps nowhere more clearly and concisely illustrated than in his preface to the *Book of Common Prayer.* In a sense, his entire enterprise is disclosed in his opening sentence, both in what it says and what it references. Cranmer bursts out of the liturgical gate: "There was never any thing by the wit of man so well devised, or so surely established, which (in continuance of time) hath not been corrupted: as (among other things) it may plainly appear by the common prayers in the Church."[1] Sixteenth-century clerics and scholars attuned to contemporaneous liturgical revisions taking place in the Roman Catholic Church on the Continent may very well have recognized this sentence of Cranmer's as not original to him. It is lifted (with a significant surgical cut-and-stitch) from the opening lines of the 1536 preface of a Breviary revision made by the Spanish Cardinal Francisco de Quiñones. The Quignon Breviary, as it is called, reads, "There was never anything by the wit of man so well devised which could not later be rendered more perfect by the added insight of many."[2] Comparing Cranmer with Quiñones summarizes, in essence, the difference between the theological outlook of Rome and that of the Reformers. Instead of a preface which highlights the "perfectability" of humanity, Cranmer offers exactly the opposite sentiment, which is telling of his commitment to *sola fide* and resulting liturgical agenda. What is foregrounded right at the beginning is the depravity of humanity and (therefore) the necessity of a grace that is found by faith alone in Christ alone. We could say that the way Cranmer edited Quiñones's preface would be the way he would go about redacting all liturgical content—saying no to the "I," and yes to Christ.

THEOLOGICAL LANGUAGE AND THE GRAMMAR OF *SOLA FIDE*

We observe first, broadly, that the Reformers were concerned about words and how their usage and context impacted people pastorally. We hear in their arguments the kind of thinking which showed how the grammar of *sola fide* would become a theological governor for language. We read this, for instance, in Luther's lectures on Romans when we see *sola fide* governing how he chooses

---

[1]Joseph Ketley, ed., *The Two Liturgies, A.D. 1549, and A.D. 1552* (Cambridge: Parker Society, 1844), 18.
[2]Translated by Geoffrey Cuming, *The Godly Order: Texts and Studies Relating to the Book of Common Prayer* (London: SPCK, 1983), 2. Original Latin: "*Nihil enim humano elaboratum ingenio tam exactum initio unquam fuit quin postea multorum accedente iudicio perfectius reddi possit.*" See J. Wickham Legg, ed., *The Second Recension of the Quignon Breviary*, vol. 1 (London: Harrison and Sons, 1908), xxiii.

to translate ἀφωρισμένος εἰς εὐαγγέλιον θεοῦ ("set apart for the gospel of God") in the first verse of Paul's epistle. *Sola fide* would govern vocabulary to such an extent that Luther would feel compelled to argue that ἀφωρισμένος must not be translated "sanctified," but "separated" or "set apart." Luther's reasoning: "It is more unpretentious and more modest to call himself 'separated' rather than 'sanctified,' lest he speak boastfully of himself."[3] Behind this for Luther is more than Paul's sinful pretention, for Paul would use the concept of boasting elsewhere to draw the very kinds of distinctions that *sola fide* makes (1 Cor 1:26-31). *Sola fide* grammatically excludes boasting precisely because faith *alone* is that which trusts *wholly* in the work of Christ. *Sola fide* therefore dismisses "sanctified" as a word choice, lest some misunderstandings creep in of what sanctified *could* mean (i.e., more holy, more morally pure).

Cranmer would share this meticulous concern for wording. We have already cited above the Archbishop's pushback against Henry's desire to add "chiefly" and "only" in order to temper (and ultimately dismantle) the radically disjunctive nature of *sola fide*. Elsewhere in his annotations to Henry's corrections of the Bishops' book, Cranmer spends lengthy passages setting up the argument for why he would desire to eliminate the conditional phrases and language inserted by Henry. For several paragraphs, the Archbishop asserts the theological outlook of Paul and James, where Cranmer and Henry can agree—true faith inevitably produces good works:

> If the profession of our faith of the remission of our own sins enter within us into the deepness of our hearts; then it must needs kindle a warm fire of love in our hearts towards God, and towards all other for the love of God—a fervent mind to seek and procure God's honour, will, and pleasure in all things . . . *in summa*, a firm intent and purpose to do all that is good, and leave all that is evil.[4]

But Cranmer would reason that if faith *alone* does this,

> In my judgment it shall not be necessary to interline or insert in many places, where we protest our pure Christian faith, these words or sentence, that be newly added, namely, "I being in will to follow God's precepts;" "I rejecting in my will and heart the Devil and his works;" "I willing to return to God;" "If I

---

[3]Luther, "Lectures on Romans," (*LW* 25, 144).
[4]Cranmer, "Corrections," in John Edmund Cox, ed., *The Works of Thomas Cranmer*, vol. 2 (Cambridge: The University Press, 1846), 86.

continue not in sin;" "If I continue a Christian life;" "If I follow Christ's precepts;" "We living well;" "If we order and conform our wills in this world to his precepts;" "If we join our wills to his godly motions;" and other such like sentences and clauses conditional, which to the right faith need not be added: for without these conditions is no right faith.[5]

What Cranmer is saying is that the use of conditional clauses to surround statements of faith and the gospel is unnecessary. Underneath this concern is the Archbishop's greater burden that conditional statements like these actually serve to muddy the waters of *sola fide*, reintroducing the commingling of faith and works that justification has set out to distinguish. Cranmer was therefore arguing that it is precisely the *unconditioned* gospel of grace which has the power to change us within "the deepness of our hearts" and produce the good works that the conditionality demands. This line of argumentation, down to the concern for words and phrases, will be (implicitly) employed time and again as Cranmer translates and redacts the received liturgies and forms them into the gospel-proclamation that is the 1552 Book of Common Prayer. Sometimes, the grammar of *sola fide* necessitates the subtraction of words and phrases—other times, addition. Yet other times, whole prayers and liturgical sections need to be demolished and built from the ground up. We will observe all these techniques employed by Cranmer.

SOLA FIDE IN THE COLLECTS

Cranmer's Collects are perhaps the most overt place where this kind of theological distinction happens on the level of terminology. That the Collects of Western Christianity were in need of theological revision was felt by other Reformers. Luther, for instance, urged that the Collects (along with the Antiphons and Responsories) be shelved "until they have been purged, for there is a horrible lot of filth in them."[6] Interestingly enough, many of the most ancient Collects, in their original form, seem to operate along the grammar of *sola fide*. This may very well be due to the fact that not a small amount of them were forged in the controversies of the Pelagian heresy, where it became important for the church to clarify the gospel by insisting on humanity's

---

[5]Cranmer, "Corrections," in Cox, *Works*, vol. 2, 86.
[6]Martin Luther, "Concerning the Order of Public Worship," (*LW* 53, 14).

helplessness apart from the work of God.[7] The so-called Gelasian Sacramentary, named after the fifth-century bishop of Rome, Gelasius, contains some of the early Collects that appear to have been composed in the wake of Augustine's anti-Pelagian debates, as they echo the Bishop of Hippo's sharp faithworks distinction.[8] Even so, good as they were, Cranmer "took no chances"[9] in those Gelasian Collects when it came, for instance, to the translation of the word *mereamur,* "to merit" (see fig. 5.1).

GELASIAN SACRAMENTARY[10]	BOOK OF COMMON PRAYER, 1549[11]
Almighty and everlasting God,	Almighty and everlasting God, **which of thy tender love toward man, hast sent**
our Saviour Jesus Christ	our Saviour Jesus Christ,
took upon him our flesh	to take upon him our flesh,
and suffered death upon the cross,	and to suffer death upon the cross,
that all mankind should follow the example of his humility,	that all mankind should follow the example of his great humility:
grant that we may	**mercifully** grant, that we
both follow the example of his patience,	both follow the example of his patience,
and also may merit (*mereamur*) the partaking	and ~~also may merit the partaking~~ **be made partakers**
of his resurrection; through the same Lord.	of his resurrection; through the same Jesus Christ our Lord.

Figure 5.1. Cranmer's translation of the Collect for the Sunday next before Easter

[7]James A. Devereux, "Reformed Doctrine in the Collects of the First *Book of Common Prayer,*" *Harvard Theological Review* 28, no. 1 (January 1965): 49-50: "The doctrine of justification was, genetically at least, the principal theological issue of the Reformation; yet its effects on the translation of the collects, though clearly discernible, were not revolutionary. This was chiefly because the notion of grace implied in them was, on the whole quite acceptable to the English Reformers."

[8]See L. E. H. Stephens-Hodge, *The Collects: An Introduction and Exposition* (London: Hodder and Stoughton, 1961), 26-27. However, for more accurate dating and the complex history of authorship, composition, and use of the Gelasian Sacramentary, see Cyril Vogel, *Medieval Liturgy: An Introduction to the Sources,* trans. and rev. William Storey and Niels Rasmussen (Portland, OR: Pastoral Press, 1986), 64-70.

[9]Devereux, "Collects," 49.

[10]This translation, along with all subsequent translations, are the author's unless otherwise noted. Note that the translations favor paralleling Cranmer for the ease of analysis. Latin: "*Deus, qui humano generi ad imitandum humilitatis exemplum, Salvatorem nostrum carnem sumere et crucem subire fecisti: concede propitius, ut et pacientiae eius habere documentum et resurrectionis eius consortia mereamur,*" taken from Leo Cunibert Mohlberg (ed.), *Liber Sacramentorum Romanae Aeclesiae Ordinis Anni Circuli (Cod. Vat. Reg. lat. 316/Paris bibl. Nat. 7193, 41/56) (Sacramentarium Gelasianum)* (Rome: Herder, 1960), 53 (no. 329).

[11]Ketley, *Liturgies,* 51.

For the Reformers, *mereamur* was perhaps "the most offensive word in the Roman doctrine of grace,"[12] prompting a move that Cranmer would make time and again throughout his liturgy—a move that captures the heart of *sola fide*: human merit is excised, and in its place is put the work of God. Cranmer uses the passive voice often in these theological shifts: we are "made partakers." When faith is *alone* we are not agents in our salvation but recipients of divine agency. In the most classic example, merit is simply excised. Here is the Collect for Purity (fig. 5.2).

SARUM MISSAL[13]	BOOK OF COMMON PRAYER, 1549[14]
God, unto whom every heart is open, and all desires known, and from whom no secrets are hid: cleanse the thoughts of our hearts, by the infusion of thy Holy Spirit: that we may perfectly love thee, and, meritoriously (*mereamur*), worthily magnify thee . . .	Almighty God, unto whom all hearts be open, and all desires known, and from whom no secrets are hid: cleanse the thoughts of our hearts, by the ~~infusion~~ **inspiration** of thy Holy Spirit: that we may perfectly love thee, and ~~meritoriously~~ worthily magnify thy holy name . . .

Figure 5.2. Cranmer's translation of the Collect for Purity

Additionally, we might notice that Cranmer transposes *infusionem* into the key of *sola fide* by translating it as "inspiration," in order to avoid the medieval notion of merit based on "infused grace." Another instance of the excision of *mereamur* is in his Collect for the fourteenth Sunday after Trinity (see fig. 5.3).

SARUM BREVIARY[15]	BOOK OF COMMON PRAYER, 1549[16]
Almighty and everlasting God, give unto us the increase of faith, hope, and charity, and that we may merit (*mereamur*)	Almighty and everlasting God, give unto us the increase of faith, hope, and charity: and, that we may ~~merit~~ **obtain**

---

[12]Devereux, "Collects," 50.

[13]Latin: "*Deus cui omne cor patet et omnis voluntas loquitur, et quem nullum latet secretum; purifica per infusionem sancti spiritus cogitationes cordis nostri, ut te perfecte diligere et digne laudare mereamur*," taken from F. E. Brightman, *The English Rite: Being a Synopsis of the Sources and Revisions of the Book of Common Prayer*, vol. 2 (London: Rivingtons, 1915), 640.

[14]Ketley, *Liturgies*, 77.

[15]Latin: "*Omnipotens sempiterne deus, da nobis fidei spei & charitatis augmentum: et ut mereamur assequi quod promittis: fac nos amare quod precipis*," taken from Brightman, *English Rite*, vol. 2, 510.

[16]Ketley, *Liturgies*, 64.

SARUM BREVIARY	BOOK OF COMMON PRAYER, 1549[18]
that which thou dost promise: make us to love that which thou dost command.	that which thou dost promise, make us to love that which thou dost command.

Figure 5.3. Cranmer's translation of the Collect for the fourteenth Sunday after Trinity

Paralleling what we observed in the previous chapter with respect to Cranmer's careful use of the language of "only, chiefly," the Collect for the thirteenth Sunday after Trinity makes even more explicit what the original author of the Collect in the Gelasian Sacramentary had purposed (see fig. 5.4).

GELASIAN SACRAMENTARY[17]	BOOK OF COMMON PRAYER, 1549[18]
Almighty and merciful God, of whose gift it cometh, that thy faithful people do unto thee true and laudable service: grant we beseech thee, that we may, without offense, run to thy promises, Through our Lord.	Almighty and merciful God, of whose **only** gift it cometh, that thy faithful people do unto thee true and laudable service: grant, we beseech thee, that we may ~~without offense~~ so run to thy heavenly promises, that we fail not finally to attain the same: Through Jesus Christ our Lord.

Figure 5.4. Cranmer's translation of the Collect for the thirteenth Sunday after Trinity

Cranmer seems aware that the lack of "only" could leave the door open to medieval understandings of grace joined with our works. "Only" does the work of *sola fide*, categorically distinguishing grace as a *total* gift. Cranmer shows how a single word carries a freight of theological import. Notice, too, that "without offense" is removed. Perhaps the Archbishop desires to make clear that even *as* we offend God, "even while we were yet sinners" (Rom 5:8), we still flee to his promises.

The Second Collect for Evensong provides another important look into Cranmer's process, as it went through several English translations before

---

[17]Latin: "*Omnipotens et misericors deus, de cuius munere venit ut tibi a fidelibus tuis digne & laudabiliter serviatur: tribue nobis quesumus, ut ad promissiones tuas sine offensione curramus. Per dominum*," taken from Brightman, *English Rite*, vol. 2, 504.

[18]Ketley, *Liturgies*, 64.

Cranmer got a hold of it. It is telling that Cranmer did not simply parrot those translations (one of which was almost fifteen years old) but opted for redaction according to *sola fide* (see fig. 5.5).

REDMAN'S PRIMER, 1535	KING'S PRIMER, 1545	BOOK OF COMMON PRAYER, 1549[19]
O God,	O God,	O God,
from whom all holy desires,	from whom all holy desires,	from whom all holy desires,
all good counsels,	all good counsels,	all good counsels,
and all just works do	and all just works do	and all just works do
proceed,	proceed,	proceed:
give unto us	give unto **thy servants**	give unto thy servants
the same peace	that same peace,	that peace,
which the world cannot give	which the world cannot give,	which the world cannot
that our hearts	that our hearts	give;
being obedient	being obedient	that both our hearts
to thy commandments	to thy commandments,	may **be set to obey**
		thy commandments,
(and fear of our enemies	and the fear of our enemies	and also that **by thee**, we
be taken away)	taken away,	**being defended from the fear** of our enemies,
our time may be peaceable	our time may be peaceable	may pass our time in **rest**
through thy protection.	by thy protection.	**and quietness**:
By Christ our Lord. Amen.	Through Christ our Lord,	through **the merits of**
	Amen.	**Jesus** Christ our Savior.
		Amen.

Figure 5.5. Cranmer's translation of the second Collect for Evensong[20]

Here we notice the *King's Primer* adding "thy servants," which comes as no surprise considering Henry's desire, above all, that England be filled with loyal subjects (therefore, the rise of the language of servitude is very much a part of the Henrician agenda across the board). But once we move on to Cranmer's Collect, we see again the negation of our own obedience ("not I"), switching activity through the divine passive voice ("but Christ"). And it appears that because the Collect could be read as our obedience *leading to* the fear of our enemies being taken away, Cranmer makes doubly clear that it is done "by thee," and with yet another divine passive, "being defended."

---

[19]Ketley, *Liturgies*, 37-38.
[20]The following excerpts from Redman's Primer and the *King's Primer* are taken from Cuming, *Godly Order*, 51. It is interesting that though Cuming sets these prayers in juxtaposition, he makes no mention or analysis of Cranmer's distinctive redactions.

And, as Cranmer does elsewhere, he makes explicit what about Jesus all this power is "through": it is by his "merits."[21]

Similarly, Cranmer is found in several places excising language from the *propit-* word-group so as to avoid any idea of the mass as a propitiatory sacrifice.[22] In one instance, he replaces it with a term loaded with significance when it comes to the clarity of *sola fide* in his context. Consider his work on the Collect for the fourth Sunday in Advent (see fig. 5.6).

GELASIAN SACRAMENTARY[23]	BOOK OF COMMON PRAYER, 1549[24]
Lord raise up, we pray thee, thy power, and come, and with great might succor us,	Lord raise up (we pray thee) thy power, and come among us, and with great might succor us,
that whereas through our sins	that whereas through our sins **and wickedness**
we are hindered,	we be **sore let and** hindered,
thy bountiful grace,	thy bountiful grace **and mercy**,
by your propitiation (*propitiationis*)	through **the satisfaction of thy Son our Lord**,
may speedily deliver us.	may speedily deliver us.

Figure 5.6. Cranmer's translation of the Collect for the fourth Sunday in Advent

In addition to three expansions of "Erasmian doublets," Cranmer's big change is to make "*tue propitiationis*" even more overt with a word carrying heavy freight: "satisfaction." Ashley Null explains the significance of this word for medieval Christian piety:

> An act of mortal sin incurred a liability for both eternal damnation (*culpa*) and temporal punishment (*poena*), with contrition remitting the former and satisfactions the latter. In Scotist teaching, however, divine pardon merely commuted *culpa* to *poena*, since God had ordained that sin must be punished, either

---

[21]Cranmer adds the "merits of Jesus Christ" to one other collect (Whitsunday), a double-dose in the 1549 Communion liturgy's Prayer of Oblation ("not weighing our merits, but pardoning our offenses"; "that by the merits and death of thy Son Jesus Christ") (Ketley, *Liturgies,* 89), and a retaining of the phrase in the re-placed post-Communion prayer of 1552 ("that by the merits and death of thy Son Jesus Christ") (Ketley, *Liturgies,* 280). Based on *sola fide*, for Cranmer, "merit" seems to be a word wholly inappropriate for self-attribution, except in our failure.

[22]See Devereux, "Collects," 56-57.

[23]Latin: "*Excita quaesumus domine potentiam tuam et veni, & magna nobis virtute succurre: ut per auxilium gratie tue quod nostra peccata prepediunt: indulgentia tue propitiationis acceleret,*" taken from Brightman, *English Rite,* vol. 1, 213-14.

[24]Ketley, *Liturgies,* 42.

by himself on the day of judgement or by the *viator*. Therefore, after a penitent had been loosed from his debt of eternal punishment through the infusion of grace, he still remained bound to work off his debt of temporal punishment through the penance [i.e., satisfactions] which his confessor had assigned him.[25]

That Cranmer here attributes "satisfaction" to the work of Christ is yet another instance of a stark "not I, but Christ" distinction, drawing lines that were blurred in his day and age. Cranmer uses the prayer to retell the doctrine of satisfaction through the grammar of *sola fide*.

Here is another prayer where Cranmer's redaction is found negating the "I" (see fig. 5.7).

GREGORIAN SACRAMENTARY[26]	BOOK OF COMMON PRAYER, 1549[27]
Lord we beseech Thee, receive the prayers of thy holy, heavenly people who follow thee: and grant that they perceive what things they ought to do, and also have power faithfully to fulfill the same.	Lord we beseech Thee, **mercifully** to receive the prayers of thy ~~holy, heavenly~~ people **which** ~~follow~~ **call upon** thee: and grant that they may both perceive **and know** what things they ought to do, and also have **grace and** power faithfully to fulfill the same.

Figure 5.7. Cranmer's translation of the Collect for the first Sunday after Epiphany

Holy and heavenly? "Not I," says Cranmer. Do I follow God wholeheartedly? "Not I," says Cranmer, "but I certainly *call upon* God." And if we are to do what we "ought to do," we must not only have power. We must also have "grace." Take note, as well, that "call upon" is a phrase that pervaded the Psalms in Cranmer's English Bible,[28] used specifically in contexts of utter helplessness and dependence, sometimes of repentance. No doubt this word choice carries those strong connotations of the grammar of *sola fide*. What does a person with nothing do? They "call upon" the Lord.

---

[25] Ashley Null, *Thomas Cranmer's Doctrine of Repentance: Renewing the Power to Love* (Oxford: Oxford University Press, 2000), 55.

[26] Latin: "*Vota quesumus domine supplicantis populi celesti pietate prosequere: ut & que agenda sunt videant: et ad implenda que viderint convalescant,*" taken from Brightman, *English Rite*, vol. 1, 252.

[27] Ketley, *Liturgies*, 46.

[28] In the 1539 Great Bible, "call upon" is present fifteen times (Ps 14:4; 17:6; 18:2 [18:3]; 31:19 [31:17]; 50:15; 53:4; 79:6; 80:18; 86:5, 7; 88:9; 99:6 [twice]; 105:1; 141:1). (Brackets refer to references in modern translations.)

In the third Collect for Evensong (also known as the Inlumina Prayer), we find the grammar of *sola fide* in this instance not only subtracting and replacing, but adding. The work of Christ is made more explicit (see fig. 5.8).

GELASIAN / GREGORIAN SACRAMENTARIES[29]	BOOK OF COMMON PRAYER, 1549[30]
Illumine, we beg you, Lord, our darkness and kindly drive away all the snares of the night: through Jesus Christ.	Lighten our darkness we beseech thee, O Lord; by **thy great mercy** **defend us** from all perils **and dangers** of this night; **for the love of thy only Son, our Savior** Jesus Christ.

Figure 5.8. Cranmer's translation of the Inlumina Prayer

In yet other instances, the grammar of *sola fide* demanded the abandonment of whole sections of prayers, as in the Collect for the twelfth Sunday after Trinity (see fig. 5.9).

GELASIAN / GREGORIAN SACRAMENTARIES[31]	BOOK OF COMMON PRAYER, 1549[32]
Almighty and everlasting God, who dost exceed the merits (*merita*) and prayers of thy suppliants; Pour down upon us thy mercy	Almighty and everlasting God, ~~who dost exceed the merits (merita)~~ ~~and prayers~~ ~~of thy suppliants;~~ **which art always more ready to hear than we to pray; and art wont to give** **more than either we desire or deserve:** Pour down upon us **the abundance of** thy mercy,

---

[29]Thomas A. Krosnicki, "How Dark the Night: The 'Inlumina' Prayer," *Worship* 85, no. 5 (September 2011): 447, indicates that the prayer, though found in the Gelasian and Gregorian Sacramentaries, predates those collections and is of obscure origin. This English translation is Krosnicki's, with altered word order to parallel Cranmer for ease of reading. Krosnicki provides the original Latin: "*Inlumina, quaesumus, domine, tenebras nostras et tocius noctis insidiis repelle propicius: per.*"

[30]Ketley, *Liturgies*, 38.

[31]Translation is a combination of mine and that of Cuming, *Godly Order*, 59. Latin: "*Omnipotens sempiterne deus: qui abundantia pietatis tue et merita supplicum excedis et vota, effunde super nos misericordiam tuam: ut dimittas que conscientia metuit: et adijcias quod oratio non presumit. Per,*" taken from Brightman, *English Rite*, vol. 2, 502.

[32]Ketley, *Liturgies*, 63.

GELASIAN / GREGORIAN SACRAMENTARIES	BOOK OF COMMON PRAYER, 1549
forgiving us those things whereof our conscience is afraid, and giving unto us that that our prayer dare not presume to ask.	forgiving us those things whereof our conscience is afraid, and giving unto us that that our prayer dare not presume to ask.

Figure 5.9. Cranmer's translation of the Collect for the twelfth Sunday after Trinity

And even in other times, Cranmer jettisoned entire prayers, opting for wholesale replacement, not only because of what they said, but because of the tenuous nature of their context in the light of the doctrine of justification. The classic example is the Collect for the first Sunday in Lent, a season in medieval Christianity especially prone to penitential acts of merit on the part of earnest Christians (see fig. 5.10).

GREGORIAN SACRAMENTARY[33]	BOOK OF COMMON PRAYER, 1549[34]
God, who didst purify thy Church by the yearly observance of Lent, help your family strive toward abstinence, and flawless good works.	~~God, who didst purify thy Church by the yearly observance of Lent, help your family strive toward abstinence, and flawless good works.~~ **O Lord, which for our sake, didst fast forty days and forty nights: Give us grace to use such abstinence, that, our flesh being subdued to the Spirit, we may ever obey thy godly motions in righteousness, and true holiness, to thy honor and glory.**

Figure 5.10. Cranmer's New Collect for the first Sunday in Lent

Apparently, Cranmer felt the need, both for the sake of the prayer and for the sake of the season, to clarify the distinctions made by *sola fide* on the front end of what could otherwise be a forty-day feast for the Old Adam's delight in confusing faith and works. Notice the divine passive ("our flesh being

---

[33]The translation is admittedly a bit wooden for the sake of bringing out some of the terminology. Latin: "*Deus qui ecclesiam tuam annua quadragesimali observatione purificas: presta familie tue ut quod a te obtinere abstinendo nititur: hoc bonis operibus exequatur,*" taken from Brightman, *English Rite,* vol. 1, 294.

[34]Ketley, *Liturgies,* 49.

subdued") and that we are not obeying God's commands but rather obeying the "Godly motions" of the Spirit in us.[35] And, most significantly, notice where Cranmer puts the emphasis of the Lenten fast—*not* on our fasting ("not I"), but on Jesus' forty days and forty nights ("but Christ").

Finally, we can see how in translation Cranmer in some instances traded a less precise English word for a more precise one when it came to making *sola fide* more clear. Evidently, Cranmer felt that the definition of faith was at stake in how one translated the Latin word *spero*, typically translated as "hope" in the English. Observe Cranmer's work in the first Sunday after Trinity (see fig. 5.11).

GREGORIAN SACRAMENTARY[36]	BOOK OF COMMON PRAYER, 1549[37]
God, the strength of all them that hope in thee,	God, the strength of all them that ~~hope~~ **trust** in thee,
mercifully accept our prayers:	mercifully accept our prayers;
And because the weakness of our mortal nature	And because the weakness of our mortal nature
can do nothing without thee,	can do ~~nothing~~ **no good thing** without thee,
grant us the help of thy grace,	grant us the help of thy grace,
that in keeping of thy commandments,	that in keeping of thy commandments,
we may please thee both in will and deed.	we may please thee both in will and deed.

Figure 5.11. Cranmer's translation of the Collect for the first Sunday after Trinity

We notice the clarity of translating *spero* as "trust" instead of "hope." Hope insinuates possibility, whereas trust is more explicitly believing in the veracity of an external word or promise. Faith as hope might be understood as believing that God's promises *could be* true. Faith as trust must be understood as believing that God's promises *are* true. In his Homily on Faith Cranmer pairs trust and hope with the former tied to "confidence": "[Faith] is . . . a sure trust and confidence of the mercy of God, through our Lord Jesus Christ, and a steadfast hope of all good things to be received at God's hand."[38] As

---

[35]Ketley notes the variant, "monitions" (*Liturgies*, 49n7).

[36]Latin: "*Deus in te sperantium fortitudo, adesto propitius invocationibus nostris: & quia sine te nichil potest mortalis infirmitas: presta auxilium gratie tue: ut in exequendis mandatis tuis, et voluntate tibi & actione placeamus,*" taken from Brightman, *English Rite*, vol. 2, 462.

[37]Ketley, *Liturgies*, 60.

[38]Roland B. Bond, ed., *Certain Sermons or Homilies (1547) and A Homily Against Disobedience and Wilful Rebellion (1570): A Critical Edition* (Toronto: University of Toronto Press, 1987), 92.

Devereux observes here, "The Lutheran cast of this definition should be evident. Here, although 'trust' and 'hope' are paralleled, they are clearly distinguished."[39] Note additionally in the Collect that Cranmer puts a particularly moral spin on "can do nothing without thee," highlighting that it is particularly in the doing of righteous deeds that we can claim "no" ground. *Sola fide*, once again, says no to the not-gospel of works-righteousness. As we can see, the Collects above, along with others,[40] become windows for viewing all the different ways that theological and terminological redaction will take place throughout the Prayer Book—translation, transposition, addition, subtraction, reordering, and more. The Collects, then, serve as a helpful microcosm for the kind of content-redaction taking place throughout the entire liturgy. The following sections will take the kinds of work we have observed in the Collects, categorize them, and observe them in the rest of the liturgy.

SOLA FIDE IN WORDS AND THEIR SUBJECTS AND OBJECTS

Throughout the Prayer Book, we find Cranmer's method of redaction meticulously consistent in certain instances, especially when it comes to specific words and how they are employed alongside their subjects and objects. In this way, we witness the grammar of *sola fide* looking most literally like a grammar, theologically determining where words are positioned in the construction of liturgical sentences. Let us closely examine how *sola fide* informs three terms in the Book of Common Prayer: oblation, sacrifice, and satisfaction.

"Oblation" and "sacrifice" underwent severe scrutiny by Cranmer. We observed above how the grammar of *sola fide* insisted that, structurally, any *self*-oblation happens only after receiving the grace of the gospel through the reception of the bread and wine. Likewise, *self*-sacrifice could only happen

---

[39]Devereux, "Collects," 55.

[40]There are more Collects to observe and dissect: (a) Epiphany 1's expansion of *convalescent* to "have grace and power"; (b) Septuagesima's added phrase, "by thy goodness"; (c) Trinity 7's translation of *que sunt bona nutrias* as "nourish us with all goodness," in order to avoid any idea of "congruent merit" as articulated by Ockham and Biel. See comments on these in Devereux, "Collects," 51. We also observe (d) Trinity 19's reversal of the Gelasian Collect's ordering so that the acknowledgment of our inability precedes the mention of God's mercy directing and ruling our hearts. See brief comments in C. Frederick Barbee and Paul F. M. Zahl, *The Collects of Thomas Cranmer* (Grand Rapids, MI: Eerdmans, 1999), 106.

in the same position. But both words also needed proper grammatical usage in the liturgy leading up to reception for the distinction of faith and works to be made clear. Cuming observes Cranmer at work:

> In the pursuance of his objective of ejecting all offering of the elements, Cranmer almost at once replaces "*haec dona, haec munera, haec sancta sacrificia illibata*" by "these our prayers." Since he could not allow any suggestion that the redemption and salvation of men's souls could be achieved by offering a sacrifice of praise, whatever content was attached to that phrase, . . . he naturally finds the section *Memento Domine* largely useless, and replaces it by detailed intercession. . . . Again, when God is asked to bless and sanctify the bread and wine, they are not referred to as "this oblation," but as "these thy gifts and creatures." Still less, after the Institution Narrative, can the bread and wine be called "a pure, holy, immaculate victim . . . a holy sacrifice;" they are still "these thy gifts," though now qualified as "holy." . . . Above all, Cranmer could not offer "the holy bread of eternal life and the cup of everlasting salvation;" these are benefits which God offers to us, not we to him.[41]

What Cuming observes is that in Communion, *sola fide* governs what subject and object oblation can take. *Sola fide* tells us that God is always the first subject of offering and oblation, and we are the objects. We do not offer and present to God anything of worth without God first giving himself to us "by his one oblation of himself once offered." This is furthermore why Cranmer excludes the words "Offertory" and "oblations" before the Intercessions prior to Communion, nor are those financial "offerings" (the language of the rubric) to be placed at or by the table, but simply "into the poor-men's box."[42] Because grace is received by faith alone, our oblations must be completely disassociated with the table, to say no to ourselves and yes to Christ's one oblation of himself once offered.

Tied to the language of Christ as the subject of sacrifice is the emphasis on it being one and once. Cranmer's concern was that if Christ's sacrifice were either repeatable or re-presentable, an opportunity for our participation as the subject of the sacrifice could sneak in, making unclear *whose* sacrifice

---

[41]Cuming, *Godly Order*, 93-94.
[42]See Andrew Atherstone, "The Lord's Supper and the Gospel of Salvation: Grace Alone and Faith Alone in the Book of Common Prayer," in *Feed My Sheep: The Anglican Ministry of Word and Sacrament*, ed. Lee Gatiss (Watford: Lost Coin Books, 2016), 82.

it was, and therefore blurring the distinction between faith and works insisted upon by *sola fide*. Cranmer further insisted that said sacrifice was "made there," on the cross, as opposed to here, at the table. The sacrifice is further punctuated as "full, perfect, sufficient." The persistent totalizing language, combined with careful parsing of *who* is the subject of the sacrifice, serves to clarify the gospel, separating it from the not-gospel which combines Christ's sacrifice with our faithful re-presentation of it. Works must not sneak into our salvation.[43] Though we will not spend much time analyzing Cranmer's 1550 Ordinal, it is notable for this discussion that it is the medieval understanding of the sacrificial priesthood (in other words, humanity as the subject of sacrifice) that led Cranmer to an "almost total rejection of the wording of medieval rites" in his architecture of the ordination liturgies for the Church of England.[44]

Likewise, as we observed in the Collects, "satisfaction" required proper delineation of subject and object. Departing from Rome, *sola fide* insists that the only proper subject of satisfaction is Christ himself. Cranmer argues for

---

[43]The argumentation just offered is why I have a hard time supporting George Sumner's noble efforts to help modern American priests understand the tensions exposed in the current liturgies regarding priesthood and sacrifice. Emphasizing Victor Turner's contrast between structure and anti-structure, Sumner quite thought-provokingly proposes that Cranmer's liturgy places the priest in the ironic situation of undermining their own mediatorial role and pointing to Christ. In this instance of "ritual evisceration of meaning," Cranmer's priest "proceeds . . . to deny that any offering or sacrifice is being made, that in fact the one, true, only 'sacrifice, oblation, and satisfaction' has already been accomplished on the cross of Christ. Having made this abundantly and repeatedly clear, the priest confirms that the people are making a sacrifice, one of responding praise and thanksgiving" (Sumner, *Being Salt: A Theology of an Ordered Church* [Eugene, OR: Cascade, 2007], 23-24). Sumner goes on to describe the priest's continuing consecration prayer (of 1549, not 1552) in a similar manner, concluding that the priest's prayer "plays a kind of spiritual shell-game, giving and taking away the language of sacrifice and offering. The person at the table looks and acts priestly, and does seemingly priestly things (e.g., spreading hands over the gifts) even as he or she reiterates its denial" (Sumner, *Salt*, 24). What Sumner does not make clear, though, is that Cranmer's priest is not using Cranmer's (1552) liturgy, but the American liturgy, drawn ultimately from the 1549 rite which Cranmer saw fit to revise. In fact, it is precisely this "spiritual shell-game," this "giving and taking away the language of sacrifice and offering" of 1549 that Cranmer attempted to rectify and disambiguate in 1552. So while this construction of Cranmer's vision of the priesthood is intriguing, and may even be a satisfying workaround for many American priests who feel the tension of their current liturgy, we cannot say that this vision is of a "Cranmerian priest." Rather, it is of a Protestant priest attempting to be faithful with an ultimately non-Cranmerian liturgy.

[44]Bryan Spinks, "German Influence on Edwardian Liturgies," in *Sister Reformations [Schwesterreformationen]*, ed. Dorothea Wendebourg (Tübingen: Mohr Siebeck, 2010), 186. See also Paul Bradshaw, *The Anglican Ordinal: Its History and Development from the Reformation to the Present Day* (London: SPCK, 1971), 24.

this theological parsing in his response to Henry's regarding the Bishops' book. There Henry had "corrected" the Bishops' book by removing "satisfaction" as a term applied to Christ and his work. Cranmer insisted that it must be added back in:

> "Satisfaction," which is put out meseemeth in any wise should stand still, to take away the root, ground, and fountain of all the chief errors, whereby the bishop of Rome corrupted the pure foundation of Christian faith and doctrine. For upon this satisfaction did he build sticks, hay, and straw, and satisfactory masses, trentals, *scala coeli,* foundations of chantries, monasteries, pardons, and a thousand other abuses.[45]

We see clearly here that for Cranmer, the subject of "satisfaction" makes or breaks the very idea of faith. The result of this is that, when it comes to God, he must be both the subject and object of satisfaction.[46] We must not be included. At the one moment of the liturgy, therefore, where satisfaction is rendered to God, it is rendered by Christ's "full, perfect, and sufficient sacrifice, oblation, and satisfaction." The only place we factor into this equation is as sinners who are the recipients of the gracious benefits of that transaction between the Son and the Father. It is of note that the Sarum Missal contained *no* reference to satisfaction. It is as though Cranmer was going out of his way to make his doctrinal point, holding up Holy Communion as a locale for the proclamation of the gospel through justification by faith alone.

---

[45]Cranmer, "Corrections," in Cox, *Works,* vol. 2, 93. A "trental" is a mass for the dead on the thirtieth day after burial. *Scala coeli* ("ladder to heaven") was the name for a vision of St. Bernard's at the Santa Maria (Scala Coeli) church in Rome where he saw the souls of those he prayed for, ascending to heaven. "This legend was the basis for an indulgence, applicable to the dead, attached to requiem Masses celebrated in the church. In due course this indulgence was made available in specially nominated churches outside Rome. In May 1500 Henry VII secured the "Scala Coeli" indulgence for requiem masses celebrated in his new chapel in Westminster Abbey" (Eamon Duffy, *The Stripping of the Altars: Traditional Religion in England 1400–1580* [New Haven, CT: Yale University Press, 1992], 375-76).

[46]Note carefully that "satisfaction" is used in one other place in the Communion liturgy, and it is indeed used with humanity as the subject. However, the recipient of that satisfaction is not God, but other people. In preparation for Communion, the second exhortation urges believers to deal with their grievances with others: "Ye shall reconcile yourselves unto them, ready to make restitution and satisfaction, according to the uttermost of your powers."

SOLA FIDE IN WORD USAGE AND TRANSLATION

When it came to the grammar of *sola fide* it appears that Cranmer's calibration was even more finely tuned than other Protestants who were developing liturgies in his time. We have already noted Cranmer's indebtedness to Archbishop Hermann von Wied's liturgy for Cologne, titled in English, *A Simple and Religious Consultation*. But observant historians note that Cranmer's usage of such liturgies was never slavish.[47] He was always editing. A powerful illustration of this is found in Cranmer's usage of Hermann's Confession[48] for Holy Communion, paralleled with the same prayer in the 1552 Prayer Book (see fig. 5.12).

HERMANN VON WIED, COLOGNE LITURGY, 1543[49]	BOOK OF COMMON PRAYER, 1552[50]
Almighty, everlasting God,	Almighty God,
the Father of our Lord Jesus Christ,	father of our Lord Jesus Christ,
the maker of all things, the judge of all men,	maker of all things, judge of all men,
we acknowledge and we lament	we knowledge and bewail
that we were conceived and born in sins,	our manifold sins and wickedness,
and that therefore we be prone to all evils,	
and abhor from all good things;	
that we also have transgressed thy holy	
commandments	
without end and measure,	
in despising thee and thy word, in	
distrusting thy aid,	
in trusting ourselves and the world,	
in wicked studies and works,	which we from time to time
wherewith we have most grievously	most grievously have committed,
offended	by thought, word, and deed, against thy
thy majesty and hurted our neighbors.	divine Majesty:
	provoking most justly thy wrath
Therefore we have more and more buried	and indignation against us:
and lost ourselves into eternal death.	
And we are sorry for it with all our hearts,	we do earnestly repent, and be heartily sorry
and we desire pardon of thee for all the things	for these our misdoings:

---

[47]Spinks makes this observation when comparing Cranmer's liturgical creativity to Calvin's more slavish usage of previous rites. See Spinks, "German Influence," 186.

[48]Bucer was significantly behind Hermann's liturgy, and while we here call it Hermann's work as overseer and patron, we are reminded that these prayers are most likely composed by Bucer. For instance, language from Bucer's 1537 Strassburg liturgy appears in this Confession.

[49]Taken from Geoffrey Cuming, *A History of Anglican Liturgy* (London: MacMillan, 1969), 342.

[50]Ketley, *Liturgies*, 90-91.

HERMANN VON WIED, COLOGNE LITURGY, 1543	BOOK OF COMMON PRAYER, 1552
that we have committed against thee; we call for thy help against sin dwelling in us, and Satan the kindler thereof; keep us that we do nothing hereafter against thee, and cover the wickedness that remaineth in us with the righteousness of thy Son, and repress it in us with thy Spirit, and at length purge it clean out.	the remembrance of them is grievous unto us, the burden of them is intolerable:
<u>Have mercy upon us, most good and gentle Father, through thy Son our Lord Jesus Christ.</u>	<u>have mercy upon us</u>, have mercy upon us, <u>most</u> merciful <u>father</u>, for <u>thy son our Lord Jesus Christ</u>'s sake: forgive us all that is past,
<u>Give</u> and increase thy Holy Spirit in us, who may teach us to acknowledge our sins truly and thoroughly, and to be pricked with a lively repentance of the same, and with true faith to apprehend and retain remission of them in Christ our Lord; that, dying to sin daily more and more, <u>we may serve and please thee in a new life, to the glory of thy name</u> and edifying of thy congregation.	and <u>grant</u> that we may ever hereafter <u>serve and please thee, in newness of life, to the</u> honor and <u>glory of thy name</u>:
For we acknowledge that thou justly requirest these things of us, wherefore we desire to perform the same.	
Vouchsafe thou, O Father of heaven, which hast given us a will, to grant us also that we may study to those things with all our hearts which pertain to our health, <u>through our Lord Jesus Christ.</u>	<u>Through Jesus Christ our Lord</u>.

Figure 5.12. Cranmer's redaction of Hermann's Cologne Confession

We see here that Cranmer seems to value simplicity and clarity above an overly wordy Confession, and this apparent desire may be driving the shortening of the prayer. In a brilliant move which would remain enduringly memorable, Cranmer compacts Hermann's long-winded litany of sin with the all-encompassing trio, "thought, word, and deed."[51] But notice, too, some of the language Cranmer chooses to leave out, particularly in the second half of Hermann's prayer. Perhaps it is that though Cranmer could agree with Hermann's theology about the new life granted by the Holy Spirit, he is still reticent to spend any time praying, at this liturgical moment, about anything that speaks of *our* works for God—the Confession is a clear place where the grammar of *sola fide* should clearly distinguish faith and works by emphasizing the *not* of "not I." This could very well be why Cranmer excises any opportunity to inflate the "I" through the "apprehend(ing) and retain(ing)" of forgiveness (even if it is qualified with an origination in "true faith"), or through "dying to sin more and more." Except for Cranmer's final line ("and grant"), the confessing believer is not the subject of any action save sinning and repenting: *we* acknowledge sin; *we* grievously commit it; *we* provoke God's wrath; *we* repent and are sorry. Likewise, Cranmer also seems hesitant to place the "I" as the subject of "desiring" to do that which God requires of us, so that section is left out. Similarly, Cranmer's understanding of the bondage of the will[52] (shared with Luther and Melanchthon) offers a good explanation as to why he leaves out even that final set of prayers. Hermann does acknowledge the will as "given" and would certainly understand this as the new will restored to us by God's grace and empowered by the Spirit, but Cranmer's grammatical filter evidently seeks to strain out *any* ambiguity which would

---

[51]It is also interesting to note that Cranmer does not keep Hermann's duo of those sinned against—namely, "thy majesty" and "our neighbors"—opting for the singular offense "against thy divine majesty." Though Cranmer would have no doubt agreed with Hermann's hamartiology, he seems to choose a more deliberate echo of Ps 51:4: "Against you, you only, have I sinned." Lending credence to the idea that Cranmer's choice was purposeful is that in Hermann's litany of sins there are several echoes of the same psalm (e.g., "conceived and born in sins" and "prone to all evils" [51:5]), which may have kept David's great confession psalm at the front of Cranmer's mind.

[52]We see Cranmer's understanding of the bondage of the will in action in one of Cranmer's annotations to Henry's corrections to the *Institution*, where the Archbishop challenges the king's desire to insert "applying our will to his motions" in order to qualify how it is that "we be in the favor of God." Cranmer's bold response to Henry's proposal was that such an action "were the ready way unto desperation," not God's favor. Cranmer then proposed an alternate correction that made clear *who* does the willing in the divine-human economy: "That we, which be renovate by the same Spirit, and do convert our lives from following *our own carnal wills* and pleasures, and repenting us that we have followed the same, and now apply our minds to follow *the will of that Holy Spirit*, be in the favour of God." See Cranmer, "Corrections," in Cox, *Works*, vol. 2, 94; emphasis added.

confuse "not I, but Christ." This comparison is important because it shows how Cranmer's application of the grammar of *sola fide,* over against that of another Protestant's, is more surgically exacting.

Another similar comparison may be found in juxtaposing Cranmer to Luther himself in the evolution of Luther's 1526 baptismal rite, his *Taufbüchlein,* through the changes in Cranmer's 1549 and 1552 liturgies. We examine, in particular, the final lines of what has been traditionally called the "Flood Prayer" (see fig. 5.13).

LUTHER'S TAUFBÜCHLEIN, 1526[53]	BOOK OF COMMON PRAYER, 1549[54]	BOOK OF COMMON PRAYER, 1552[55]
. . . that he may be separated from the unfaithful, preserved in the holy ark of Christendom dry and safe, and ever fervent in spirit	. . . that they, being delivered from thy wrath, may be received into the ark of Christ's church, and so saved from perishing: and being fervent in spirit, steadfast in faith,	. . . that they, being delivered from thy wrath, may be received into the ark of Christ's church, and being steadfast in faith,
and joyful in hope	joyful through hope, rooted in charity,	joyful through hope, and rooted in charity,
serve thy name,	may ever serve thee:	**may so pass the waves of this troublesome world,**
so that he with all the faithful	(*with all thy holy and chosen people).	
may be worthy to inherit	And finally attain	**that finally they may come**
thy promise of eternal life,	to everlasting life, (*)	to the land of everlasting life, there to reign with thee, world without end,
through Christ our Lord.	This grant us we beseech thee, for Jesus Christ's sake our Lord.	through Jesus Christ our Lord.
	* *This section moved up to parallel Luther more closely.*	

Figure 5.13. Cranmer's redaction of Luther's *Taufbüchlein*: The Flood Prayer

---

[53]This English translation of Luther's Second *Taufbüchlein* (1526) is taken from Gordon Jeanes, *Signs of God's Promise: Thomas Cranmer's Sacramental Theology and the Book of Common Prayer* (London: T&T Clark, 2008), 252.

[54]Ketley, *Liturgies*, 108.

[55]Ketley, *Liturgies*, 285.

We observe two key small but significant changes in 1552. First, Cranmer removes the prayer that the baptismal candidate would, in the future, "serve thy name" (Luther) and "ever serve thee" (1549). Interestingly, Cranmer opts for something more passive: "May so pass the waves of this troublesome world," expanding on the maritime metaphors, and perhaps even offering an (ironically Lutheran) image of the *vita passiva*, trading active "service" of God for a more modest suffering through "the waves of this troublesome world."[56] It reminds one of the description Luther's *vita passiva* offered by Oswald Bayer: "Faith is thus the work of God, through and through, with nothing accomplished by the human being; rather, it can only be received and suffered."[57]

Second, Cranmer changes Luther's "may be worthy to inherit thy promise of eternal life" to "finally attain to everlasting life" in 1549. As we saw with the Collects above, the concern about merit will often extend into language about being "worthy" to receive something from God. But we note that Cranmer even eventually shies away from the idea that we "attain to everlasting life," for in 1552, the language is again far more passive: "That finally they may come to the land of everlasting life." Not only does Cranmer here yet again extend the oceanic metaphor, he opts for a verb "come" which drains all effort from the action. Again, we witness *sola fide* functioning like a filter, sifting out the "I" so that only the pure gold of "but Christ" is left alone.[58]

It is becoming clear that when it comes to the grammar of *sola fide*, individual words matter. We observed in the Collects the sensitivity with which Cranmer translated, transposed, or simply removed loaded Latin ideas like

---

[56]It is interesting that of the observations made by Bryan Spinks in comparing the Flood Prayers of 1549 and 1552 (and how, in his words, 1552 had been "Cranmerized"), he does not note this difference but instead focuses on how Cranmer responds to Bucer's critique in the *Censura* and expands with "kindred imagery" the oceanic metaphor. See Bryan Spinks, "Treasures Old and New: A Look at Some of Thomas Cranmer's Methods of Liturgical Compilation," in *Thomas Cranmer: Churchman and Scholar*, ed. Paul Ayris and David Selwyn (Woodbridge: Boydell, 1993), 184.

[57]Oswald Bayer, *Martin Luther's Theology: A Contemporary Interpretation* (Grand Rapids, MI: Eerdmans, 2003), 43.

[58]I ask this question modestly: Could it be that Cranmer was more intentional about applying the doctrine of *sola fide* to liturgical reform than Luther himself? Perhaps intentionality is too strong an idea. The German reformer and the Archbishop of Canterbury were serving different contexts which in various seasons were more and less ripe for quick change. Between this and probably slightly different pastoral views on change and its pace, it may be a bit unfair to so easily compare Cranmer and Luther. Still, I find the question fascinating, and it keeps coming around to me in comparative research such as this.

mereamur, spero, and *propitius*,[59] But we also see general statistical upticks in the usage of certain terms that keenly express the doctrine and fruit of *sola fide*. As we noted in chapter three, "comfort" is one of those terms. But we might also observe with Geoffrey Cuming that "'mercy' and its cognates appear a good deal more often than the Latin warrants" in Cranmer's liturgy.[60] In 1552, the word-group appears seventeen times in Morning Prayer, four times in Evening Prayer, ten times in baptism, and sixteen times in the Collects,[61] and, most tellingly, thirty-four times in Holy Communion (compared with thirteen in the Sarum Missal). Similarly, Sykes notes the repeated language of reception in the baptism liturgy as it pertains to the baptismal candidate being "received" into the church, by the priest, and ultimately by Jesus himself, culminating in the liturgy's affective climax in "the emotionally powerful image of the child being embraced in the arms of Jesus' mercy," ceremonially enacted in the priest receiving the child into his arms just before the baptism.[62] Sykes concludes that the liturgy is "by reason of its structure, drama, and repetitions, a liturgy proclaiming Christ's reception of little children."[63] In other words, the repetition of "receive" serves the gospel narrative of God's one-way love to the undeserving.[64]

SOLA FIDE IN THE LECTIONARY

The aforementioned prevalence of the "mercy" word-group segues into another way Cranmer amplified the voice of *sola fide:* the Lectionary "to be used at the celebration of the Lord's Supper and Holy Communion through the year."[65] In the assigned readings, the word-group appears forty-one times.

---

[59]We might, with Devereux, add to this list *praevenire.* See Devereux, "Collects," 53-54.

[60]Geoffrey Cuming, "Thomas Cranmer: Translator and Writer," in *Language and the Worship of the Church,* ed. David Jasper and R. C. D. Jasper (New York: St. Martin's Press, 1990), 113.

[61]A large concentration of "mercy" and its cognates (eleven out of the total sixteen) are located in Epiphany through Lent.

[62]Stephen Sykes, "Baptisme Doth Represente unto Us Oure Profession," in *Thomas Cranmer: Essays in Commemoration of the 500th Anniversary of His Birth,* ed. Margot Johnson (Durham: Turnstone, 1990), 130. Sykes counts ten uses of "receive" and its cognates in the 1552 baptism liturgy, excluding rubrics (132).

[63]Sykes, "Baptisme," 132.

[64]On the idea of "one way love" as an explication of the gospel of justification by faith alone, see Paul F. M. Zahl, *Grace in Practice: A Theology of Everyday Life* (Grand Rapids, MI: Eerdmans, 2007) and Tullian Tchividjian, *One Way Love: Inexhaustible Grace for an Exhausted World* (Colorado Springs: David C. Cook, 2012).

[65]Ketley, *Liturgies,* 239.

But Cranmer's editorial eye took watchful care over more than word counts. Sometimes, Cranmer appears to have expanded the lectionary's readings where the gospel can be proclaimed. For instance, the original lectionary reading for Easter Tuesday only included the first half of Acts 13. Cranmer calls for a reading of the whole chapter, which now includes the announcement of "forgiveness of sins is proclaimed to you" (13:38); the distinction between law and gospel in the freedom of Christ versus bondage of the law (13:39); urging of continuance in the grace of God (13:43); the outpouring of the "word of the Lord" (13:44, 48). This all resulted in abounding faith (13:48) and the disciples being "filled with joy and with the Holy Spirit" (13:52).[66] Quite interestingly, Cranmer makes a specific move on the fifteenth Sunday after Trinity, which Cuming calls a "single unaccountable change," as "both passages are worth reading, but in a context of little change, the present substitution seems surprising."[67] However, the substitution is only surprising if one does not account for Cranmer's passion for the clarity and centrality of justification by faith alone. The originally assigned passage, Galatians 5:25–6:10, pulls Paul's string of admonitions (the voice of the law) out of the context of his epistle. So instead, Cranmer replaces the reading with what follows in Galatians 6:11-18, which renounces boasting in the flesh (6:12-13), urges boasting in Christ alone (6:14), and is punctuated by "the grace of our Lord Jesus Christ" (6:18). It seems that Cranmer would rather platform a passage that clearly distinguishes law from gospel and faith from works than remain in the ambiguities of moral injunctions divorced from those distinctions.

On St. John the Baptist, Cranmer would interestingly swap out the original reading of Isaiah 49:1-7 for the new reading of Isaiah 40 in 1552.[68] The former is highlighted in Luke 2:32 as pertaining to the salvation of the world through Jesus Christ. The latter is a more explicit reference to John the Baptist, as Isaiah's words are quoted in all four Gospels (Mt 3:3; Mk 1:2; Lk 3:4; Jn 1:23). But not to be missed is the new passage's emphasis on some of Cranmer's favorite language of the gospel's consolation reminiscent of his own first comfortable word and his concern for a "hearty" liturgy: "*Comfort* my people

---

[66]See Cuming, *Godly Order,* 65, though Cuming does not make the theological observation we have made.
[67]Cuming, *Godly Order,* 65.
[68]Ketley, *Liturgies,* 261.

(O ye prophets) *comfort* my people, sayeth your God, *comfort* Jerusalem *at the heart*, and tell her: that her *travail* is at an end that her offence is pardoned, that she hath received of the Lord's hand sufficient correction for all her sins."[69] Even in his lectionary revisions, the Archbishop appears to have sought out opportunities to proclaim the gospel and speak its comfort.

SOLA FIDE IN NEWLY COMPOSED PRAYERS

As hinted at with the emergence of new theological emphases through the rise in words such as mercy, we also observe that Cranmer's wholly original contributions to the liturgy do some of the strongest work in the grammar of *sola fide*. We therefore want to look at two new prayers in the Communion liturgy—the Prayer of Humble Access and the Post-Communion Prayer. Though unprecedented, as we find with much of Cranmer's best work, both prayers together appear to be a reaction to the language and theology of medieval public piety. Eamon Duffy records a popular prayer in medieval England, found regularly throughout early sixteenth-century primers devoted to preparing the faithful Christian for receiving Communion.[70] Setting a portion of this prayer known as the *Salve salutaris hostia* alongside both of Cranmer's new prayers illumines the theological clarity with which Cranmer sets forth *sola fide* (see fig. 5.14).

SALVE SALUTARIS HOSTIA[71]	THE PRAYER OF HUMBLE ACCESS[72]	THE POST-COMMUNION PRAYER[73]
. . . **I may be worthy to be incorporated into your body, which is the Church**.	We do not presume to come to this thy table, O merciful Lord, trusting in our own righteousness,	Almighty and everliving God, we most heartily thank thee, for that thou dost vouchsafe to feed us,

---

[69]From *The Byble in Englyshe* (London: Edward Whitchurch, 1540), accessed November 28, 2021, archive.org/details/GreatBible1540/page/n269/mode/2up?view=theater. Spelling modernized, and emphasis added.

[70]Duffy, *Altars*, 92-93.

[71]This prayer is different from the Aquinas hymn by the same title, often translated "O Saving Victim, Open Wide." It is found in *Horae Eboracenses: the Prymer or Hours of the Blessed Virgin Mary, According to the Use of the Illustrious Church of York*, ed. C. Wordsworth (Durham: Andrews & Co.; London: Bernard Quaritch, 1920), 73. This translation is from Duffy, *Altars*, 93.

[72]Ketley, *Liturgies*, 92, 278.

[73]Ketley, *Liturgies*, 280.

SALVE SALUTARIS HOSTIA	THE PRAYER OF HUMBLE ACCESS	THE POST-COMMUNION PRAYER
May I be one of your members, and may you be my head, **that I may remain in you, and you in me,** so that in the resurrection **my lowly body may be conformed to your glorious body,** according to the promise of the Apostle, **so that I may rejoice in you and your glory eternally.**	but in thy manifold and great mercies: **we be not worthy,** so much as to gather up the crumbs under thy table: but thou art the same Lord whose property is always to have mercy: grant us therefore (gracious Lord) so to eat the flesh of thy dear son Jesus Christ, and to drink his blood, **that our sinful bodies may be made clean by his body, and our souls washed through his most precious blood, and that we may ever more dwell in him, and he in us.**	which have duly received these holy mysteries, with the spiritual food of the most precious body and blood of thy son our savior Jesus Christ, and dost assure us thereby of thy favor and goodness toward us, and that **we be very members incorporate in thy mystical body, which is the blessed company of all faithful people, and are also heirs, through hope, of thy everlasting kingdom,** by the merits of the most precious death and Passion of thy dear son. . ...

Figure 5.14. *Salve salutaris hostia* and Cranmer's New Communion Prayers

Though it would be a stretch to say that Cranmer's new prayers were recasting the *Salve* prayer or other prayers like it, what we can say is that the changes in language along with new sentences illumine how Cranmer's theology resulted in a reshaping of common euchological language around the table. What we see clearly here is how *sola fide* serves to form language that draws distinctions, rather than blurs them. In the lines of the *Salve* prayer preceding what we have displayed here, the supplicant asks to be made worthy by God in order to "merit" (*merear*) incorporation into the death and resurrection of Christ.[74] Though the one praying is found initially seeking this worth from God, the underlying theology and thrust of the prayer is that they are asking to be made *intrinsically* righteous and to bring *that* righteousness to the table. The *Salve* prayer therefore predicates coming to the table on the

---

[74]Latin: *Fac me, Domine, ita ea ore et corde precipere, atque fide et affectu sentire: ut [per] eorum virtutem merear confirmari similitudini mortis et resurrectionis tue* (*Horae*, 73).

worthiness of the supplicant to be incorporated into the body of the church ("I may be worthy"), while the Prayer of Humble Access claims a clear "not I" in "we be not worthy." It makes clear that we are not "trusting in our *own* righteousness." The post-Communion prayer likewise does not place this incorporation into Christ's body in the sphere of worthiness, but in the sphere of assurance because of the worthiness ("the merits") of Christ. Also noteworthy, the *Salve* prayer's closing of "rejoicing in you eternally" remains subsumed under the (intrinsic) worthiness of the supplicant, while the post-Communion prayer subsumes eternal life under assurance. In the former, eternity is earned (faith and works together). In the latter, eternity is given (faith and works distinguished).[75]

While the *Salve* prayer requests "May I be one of your members," the post-Communion prayer yet again assures us that, because of Christ, we simply *are* members. Whereas the *Salve* prayer emphasizes the resurrection as the place where our "lowly body" will be "conformed" to his "glorious body" (which is certainly true), the Prayer of Humble Access emphasizes in its body-comparison the radical disjunction between our sinfulness and Christ's righteousness: our "sinful bodies" are cleansed by his (pure) body, and our souls are washed through his blood. It is as though the Prayer of Humble Access here takes every possibility for the confusion of faith and works in medieval eucharistic piety and recasts each moment in order to claim, "not I, but Christ." Finally, we notice that the Prayer of Humble Access uses the language of "mercy" three times. We might say in summary that the *Salve* prayer centralizes eucharistic piety around our worthiness to receive the grace of God ("both I, and Christ"), whereas Cranmer's prayers centralize the devotion of the table around our *un*worthiness being met by the assurance of *Christ's* merits and his benefits for us ("not I, but Christ").

We should take further note of how the post-Communion prayer's whole notion of assurance may be offering a not-so-subtle critique of medieval piety as the prayer operates according to the grammatical rules of *sola fide*. Duffy's extensive inquiry into the devotion of the Middle Ages argues persuasively that for Christians of that time, being remembered after death was key to

---

[75]It is important to point out here that, like "merit," the terminology around "worth" and "worthiness" was a point of debate in the Reformation, particularly with respect to the sacraments. See Bayer, *Luther's Theology*, 96.

one's eternal security. Indeed, this remembrance was one of the principal ways a believer before death was offered assurance of heaven after death. This was the theology (indeed, the soteriology) behind prayers for the dead. Devotional and doxological practices developed around these beliefs, most especially the "bede-roll"—a catalog of the souls of the dead to be prayed for. As Duffy summarizes, "The most straightforward, and the cheapest, way of securing the perpetual recollection of one's name in the course of the worship of the parish was to have it entered on the bede-roll." The annual recitation of this bede-roll "gave parishioners a vivid sense of the permanence and security of their own place, large or small, within the community of the parish"[76] and, by virtue of that, their place within the mystical body of the communion of saints. In other words, the bede-roll became a significant anchor and ceremony to *assure* people that they were truly members of Christ's church. This outlook, to put it bluntly, allowed a person to literally purchase their assurance of eternal salvation. For Cranmer and the other Reformers, the doctrine of *sola fide* would say no to this confusion of faith and works.

This would in turn give rise to the rediscovery of the sacraments themselves as places of assurance by faith apart from works. Whereas in medieval piety the bede-roll along with other similar devotions located assurance in the act of joining faith and works, the Reformers would exposit the sacraments as the location of assurance precisely because they were proclamations of the gospel by distinguishing works from faith. Listen carefully, for instance, to Melanchthon's language surrounding baptism and the Lord's Supper:

> We should always be most certain of the forgiveness of sin and God's goodwill toward us who have been justified. Therefore, sacraments or signs of God's mercy have been added to the promises, . . . and they give a most certain testimony that God's goodwill applies to us. . . . The signs of Baptism and participation in the Lord's Supper have been added to the promises as autographs of Christ, so that Christians may be certain that their sins are forgiven.[77]

---

[76]Duffy, *Altars*, 334-35.
[77]Melanchthon, *Commonplaces*, 147.

> In the Scriptures signs are added to the promises as seals, both to remind us of the promises and to serve as sure testimonies of God's goodwill towards us, confirming that we will certainly receive what God has promised.[78]

Cranmer's post-Communion prayer would strongly echo these sentiments. At the table, God "dost *assure* us thereby of thy *favor and goodness towards us*." And what assures us that we are secured as "very members incorporate in thy mystical body" and that we are "heirs through hope of thy everlasting kingdom" is not that we have purchased for ourselves a place on the bede-roll, but that Christ has purchased a place for us through "his most precious body and blood." In other words, it is the promise of God, spoken through tangible means of bread and wine, which assure believers of their place in eternity. The gospel preached in Communion and received by faith alone is Cranmer's "bede-roll," given, not earned.

We have spent significant time examining the text of the liturgy—words and phrases. We now move on to the equally important content located not in the liturgical text but the liturgical practice. Though less immediately tangible, ceremonies—liturgical action and its assisting tools—are no less formative and persuasive, and just as with words, Cranmer knew that ceremonial carried power to either proclaim or obscure the gospel.

---

[78]Melanchthon, *Commonplaces*, 167.

6

"NOT I, BUT CHRIST" CEREMONIALLY

SOLA FIDE IN CRANMER'S LITURGICAL ACTIONS AND ASSISTING TOOLS

UP TO THIS POINT, we have examined liturgical words. However, the words of the liturgy are only a portion of the content being conveyed in a worship service. The actions of the service's leaders and participants, along with the spaces in which those actions take place and the accompaniment of assisting tools,[1] carry their own doctrinal freight. In fact, as Gordon Jeanes has argued, actions carry the power to *reinterpret* any verbal liturgical content, resulting in newly created meaning—even meaning contrary to the explicit liturgical text—proving the axiom that a picture is worth a thousand words.[2] The power of ceremonial reinterpretation of the explicit text is precisely the issue at play in the controversies following the ratification of the 1549 Prayer Book. While theoretically more "Protestant," the 1549 liturgy was still vulnerable to ceremonial reinterpretation in the spirit of the Sarum rite, which is why conservatives like Stephen Gardiner could consent to its use. Ceremony preaches,[3] and Cranmer knew it.

---

[1]The phrase "assisting tools" as opposed to merely "tools" is deliberate and owes its specificity to Juan Oliver's important observation that people, not items, are in fact the chief instruments being used by God in the rituals of the liturgy. In this sense, the worshipers themselves are the primary "tools" of worship, while "our texts, music, décor, ceremonial, sacred objects, etc., all *assist* us as an assembly in our work of embodying and rehearsing life in the Reign of God" (Juan M. C. Oliver, "Worship, Forming and Deforming," in *Worship-Shaped Life: Liturgical Formation and the People of God*, ed. Ruth Meyers and Paul Gibson [Norwich: Canterbury Press, 2010], 9; emphasis original).

[2]Gordon Jeanes, "Liturgy and Ceremonial," in *Liturgy in Dialogue*, ed. Paul Bradshaw and Bryan Spinks (London: SPCK, 1993), 26-27.

[3]This certainly connected with the idea that ritual is a means through which human beings are shaped and interpellated. Cf. e.g., Catherine Bell, *Ritual Theory, Ritual Practice* (New York: Oxford University Press, 1992), 19-29.

Ramie Targoff observes that the English Reformers inherited from Augustine a skepticism about being able to properly assess internal disposition based on outward action.[4] Grounded in Christ's teaching on the Sermon on the Mount, this understanding of the mysterious internality of Christian devotion became the reflective backdrop on which Cranmer would stage ceremonial in worship: How do we avoid Christ's accusation of hypocrisy? How do we engage ceremonial sincerely? We make it plain, clear, and disambiguated, the English Reformers would argue.

Yet these thoughts were not shared merely by the *English* Reformers. Across the channel, the Continental Reformers understood the doctrinal import of ceremonial. Calvin would argue that ceremonial should clarify, not obscure, the gospel: "Shall no ceremonies then . . . be given to the ignorant to help them in their inexperience? I do not say that. For I feel that this kind of help is very useful to them. I only contend that *the means ought to show Christ, not to hide him.* Therefore, God has given us a few ceremonies, not at all irksome, to *show Christ present.*"[5] Melanchthon stated similarly, "When traditions obscure faith . . . they should be violated."[6] Vilmos Vajta summarizes Luther's take with particular respect to the ceremonies of Holy Communion, but applicable to all liturgical ceremonial:

> Jesus had observed such stark simplicity at the institution of the mass, because he meant to abolish ceremonial laws completely and to preserve the unity of his church through the gospel alone. This shows that Luther's criticism of outward ceremonies sprang not, as has been charged so often, from indifference toward liturgical forms, but from his concern for the Christian conscience cramped and threatened by ceremonial laws. . . . Where the ceremonial laws tried to supplant the gospel (Christ's original institution), they had "intruded into heaven," where they had no right, and must be ejected.[7]

---

[4]Ramie Targoff, *Common Prayer: The Language of Public Devotion in Early Modern England* (Chicago: University of Chicago Press, 2001), 7.

[5]Calvin, *Institutes*, 1192 (IV.10.14); emphasis added.

[6]Melanchthon, *Commonplaces*, 85. In this instance, he cites the traditions of penance and satisfaction, which appear to have been birthed out of the Council of Nicaea. Even that council, according to Melanchthon, is subject to Scripture. The cutting edge of Melanchthon's criticism is that "the very power of the Gospel has been obscured by this tradition" (*Commonplaces*, 86).

[7]Vilmos Vajta, *Luther On Worship: An Interpretation* (Minneapolis: Fortress, 1958), 29.

We carefully observe here not a kind of "ceremonial iconoclasm" but a strong prioritization of the clarity of the gospel over ceremonial tradition. This was certainly Cranmer's opinion. Cranmer's brief explanation at the beginning of the prayer books ("Of Ceremonies, Why Some Be Abolished and Some Retained") shares the ultimate concern with Luther that the excess of ceremonies ultimately served to "burden men's consciences without any cause" precisely because "they did more to confound and darken, then declare and set forth Christ's benefits unto us."[8] Even before the dawn of the prayer books, Cranmer relayed to Henry the content of a sermon he preached in Canterbury in 1536:

> I spoke as well of the ceremonies of the Church . . . that they ought neither to be rejected or despised, nor yet to be observed, with this opinion, that they of themselves make men holy, or that they remit sin. For seeing that our sins be remitted by the death of our Savior Christ Jesus, I said it was too much injury to Christ to impute the remission of our sins to any laws or ceremonies of man's making.[9]

Cranmer's 1549 injunctions for his visitation to Norwich—which, far from an isolated incident would be a pacesetter for future enforcement throughout England[10]—reveal a concern for ceremonial not simply because ceremonial is inherently bad (an iconoclastic perspective), but because, in Cranmer's words, people are led to "put their trust" in such things.[11] Therefore, headed into 1552, the Archbishop-Reformer was convinced that *sola fide* had more ground to plow. The second Prayer Book of Edward VI would thus seek to filter even ceremony—rubrics, language, actions, furniture, architecture—through its fine-meshed evangelical gold-pan.

---

[8]Joseph Ketley, ed., *The Two Liturgies, A.D. 1549, and A.D. 1552* (Cambridge: Parker Society, 1844), 157, 156, respectively.

[9]Henry Ellis, *Original Letters Illustrative of English History*, Series III, vol. 3 (London: Richard Bentley, 1846), 26; English modernized.

[10]See Diarmaid MacCulloch, *Tudor Church Militant: Edward VI and the Protestant Reformation* (London: Penguin, 1999), 96-99.

[11]"[Inquire] whether they have counseled or moved their parishioners rather to pray in a tongue not known, then in English, or to put their trust in any prescribed number of prayers, as in saying over a number of beads, or other like" (quoted in Paul Ayris, "The Public Career of Thomas Cranmer," *Reformation and Renaissance Review* 4 [2000]: 121; English modernized). Recall our earlier discussion on the significance of the word *trust* in Cranmer's thought. See chap. 5.

SOLA FIDE AND CONGREGATIONAL PARTICIPATION

The most obvious could be easily missed. Translating the liturgy into English was not merely motivated by the humanist agenda of contextualizing into the vernacular. We detect that Cranmer's impulse was not only propelled by a desire for the English people to understand the liturgy but to participate in it. In putting the liturgy into the vernacular, Cranmer shifted the center of ceremonial action away from the priests and onto the people, effectively removing the extra middleman between worshipers and God the Father (this theme will appear again and again in Cranmer's ceremonial changes). By taking the liturgy out of the mouth of the priest and putting it more into the mouths of the people, Cranmer was attempting to pave a more direct access to God through Christ. This ceremonial shift would certainly aid an environment which said no to the not-gospel of human priestly mediators, and yes to the gospel of Christ's high priestly mediation.

With this move comes the residual effect, no less in line with the grammar of *sola fide*, of allowing for fewer ceremonial opportunities for people to place their trust in the meritorious actions of a human priest and instead fix their eyes on Christ. For instance, what was once a priest's private pre-service prayer in Latin—the Collect for Purity—became the minister's public words in English at the start of the Communion liturgy.[12] It would be important for Cranmer that priests not engage in what would appear to the people as quiet, secretive, and mysterious liturgical action. Therefore, in 1552, we observe a host of rubrical notes dedicated to the clarity of the minister's words. In the Communion liturgy, the minister is to "rehearse distinctly" the Ten Commandments.[13] Morning Prayer emphasizes at the beginning that "the minister shall so turn him, as ye people may best hear,"[14] and several times later notes that the minister should lead the liturgy "with a loud voice."[15] This too accounts for why Cranmer sought to downplay the role of the choir specifically and

---

[12]It should be noted that for the upper classes of the laity, a version of this prayer would have been available in English by the mid-fourteenth century to readers of the popular devotional book of mystical piety, *The Cloud of Unknowing*. See Sykes, "Cranmer on the Open Heart," in *This Sacred History: Anglican Reflections for John Booty*, ed. Donald S. Armentrout (Cambridge: Cowley, 1990), 2.

[13]Ketley, *Liturgies*, 266.

[14]Ketley, *Liturgies*, 217.

[15]Ketley, *Liturgies*, 219, 220, 224, 225.

music generally in the worship service. In his day, these ensembles and compositions created an unhelpful and ambiguous layer of mystery. The musical rubrics are scant in 1552,[16] but we do find Morning Prayer encouraging the people to sing "in a plain tune after the manner of distinct reading."[17] But even in 1549, we find rubrics which encourage priests to "sing plainly and distinctly"[18] as opposed to singing with lots of flourish or employing complex musical forms, which would obscure the texts of the prayers.[19] Audibility and visibility were important precisely so the Word would be freed to do its work in the liturgy and so sinful imaginations might not be tempted to fill up ambiguous ceremonial spaces with a mysterious wonderment about what the priest was doing. Ironically, the audibility and visibility of the minister's words and actions would serve to get him out of the way, as it were, and shorten the "ceremonial distance" between the laity and Christ himself. Cranmer's net effect with these changes was to create "hearing aids" for the gospel.[20]

SOLA FIDE AND ARCHITECTURE AND ARTIFACTS

Liturgical theologian Nathan Jennings observes the inevitability of worshipers' culture-creation in the form of architecture and artifacts, which in turn shapes the worshipers:

> The physical reality arises in such a way as to incorporate the surrounding environment topologically while arranging a continuously growing material culture. That is to say, material culture becomes a kind of feedback loop within its initially formative dynamic. Thus, for example, liturgists are familiar with the old dictum, "the architecture always wins."[21]

---

[16]There is only one reference to music in the 1552 Holy Communion liturgy, just before the ending Gloria, which "shall be said or sung" (Ketley, *Liturgies*, 280). Likewise, in Morning and Evening Prayer, from 1549 to 1552, we see a significant decrease of musical references in the rubrics.

[17]Ketley, *Liturgies*, 220; retained from 1549 Matins (Ketley, *Liturgies*, 30).

[18]Ketley, *Liturgies*, 87.

[19]In a brief letter to Henry in 1544, Cranmer describes some of the editorial reasoning behind his translation and redaction of the Great Litany. There he takes time to suggest that "in mine opinion, the song that shall be made thereunto would not be full of notes, but as near as may be, for every syllable a note; so that it may be sung distinctly and devoutly" (Henry Jenkyns, *The Remains of Thomas Cranmer*, vol. 1 [Oxford: The University Press, 1833], 315-16).

[20]Hearing aids for the gospel is a metaphor I first heard in the teaching of Jonathan Linebaugh.

[21]Jennings, *Liturgy*, 44.

In this "feedback loop," architecture and furniture carry a special power to "ceremonially catechize" believers. Evidence Eamon Duffy's report about mixed-messaging in the English churches at the time of the Reformation: "Even after the iconoclastic hammers and scraping-tools of . . . Protestantism had done their worst, enough of the old imagery and old resonances remained in the churches in which the new religion was preached to complicate, even, in the eyes of some, to compromise, the new teachings."[22] Duffy would identify architectural messaging quite contrary to the gospel:

> There was about late medieval religion a moralistic strain, which could be oppressive. Churches contained not only the chancel-arch representation of the Day of Doom, with its threat of a terrifying reckoning down to the last farthing, but wall-paintings and windows illustrating the deadly sins, the works of mercy, the Commandments, Christ wounded by Sabbath-breaking, the figures of the three living and the three dead, or the related *danse macabre*.[23]

Christ depicted as apocalyptic Judge was a common scene above or behind the rood screens,[24] to the end that Duffy could say, "The whole machinery of late medieval piety was designed to shield the soul from Christ's doomsday anger."[25] Medieval worshipers caught up in this "machinery" would be hard pressed to find any motivation for faithful obedience other than guilt and fear. This is why Reformers such as Luther would identify the entire divine service as an attempted good work, with architecture aiding and abetting that gospel-veiled vision.[26] The grammatical rules of *sola fide* would expose in this messaging a failure to distinguish law from gospel: only the gospel can give and produce what the law demands. And yet, the architecture itself preached very little gospel alongside its amplification of the law's totalizing demand. It is far too simplistic therefore to coldly stamp "iconoclasm" onto the actions of the

---

[22]Eamon Duffy, *The Stripping of the Altars: Traditional Religion in England 1400–1580* (New Haven, CT: Yale University Press, 1992), 4.

[23]Duffy, *Altars*, 187.

[24]Duffy, *Altars*, 157.

[25]Duffy, *Altars*, 309.

[26]Martin Luther, "Concerning the Order of Public Worship": "Such divine service was performed as a work whereby God's grace and salvation might be won. As a result, faith disappeared, and everyone pressed to enter the priesthood, convents, and monasteries, and to build churches and endow them" (*LW* 53, 11).

Reformers in their architectural reforms. The grammar of *sola fide* clarified that the gospel was at stake in these changes, for the very Word (the law) that would declare Christ as Judge, striking terror into the hearts of humanity, would follow with the shocking revelation (the gospel) that the Judge has become the judged, for our sake, and for our comfort.

When we take a closer look at the layout and the furniture, we find the filter of *sola fide* sifting and separating in Cranmer's liturgy. We look, for instance, at the layout and positioning of the Communion table. So as to not confuse Communion with a sacrificial mass, the table must not look like a sacrificial altar. We thus find in Cranmer's 1552 rubrics no mention of a frontal, but instead a "fair white linen cloth."[27] Moreover, this table preferably "shall stand in the body of the Church" (i.e., on the floor where the pews are), "or in the chancel."[28] In not a few instances, altars were completely demolished, which included the removal of altar steps and the leveling of chancels. One such instance is recorded at All Hallows Staining between 1550 and 1551, upon the visitation of Gloucester's bishop, John Hooper. Similar articles are recorded for Salisbury Bishop John Salcot's visitation in 1553.[29] Architecturally, this all brings the experience of the body and blood of Christ much closer to the people. No longer must they take a great "upward journey" to receive the Supper (perhaps a ceremonial nod to the great effort one must make to receive the grace of God). Rather, Christ comes to the worshiper, where they are, "even while we were yet sinners" (Rom 5:8). We see in this architectural move a grammatical parsing: we arrive at the table not because we have so much journeyed to Christ, but he has journeyed to us—we arrive at the table not by works, but by faith.

Per the injunctions of Edward VI in 1547, images and art were removed from public worship spaces,[30] and as MacCulloch chronicles, the royal visitations which enforced these injunctions often went beyond the injunctions themselves.[31] It is important to our discussion to note that the walls

---

[27]Ketley, *Liturgies*, 265.

[28]Ketley, *Liturgies*, 265.

[29]See Kenneth Fincham and Nicholas Tyacke, *Altars Restored: The Changing Face of English Religious Worship, 1547–c.1700* (New York: Oxford University Press, 2007), 21.

[30]See John Edmund Cox, ed., *The Works of Thomas Cranmer*, vol. 2 (Cambridge: The University Press, 1846), 498-99.

[31]MacCulloch, *Militant*, 69-76.

were not simply whitewashed. Often in place of images were clear verses of Scripture, which, as we will note later, were viewed as the "reliquary" of the Holy Spirit—offering direct access to God through Christ, and eliminating the gospel-obscuring intermediaries of priests, saints, and their icons and images.[32]

Yet in the Middle Ages, it was not only what was in buildings, but the buildings *themselves* which would, by their very existence, preach a message contrary to the gospel. Duffy recounts the fifteenth-century surge in church building projects, especially in East Anglia: "The extensive and often sumptuous rebuilding of so many churches of East Anglia in the fifteenth century was an expression not simply of the bourgeois prosperity brought by the wool trade, but of the concern of rich graziers or cloth-merchants to *use their wealth as post-mortem fire insurance*."[33] Put plainly, funding these buildings earned the wealthy favor with God. The edifices would therefore stand, after their death, as monuments to their eternal security—"that the soul may be remembered" in a kind of architectural prayer for the dead. And the remaining public saw it this way. Patronized church buildings, then, became the wider culture's most stunning trophies of works-righteousness. Once we observe this, we can no longer hold one- or even two-dimensional views of the radical moves of architectural reform made in the sixteenth century. Part of the motivation was to clarify for troubled consciences just where our assurance lies—not in memorials and monuments bought with money (and what hope is there for the poor?), but simply in the word of promise of who Jesus is and what he has accomplished for his people.

SOLA FIDE AND LITURGICAL NOMENCLATURE

The grammar of *sola fide* would reconstruct the architecture and furniture of worship, and, as we have already seen here and there, it would alter

---

[32]Interestingly, in addition to the more well-known displays of the Decalogue, evidently 1 Tim 4:3-5 was a common text painted on church walls in Edwardian England. The text served as a call sign for evangelical liberty, particularly as it pertained to clerical marriage (see MacCulloch, *Militant*, 133). Not to be missed at the end of that passage is one of the chief appeals for a Reformation understanding of consecration—namely, "made holy by the word of God and prayer" (rather than the hands of the priest or a series of extrabiblical "incantations").

[33]Duffy, *Altars*, 302; emphasis added.

ceremonial nomenclature as well, especially in key worship-words around Holy Communion like "priest," "mass," "chalice," and "altar." In the sixteenth century, the language of "priest" would have been especially challenging to sort out in relationship to the gospel made clear by justification by faith alone. "Priest," with its Latin counterpart, *sacerdos* ("one who does the sacred act," or even "sacrificer"), would be hard to separate conceptually from a sacrificial understanding of the Lord's Supper.[34] Therefore, though for the Reformers the language of "priest" was scripturally warranted, especially as pertaining to all believers,[35] the concern was over the term's present association with those ministers who re-sacrificed or re-presented the sacrifice of Jesus through the sacramental act. Undermining both the finished nature of Christ's once-for-all sacrifice and the sole mediatorial work of Christ, "priest" became a term needing clarification and redefinition. So when it came to the liturgy and the shaping of the people, we find that as terms like these obscured the clarity of the gospel, Cranmer favored lessening or eliminating their usage. In 1549, "priest" appears forty-nine times in the Communion liturgy, mostly in the rubrics. In 1552, we find its usage reduced by more than a half, totaling twenty-one appearances.[36] And significantly, Cranmer replaces "priest" with "minister" in a few key moments, such as in the rubric before distributing the elements (see fig. 6.1).

BOOK OF COMMON PRAYER, 1549	BOOK OF COMMON PRAYER, 1552[37]
Then shall the Priest first receive the Communion in both kinds himself, and next deliver it to other Ministers, if any be there present, (that they may be ready to help the chief Minister,) and after to the people.	Then shall the **minister** first receive the Communion in both kinds himself, and next deliver it to other ministers, if any be there present (that they may help the chief minister,) and after to the people in their hands kneeling.

Figure 6.1. Cranmer's 1549 and 1552 distribution rubrics compared

[34]See H. C. G. Moule, *Our Prayer Book: Short Chapters on the History and Contents of the Book of Common Prayer* (London: Seeley and Co., 1898), 43.

[35]In 1 Pet 2:5-9, the apostle describes the entire church as a "holy priesthood, to offer spiritual sacrifices acceptable to God through Jesus Christ," and a "royal priesthood."

[36]Understandably, Colin Buchanan therefore considers this move a "half-reform . . . a reform of substance, unmatched by a reform of terminology" (*An Evangelical Among the Anglican Liturgists* [London: SPCK, 2009], 151).

[37]Ketley, *Liturgies*, 92 (1549), 279 (1552).

It is important to understand how significant this shift in nomenclature is. "Minister" was, at least by the 1540s, a polemical title. On June 20, 1540, Cranmer had signed a letter to conservative Polish diplomat, Johannes Dantiscus, as *"Thomas Ecclesiae Cantuariensis minister"* (Thomas minister of the Church of Canterbury). Dantiscus received this signature as a provocation, offering in response choice words critical of the religious changes (toward Protestantism) happening in England.[38]

Parallel to these concerns about "priest," for the simple reason that the Roman liturgy's service was known as the "Mass" and therefore carried all the above associations of priestly sacrifice, we see that Cranmer insisted on changing the title of the rite in the Prayer Book. In 1549, it was already knocked down one rung of importance in an almost parenthetical addendum when the service was titled, "The Supper of the Lord and Holy Communion, Commonly Called the Mass."[39] But by 1552, it was simply "The Order for the Administration of the Lord's Supper or Holy Communion."[40]

Cranmer would completely excise the use of "chalice" (with its sacerdotal overtones[41]) after the 1549 liturgy, replacing it entirely with "cup" in 1552, with the most striking instance being in the moment of administration where 1549 has the "priest" ministering "the sacrament of the blood" with "the chalice"[42] and now 1552 simply has "the minister that delivereth the cup"[43] speaking the simplified words of administration. Again, along the same lines, "altar" completely disappears from 1552.[44] It is telling how important an issue this particular term was for Cranmer given that in 1549, the usage of "altar" was already considerably down from its use in Sarum (see fig. 6.2).

---

[38]See Diarmaid MacCulloch, "Thomas Cranmer and Johannes Dantiscus: Retractation and Additions," *Journal of Ecclesiastical History* 58, no. 2 (April 2007): 281-86.

[39]Ketley, *Liturgies*, 76.

[40]Ketley, *Liturgies*, 265.

[41]As Moule points out, the chalice would have been a very small cup which would have only been able to serve the priest, as opposed to a congregation. See Moule, *Prayer Book*, 78n2.

[42]Ketley, *Liturgies*, 92. Interestingly, in one of our earliest eucharistic church orders, *The Apostolic Tradition,* one observes the shift from "cup" to "chalice" in some of its manuscript discrepancies. For example, in chap. 38, the earlier Sahidic text uses "cup" while the later Arabic text uses "chalice." See Paul F. Bradshaw, Maxwell E. Johnson, and L. Edward Phillips, *The Apostolic Tradition: A Commentary* (Minneapolis: Fortress, 2002), 184.

[43]Bradshaw, Johnson, and Phillips, *Tradition*, 279.

[44]Except in directly quoting 1 Cor 9:13 for one of the several options for Offertory sentences.

SARUM MISSAL[45]	BOOK OF COMMON PRAYER, 1549	BOOK OF COMMON PRAYER, 1552
"Altar" used **46** times.	"Altar" used **4** times.	"Altar" used **0** times.
34 times in the Ordinary of the Mass; 12 times in the Canon of the Mass		

Figure 6.2. The disappearance of "altar" terminology in Cranmer's liturgy

Cranmer preferred "table" and "God's board," both of which appear liberally in 1549 and 1552. Based on how thorough this change is, we can agree that Cranmer would have shared his friend Nicholas Ridley's clear articulation of the contrast. In his campaign against altars in London, Ridley claimed:

> For the use of an altar is to make a sacrifice upon it; the use of a table is to serve for men to eat upon. Now, when we come unto the Lord's board, what do we come for? To sacrifice Christ again, and to crucify him again, or to feed upon him that was once only crucified and offered up for us? If we come to feed upon him, spiritually to eat his body, and spiritually to drink his blood (which is the true use of the Lord's Supper), then no man can deny but the form of a table is more meet for the Lord's board, than the form of an altar.[46]

Ridley and Cranmer testify that a misleading liturgical and ceremonial term can have dire consequences when it comes to the clarity of the gospel for the people of God. "Altar," according to the straightforward logic, undoes *sola fide* by reversing giver and recipient. "Altar" makes *us* the giver of the sacrifice, and God the recipient (approach by works). "Table" makes *God* the host of a meal and giver of his very life, and us the recipient (approach by faith).

SOLA FIDE AND SPECIAL CEREMONIES

One wonders whether significant recognition has been given to the difference between the ceremonial outlook of the English Reformers and that of

---

[45]From a word search of *altare* and its cognates online for the Sarum Ordinary of the Mass (justus. anglican.org/resources/bcp/Sarum/Ordinary.htm) and the Sarum Canon of the Mass (justus. anglican.org/resources/bcp/Sarum/Canon.htm), accessed October 5, 2019.

[46]Nicolas Ridley, "Reasons Why the Lord's Board Should Rather Be After the Form of a Table, Than an Altar," in *The Works of Nicholas Ridley*, ed. Henry Christmas (Cambridge: Cambridge University, 1841), 322.

subsequent generations of Anglicans—that is, the High Church movement of the seventeenth-century Laudians, or the Oxford movement of the nineteenth-century Tractarians. Such a difference in outlook is not merely about who can best repristinate what is most ancient.[47] Rather, it is far more about an understanding of formation and how people are changed. The post-Reformation movements in favor of more elaborate ceremonial argue that external bodily action could excite and inspire internal desire. As Ramie Targoff points out, this is rooted in Aristotelian philosophy about the nature of *habitus* and virtue-formation: "These descriptions of the mutual dependence of body and soul in generating pious devotion, likened . . . to the exchange of heat between the skin and its woolen clothing, vividly convey what I have already described as the period's Aristotelian belief in the power of external gestures and habits to stimulate internal change."[48] Following Augustine,[49] Luther and Melanchthon fiercely opposed Aristotle on this very point—namely, that external habit has the power to change the heart.[50] But while most of these Reformers, including Cranmer, would argue that outward ceremonial did not carry power to change and form the heart, they would not have opposed all external ritual nor seen it as unbeneficial.[51]

---

[47] One hears this line of thinking especially in twentieth-century Anglican liturgical scholarship. Their argument was that subsequent generations had access to more resources from antiquity and therefore were able to more precisely repristinate the past. The classic example of this is *The Lambeth Conference 1958: The Encyclical Letter from the Bishops together with the Resolutions and Reports* (London: SPCK, 1958), 2.80: "It was Cranmer's aim to lift worship in England out of the liturgical decadence of the late medieval Church in western Christendom, and to recover as much as possible of the character of the worship of what he called the 'Primitive Church.' In this he achieved notable success, but there was not available in his day the historical material necessary for the full accomplishment of his aim."

[48] Targoff, *Common Prayer*, 10. The relevant passage in Aristotle is found in his *Ethics*, II.1-9. See Aristotle, *Nicomachean Ethics*, 2nd ed., trans. Terence Irwin (Indianapolis: Hackett, 1999), 18-30.

[49] For an account of the fundamentally different understandings of moral and ethical change between Aristotle and Augustine, see Simeon Zahl, "The Bondage of the Affections: Willing, Feeling, and Desiring in Luther's Theology, 1513-25," in *The Spirit, the Affections, and the Christian Tradition*, ed. Dale M. Coulter and Amos Yong (Notre Dame: University of Notre Dame Press, 2016), chap. 5, esp. 213-15.

[50] This is what Luther meant in his "Disputation Against Scholastic Theology" (1518) when he said, "Virtually the entire *Ethics* of Aristotle is the worst enemy of grace" (Timothy F. Lull and William F. Russell, eds., *Martin Luther's Basic Theological Writings*, 3rd ed. [Minneapolis: Fortress, 2012], 5). See Melanchthon's fuller development in *Commonplaces*, 26-36.

[51] Vajta, *Worship*, 17: "It is therefore not correct to speak of a 'dissolution of formal worship,' of 'non-cultic' worship, or of a 'de-culting' (*Entkultung*) of worship with reference to Luther. The true worship of faith is by no means incompatible with the 'external things' of the cult."

Their concern lay particularly with those special ceremonies that did not proclaim the gospel in their symbology but instead undermined the good news. *Sola fide* would be the grid that helped determine which ceremonies would pass muster.

Because of this, processions and ceremonies of *blessing*—Rogation processions, bell-ringing, blessings of salt and water every Sunday, blessing of candles at Christmas, and rituals during the baptismal ceremonies—lay particularly in the sights of the English Reformers. Duffy explains the theological significance of the medieval mindset about these special ceremonies:

> The world-view enshrined, in which humanity was beleaguered by hostile troops of devils seeking the destruction of body and soul, and to which the appropriate and guaranteed antidote was the incantatory or manual invocation of the cross or names of Christ, is not a construct of the folk imagination. Such ideas were built into the very structure of the liturgy. . . . That was the principal purpose of the processions, to drive out of the parish, with bells and banners and the singing of the litany of the Saints, the spirits "that flye above in the eyer as thyke as motes in the sonne."[52]

At first glance, it would seem that what the Reformers would be concerned with is simple superstition—too many rituals dedicated to warding off evil spirits. But the concern had more to do with the way *sola fide* would distinguish divine and human agency. These prayers and actions, as incantations, put the power of agency into the hands of the priests and the people. Here we witness a commingling of faith and works, which the grammar of *sola fide* insists must be distinguished in order to clarify the gospel against not-gospels. Not only was this underlying popular theology an affront to the supremacy of Christ, it was an unbiblical overestimation of human capability. When the Reformers therefore set out to remove special ceremonies like processions, the blessing of items, and incantatory prayers, they were ultimately attempting to urge people away from a *trust in themselves*.[53] Duffy himself admits that

---

[52]Duffy, *Altars*, 279.

[53]As a sidenote, it may have been the incantatory nature of some liturgical prayer that caused Cranmer to be leery of choirs, organs, and sung liturgies. Cranmer's oft-noted minimization of the choral tradition probably has less to do with an iconoclastic disdain for musical art in and of itself and more to do with concern that no part of the liturgy be perceived as granting human agency to

sola fide lay behind Cranmer's reforms of special ceremonies: liturgical ritual should be "reminders of the benefits of Christ, and whoever used them for any other purpose 'grievously offendeth God.'"[54]

Case in point would be Cranmer's shift in liturgical language around the ceremonial of the white robe given at baptism. The liturgy surrounding the white robe undermined the clarity of the gospel's assurance. And in this instance, he did *not* do away with the ceremony, but shifted its significance by changing the language (see fig. 6.3).

SARUM BAPTISM[55]	BOOK OF COMMON PRAYER, 1549
N, receive a white robe, holy and unstained, which thou must bring before the tribunal of the Lord Jesus Christ, that thou mayest have eternal life and life for ever and ever.	Take this white vesture for a token of innocency which by God's grace in this holy sacrament of baptism is given unto thee, and for a sign whereby thou art admonished, so long as thou livest, to give thyself to innocency of living, that, after this transitory life, thou mayest be partaker of the life everlasting.

Figure 6.3. Robing ceremonies in Sarum and the 1549 Book of Common Prayer

Gone from the ceremony is any notion of works-righteousness and that somehow one's assurance of salvation from the "tribunal of the Lord" is dependent upon what the baptismal candidate *must* do. With respect to the baptismal liturgy as a whole, whose ritual-evolution had developed elaborate ceremonial over the centuries, we see Cranmer filtering out the following practices from the 1549 liturgy headed into 1552: procession from the church door to the font, signing of the candidate's forehead and breast, exorcism of unclean spirit,[56] blessing of the font, the specification of dipping three times, clothing with chrisom, and anointing (see fig. 6.4).

---

eliciting favorable responses from God (which is precisely what incantations are). On the destruction of organs in the Edwardian era, see MacCulloch, *Militant,* 82.

[54]Duffy, *Altars,* 452.

[55]This translation is from Jeanes, "Liturgy," 20.

[56]Sykes notes that in 1552 "the demonology of [Cranmer's] service is muted" precisely because Cranmer sought to emphasize that the most significant message conveyed in baptism was cleansing from sin, not exorcism from demonic possession, as was emphasized in medieval rites. Instead, the gospel of "delivery from sin through the atoning death of Christ" is what is foregrounded in the rite (Sykes, "Baptisme," 134).

1549	1552
(at the church door)	~~(at the church door)~~
Exhortation	Exhortation
"Noah" prayer	"Noah" prayer
Naming by godparents	~~Naming by godparents~~
Signing of candidate's forehead and breast	~~Signing of candidate's forehead and breast~~
Prayer for receiving of candidates	Prayer for receiving of candidates
Exorcism of unclean spirit	~~Exorcism of unclean spirit~~
Salutation and gospel (Mark 10)	Gospel (Mark 10)
Exhortation on the gospel	Exhortation on the gospel
Lord's Prayer	
Apostles' Creed	
Prayer for the Holy Spirit	Prayer for the Holy Spirit
(processional to the font)	~~(processional to the font)~~
(at the font)	
Exhortation to godparents	Exhortation to godparents
Renunciation of devil, world, and flesh	Renunciation of devil, world, and flesh
Affirmation of Apostles' Creed (by articles)	Affirmation of Apostles' Creed (entire)
Blessing of font	~~Blessing of font~~
Petitions for those to be baptized	Petitions for candidates
Salutation and	~~Salutation and~~
Prayer for those to be baptized	Prayer for candidates
Naming of each candidate	Naming of each candidate
Dipping (three times) of each candidate	Dipping ~~(three times)~~ of each candidate
Clothing with chrisom	~~Clothing with chrisom~~
Anointing with prayer	~~Anointing with prayer~~
	Signing of the cross, reception into the congregation
	Lord's Prayer
	Prayer of thanksgiving
Exhortation to godparents	Exhortation to godparents

Figure 6.4. The structure of Baptism in 1549 and 1552[57]

In all these redactions, and in the ones we shall see below, we must hear Cranmer's caution clearly, that "although the keeping or omitting of a ceremony (in itself considered) is but a small thing, yet the willful and contemptuous transgression, and breaking of a common order and discipline, is no small offence before God."[58] Cranmer certainly understood the seriousness of

---

[57]This is a reproduction from Gordon Jeanes, "Cranmer and Common Prayer," in *The Oxford Guide to the Book of Common Prayer: A Worldwide Survey,* ed. Charles Hefling and Cynthia Shattuck (Oxford: Oxford University Press, 2006), 35.

[58]Cranmer, "Of Ceremonies," in Ketley, *Liturgies,* 155.

altering ceremonies, and yet his commitment to "declare and set forth Christ's benefits"[59] through them, in his mind, made the changes necessary.

SOLA FIDE AND THE CEREMONIAL OF PRIESTS

Given all that has been said, *sola fide* would insist on a reimagining of the priestly office and a subsequent reshaping of the various liturgies that revolved around that office. In a way, *sola fide* not only insisted on a liturgical "not I, but Christ" for the worshiper, but also for the worship leader: "Not I, the priest, but Christ, the Priest." In liturgical instances where priestly ceremonial action would either literally or figuratively position the minister "in between" God and the people, the actions are altered or removed. The omissions are telling of the theology and speak to the kind of formation Cranmer envisioned taking place by (as we said above) getting the priest out of the way of Christ and his Word.[60]

One of the clearest illustrations of this move is 1552's new instruction that the priest shall lead the beginning of the Communion liturgy "standing at the north side of the Table,"[61] instead of in front of the altar, standing between the people and the elements. This not only meant that "both verbally and visually, the medieval sacrifice had been fully superseded by a community fellowship meal."[62] It also meant that, given what we noted earlier about the table having been moved into the middle of the chancel or nave, the position of the priest is all the more striking. The north side would have been along the *long* side of the table, in the middle, rather than at the head. Further, with communicants receiving by surrounding that table, they were situated *alongside* the priest—equals in Christ, as it were. Approaching God by faith alone involved coming to the table seeking no mediator but Christ alone.

---

[59]Cranmer, "Of Ceremonies," in Ketley, *Liturgies,* 156.

[60]See George Sumner's wonderful description of the minister as "counter-sign . . . by becoming a great finger stretched away from oneself and toward the dying Jesus at the center of the Church's life" (Sumner, *Being Salt: A Theology of an Ordered Church* [Eugene, OR: Cascade, 2007], 25). He goes on to helpfully proffer a "semiotic understanding of the priesthood" (55), where the priest does not function as an icon of Christ to the Church, but rather an icon of the Church back to herself (35). This helps preserve the proper division of labor, such that "The promise is something *Christ* does, expressed characteristically in acts that the *Church* does" (84; emphasis added).

[61]Sumner, *Salt,* 265.

[62]Ashley Null, "Thomas Cranmer and Tudor Church Growth," in *Towards a Theology of Church Growth,* ed. David Goodhew (New York: Routledge, 2016), 208.

Cranmer also appears to have felt similarly about the act of confession and priestly absolution. The 1549 Prayer Book retains a single rubric in the liturgy for the visitation of the sick: "After which confession, the Priest shall absolve him after this form: *and the same form of absolution shall be used in all private confessions*."[63] The 1552 Prayer Book excises that final statement, removing any notion of private confession from England's liturgies. In the medieval mind, this would have been a significant blow to the perception of the mediatorial role of the priest—no longer were one's sins forgiven through direct encounter with a minister; one came to corporate worship to hear God's public declaration of forgiveness. This transition from private to public, and from priestly mediation to direct access, is further shown in the words added to Sarum by Cranmer to the words of forgiveness for Holy Communion originally in 1549 and carried over into 1552 (see fig. 6.5).

SARUM MISSAL[64]	BOOK OF COMMON PRAYER, 1549, 1552[65]
Almighty God,	Almighty God, **our heavenly Father, who of his great mercy hath promised forgiveness to all them that with hearty repentance and true faith turn unto him;**
have mercy upon you, and pardon all your sins, deliver you from all evil, preserve and confirm you in good, and lead you to everlasting life.	have mercy on you; pardon and deliver you from all your sins; confirm and strengthen you in all goodness, and bring you to everlasting life, **through Jesus Christ our Lord.**

Figure 6.5. The Holy Communion words of forgiveness in Sarum and Cranmer[66]

With the extra language, we witness a shift of emphasis away from the priest's direct involvement with the act of declaring forgiveness. Instead it is *God* who

---

[63] Ketley, *Liturgies*, 138; emphasis added.
[64] This translation taken from justus.anglican.org/resources/bcp/Sarum/English.htm, accessed October 5, 2019.
[65] Ketley, *Liturgies*, 91, 276.
[66] This comparison is made in Andrew Atherstone, "The Lord's Supper and the Gospel of Salvation: Grace Alone and Faith Alone in the Book of Common Prayer," in *Feed My Sheep: The Anglican Ministry of Word and Sacrament*, ed. Lee Gatiss (Watford: Lost Coin Books, 2016), 93.

has *promised* forgiveness of sins who will "have mercy on you; pardon and deliver you from all your sins." Of further significance is the fact that these very words in the Sarum rite are not given publicly to the people but privately to the priest by the other ministers that he might be prepared to serve at the altar. The fact that Cranmer gave away this special priestly act to the people is yet another illustration of attempting to get the priest out of the way of the mediatorial work "through Jesus Christ our Lord" alone, democratizing priesthood among all believers.

A significant moment in the burial rite rubrics serves as yet another example. At the actual moment of burial, when dirt is cast upon the casket, Cranmer makes a significant change (see fig. 6.6).

BURIAL RITE, 1549[67]	BURIAL RITE, 1552[68]
Then the priest casting earth upon the corpse, shall say:	*Then while the earth shall be cast upon the body, **by some standing by,** the priest shall say:*

Figure 6.6. Burial rubrics of 1549 and 1552

Following this rubric is the altered burial prayer, noted above, but here we notice that it is no longer the priest casting the earth upon the body. Instead, "some standing by" take the lead in the burial. Cranmer gives away yet another significant role of the priest to the people.

In baptism (both 1549 and 1552), it is noteworthy that before the priest administers the sacrament, the story from Mark 10 of Jesus welcoming the children is read and exposited. And then, interestingly, one detects in the following priestly actions the same sequence of events in that story of Jesus: the commanding of the children to be brought to him, embracing, laying on of hands, and blessing.[69] In a way, the priest "play-acts" as Christ himself,

---

[67] Atherstone, "Supper," 145.

[68] Atherstone, "Supper," 319.

[69] This ordering, to my eye, is a little more apparent in the public baptism of 1549 than in that of 1552, if we take the correspondence as follows: bringing of the children ("the Priest take one of the children by the hand . . . and coming into the church toward the font"); embracing ("Then the Priest shall take the child in his hands"); laying on of hands ("Then the Godfathers and Godmothers shall take and lay their hands upon the child, and the minister shall put upon him his white vesture"); the blessing ("Then the Priest shall anoint the infant"). See Ketley, *Liturgies,* 110, 111, 112, and 113, respectively.

perhaps therefore becoming quite invisible so that it is, as it were, just Jesus and the children. And, not surprisingly given what we just observed with burial, part of Jesus' actions (perhaps the part most prone to sacerdotal *mis-interpretation*) taken away from the priest and given to the Godparents: the laying on of hands.[70]

Most revealing, though, of the significant shift in the mediatorial role of the priesthood would be in the changes from the Ordinal of 1550 to that of 1552. Perhaps we could say, to borrow the language of Roman Catholic theology, that in the baptismal rite, Cranmer was comfortable with the priest play-acting *in persona Christi* (as Christ), but no such parallel was tolerable in the eucharistic rite, almost certainly because of the Roman Canon's own shifting between the priest acting *in persona Christi* and *in persona ecclesiae* (as the church): Was he acting as Christ to the people, or was he acting as the church to God? While Roman Catholic theologians (such as Aquinas) might be able to parse the role the priest is playing at what moment, experientially for the worshiper, it is hard to discern.[71] It is precisely this lack of clarity in experience that leads to the confusion about whether the priest should be perceived as Christ himself, or as a mediator. Any idea of play-acting in Holy Communion seems therefore abandoned by Cranmer. Packer's summary observation should now be obvious to us: "All suggestion that clergy were

---

[70]Gratefully, I owe this insight to Bryan Spinks, who in personal correspondence over email on March 1, 2021, pointed me to Gordon Jeanes's important article, "Reformation Treatise," where Jeanes argues for the Cranmerian authorship of an (unintentionally?) anonymous document probably from 1537–1538, titled *De Sacramentis*, currently housed in Lambeth Palace, London (ms. 1107, fos. 84-93). In this document, under "De Baptismo," we find these four sequential steps outlined and numbered: the prologue of Jesus demanding the children to come to him, then (1) accepting them into his arms; (2) laying his hands on them; and (3) blessing them (Jeanes, "A Reformation Treatise on the Sacraments," *Journal of Theological Studies* 46, no. 1 [1995]: 171). Jeanes suggests of this outline that present here is "the basic principle which will underlie the liturgical use of the story in 1549 and 1552" (Jeanes, "Treatise," 161) and then expounds on the significance and background of the ordering in much greater detail in *Signs of God's Promise: Thomas Cranmer's Sacramental Theology and the Book of Common Prayer* (London: T&T Clark, 2008), 261-68. It seems apparent therefore that the Mark 10 story is purposefully replicated ceremonially in the priest's actions in the liturgy. Sykes also has made this observation about how the priest "dramatically represents" Jesus in the "receiving and embracing of children in the arms of his mercy" (Sykes, "Open Heart," 15). See also Sykes's earlier more detailed exposition of the baptismal liturgy in his "Baptisme," 122-43.

[71]For a helpful discussion of the priest's operation in the mass *in persona Christi* and *in persona ecclesiae*, including a discussion of the teaching of Thomas Aquinas, see Dominic E. Serra, "The Roman Canon: The Theological Significance of Its Structure and Syntax," *Ecclesia Orans* 20 (2003): 121-26.

being ordained to a ministry of priestly sacrifice was eliminated from Cranmer's reformed ordinal."[72] We notice one significant ceremonial change in 1552 (see fig. 6.7).

ORDINAL, 1550	ORDINAL, 1552[73]
The Bishop shall deliver to every one of them, the Bible in the one hand, and the Chalice or cup with the bread, in the other hand, and saying:	The Bishop shall deliver to every one of them, the Bible in his hand, saying:

Figure 6.7. The rubrics for the ordination of a priest in 1550 and 1552

The 1550 ordinal already makes a significant departure from the received medieval tradition by emphasizing the Bible alongside (even ahead of) the chalice, but by 1552, the Bible is the only item given to the minister to symbolize his ministry.[74] Once the Bible is given, the priest is told by the bishop, "Take thou authority to preach the word of God, and to minister the holy Sacraments in this congregation."[75] This would stand in contrast to the vision of the priesthood cast in previous ordination liturgies, which "were so full of sacrificial language that there was little which [Cranmer] could have adopted as it stood without implying ideas about the ordained ministry [as the sacrificial priesthood]."[76] The message could not be clearer: over against a sacerdotal understanding of the priestly call, the primary task of the minister is to proclaim the Word of God—to herald Jesus Christ and his gospel.

The ordinal also presents changes in priestly dress, which we recognize from across the Prayer Book as significant of this understanding of the priesthood as revised by a commitment to *sola fide*. The reference of the priestly candidate being presented in an alb in 1550 is removed in 1552, with no mention of dress. Similarly, we see a shift in the vestments for Holy Communion. In 1549, the priest is to don "a white alb plain, with a vestment or cope," with

---

[72]J. I. Packer, introduction to *The Work of Thomas Cranmer*, ed. G. E. Duffield (Philadelphia: Fortress, 1965), xxvi.

[73]Ketley, *Liturgies*, 179 (1550), 349 (1552).

[74]Moule, *Prayer Book*, 78: "In the Second Book the Bible only was given; no doubt to shut out as much as possible the thought of a sacrificing communion."

[75]Ketley, *Liturgies*, 179, 349.

[76]Paul F. Bradshaw, *The Anglican Ordinal: Its History and Development from the Reformation to the Present Day* (London: SPCK, 1971), 24.

assisting ministers wearing "albs with tunacles."[77] By 1552, no requirement is made at all. A clear move is made to disassociate ceremonial vestments with the sacrificial priesthood. Additionally, the Ordinal made no mention of nor provision for the "minor orders," despite an Act of Parliament in 1549–1550 allowing for those rites of ordination to be drawn up.[78]

The clarification given by *sola fide* would extend even to the actual ritual and ceremonial acts of the priest during the service. Sacramentals, that is, items and actions thought to have mystical significance associated with divine presence akin to the sacraments themselves (holy water, signs of the cross, the blessing of items, etc.), are brought under severe scrutiny by Cranmer. And this was done precisely because the medieval understanding was that sacramentals such as these were utilized and enacted to "prepare the soul to receive grace." In other words, some ceremonial acts were understood by medieval Christianity *as* meritorious works. One scholar explains: "Worthy reception of sacramental grants remission of venial sin along with spiritual or material graces. . . . At the turn of the 16th century, these rituals remained popular and were considered an important aspect of Christian devotion."[79] The Ten Articles of 1536 bear witness to this perspective when, even while speaking in favor of retaining certain "customs, rites and ceremonies," they punctuate this particular section on the sacramental with this clear final line: "But none of these ceremonies have power to remit sin, but only to stir and lift up our minds unto God, by whom only our sins be forgiven."[80] As we have seen time and again, Cranmer's concern is not about superstition *as* superstition, but because the superstition is soteriological in nature. These sacramentals are untenable because they obscure the gospel by causing people *not* to hope in Christ as their minds are stirred and lifted to God, but to hope

---

[77]Bradshaw, *Ordinal*, 212.

[78]See Bradshaw, *Ordinal*, 18-19. Minor orders included the Sub-deacon, the Benet (an exorcist), and the Colet (an acolyte). When Bishop Stephen Gardiner was tried in 1550, he was required by the Privy Council to subscribe to a statement which acknowledged that "Sub-deacons, Benet and Colet, and such others as were commonly called *minores ordines*, be not necessarie by the Worde of God to be reteigned in the Churche, and be justly lefte out in the said Boke of Ordres" (Bradshaw, *Ordinal*, 19n4).

[79]Aude de Mézerac-Zanetti, "A Reappraisal of Liturgical Continuity in the Mid-Sixteenth Century: Henrician Innovations and the First Books of Common Prayer," *Revue Française de Civilisation Britannique* 22, no. 1 (2017): 6.

[80]Article IX, "Of rites and ceremonies," from the Ten Articles of 1536. See Lloyd, ed., *Formularies*, xxxi.

in the ceremonial actions performed and ceremonial items handled by the priest. Remission of sin, according to the grammar of the gospel, is the property of grace alone through faith alone.

With Luther, for instance, we find Cranmer eliminating the blessing and consecration of the baptismal water, "because all that was needed was the Divine Word, and a petition for consecration suggested lack of faith in the power of God's Word; ultimately, it was to distrust God."[81] Likewise, making the sign of the cross over the bread and the wine during the eucharistic prayer would also be concerning, as Leuenberger explains that for the medieval worshiper, the priest's making the sign of the cross effectively

> produced the presence of Jesus. This can easily lead to a calculated attitude on the part of the churchgoer by which his concentration on Jesus in the course of the liturgy is important only at brief, defined points in the course of the liturgy, in which the attention-awakening factor can be a gesture like the making of the sign of the cross over the elements. An attitude is often produced by this thinking that the churchgoer supposes, based on some particularly executed form with its associated gesture, that special blessings have been freely conferred upon him completely unconnected with any faithlike attitude upon his part.[82]

This leads us also to consider the ritualistic actions of the priest which Cranmer would pull out of the liturgy, such as the lifting up of the elements at various points in the Holy Communion liturgy. Cranmer's concern seemed to be that fixation on the elements themselves took one's gaze away from Christ, the object of faith. Cranmer articulates that this was precisely what he had in mind by drawing liturgical attention to the *sursum corda* over against the priestly action of lifting the elements. Following fifth-century church father Theodoret of Cyrrhus, the *sursum corda* was a liturgical and ceremonial signal to lift one's spiritual gaze *above* the elements, to Christ himself. As Cranmer said,

> Theodoret showeth us that the cause thereof was this, that we should not have so much respect to the bread and wine as we should have to Christ himself, in whom we believe with our hearts, and feel and taste him by our faith. . . . These

---

[81]Spinks, *Luther's Liturgical Criteria and His Reform of the Canon of the Mass* (Bramcote: Grove Books, 1982), 24.

[82]Samuel Leuenberger, *Archbishop Cranmer's Immortal Bequest: The Book of Common Prayer of the Church of England: An Evangelistic Liturgy* (Eugene, OR: Wipf & Stock, 1990), 37.

things we ought to remember and resolve in our minds, and to lift up our hearts from the bread and wine unto Christ that sitteth above.[83]

Similarly in his Ordinal, Cranmer sought to downplay any prayers associated with the laying on of hands that could be conceived as bestowing the power of the Holy Spirit through the recital of a formulaic prayer.[84] In those rites, compared with his sources, Cranmer often chose to use the language of an ordained person being "admitted" rather than "consecrated," and receiving "authority" rather than "power."[85]

With the other Reformers, Cranmer's concern was that fixation on the *stuff* of the liturgy—the items, the elements, and the priestly actions which drew attention to them—only served to veil the gospel. Cranmer's desire was that every ceremonial act and item serve as a hearing aid for the gospel, so that faith would not be in priests or their ability to perform certain rituals with precision, but in Christ alone.

SOLA FIDE AND CONSECRATION, RECEPTION, AND BLESSING OF THE ELEMENTS

Special final attention must be given to the unique editing of the shape and wording of the Communion liturgy proper. Cranmer's redaction of the Canon of the Mass here serves to illustrate the way all the above sections come together. It is the Holy Communion liturgy which most clearly illustrates how ceremonial—that is, the *way* ritual is enacted—carries theological and thus formational power. We have clearly seen from the above how cognizant Cranmer was of the doctrinal impact of the ceremonial. Cranmer seems to have believed that actions speak louder than words, and that seeing is believing.[86] Therefore, the ceremonial consecration of the bread and the wine

---

[83]Cranmer, "An Answer to a Crafty and Sophistical Cavillation devised by Stephen Gardiner," in Cox, *Works,* vol. 1, 131.

[84]Bradshaw, *Ordinal,* 28. Bradshaw notes what may be Cranmer creating deliberate ambiguity (a la the 1549 Prayer Book) around whether the laying on of hands confers grace because it was a sticking point in his debates with more Roman-leaning bishops and priests (33).

[85]Bradshaw, *Ordinal,* 30. We note, though, that Bradshaw himself doubts any significant difference in Cranmer's mind between "authority" and "power."

[86]So Luther: "Where there is no clear distinction [between the essence of the gospel and the additions of ceremony], the eyes and the heart are easily misled by such sham into a false impression and delusion" ("A Treatise on the New Testament, that is, the Holy Mass," [*LW* 35, 81]).

appears to have been the epicenter of liturgical redaction according to the grammar of *sola fide*.

In the medieval Roman rite, all priestly action, all liturgical momentum, and all assisting tools drove toward the liturgical climax of the consecration of the bread and wine, for it would be in that moment that the dramatic change would occur: ordinary bread would become Christ's true, substantial body; ordinary wine would become Christ's true, substantial blood.[87] As we have pointed out, all the ceremonial surrounding this climax served to obscure, rather than proclaim, the gospel.[88] The growth of ceremonial around Communion over time would lead Luther to conclude, "The chief thing in the mass has been forgotten, and nothing is remembered except the additions of men!"[89] In the ceremonial, the priest—not Christ—became the means of mediation. In the ceremonial, our present offering—not Christ's once-for-all offering—became the foregrounded means of expiation. In the ceremonial, our devotions, incantations, and sacramentals—not Christ's finished work— became the means of harnessing divine power. *Sola fide* would offer a decisive no to these not-gospels. Therefore, a climactic consecration that effected a transubstantiation of the elements was no longer tenable.

---

[87]Cyril of Jerusalem (c. 315–386 AD) is considered among the earliest of patristic attestation to consecratory change (via *epiclesis*) in the elements. It is interesting to note how clearly his teaching contrasts with Paul's. In his *Mystagogical Catechesis* 1.7, Cyril draws a parallel between the change which has taken place in bread and wine during the "holy invocation" (τῆς ἁγίας ἐπικλήσεως) with the change which takes place in food sacrificed to idols, which is "polluted by the invocation (ἐπικλήσει) of the unclean spirits." Cyril cites this epicletic event, even while the idol-foods remain "in their own nature plain and simple," as the reason it cannot be eaten (See F. L. Cross, ed., *St. Cyril of Jerusalem's Lectures on the Christian Sacraments: The Procatechesis and the Five Mystagogical Catechesis* [Crestwood, NY: St. Vladimir's Seminary Press, 1995], 15, 56). Paul's argument in 1 Cor 8 is very different. The food and its associations with idolatry are neither here nor there (v. 8); what matters is people and how they are loved (vv. 9-13). For Paul, the food is simply food, and no amount of pagan prayer effects a substantive change (either spiritual or physical) that would demand treating the food differently, but love of neighbor does require a different action.

[88]Though he would not come to our same conclusions, Roman Catholic liturgical theologian J. A. Jungmann exposes this obscuring (he calls it "disintegration") in his discussion of medieval worship: "It is no longer the *Anamnesis* of the work of Redemption as such, of the mystery of salvation which is in mind: a disintegration has taken place . . . the sacramental making present of the work of salvation, the Mysterium Christi which ought to enfold us, and into which we ought to enter deeper and deeper, is decidedly too little grasped" (*Pastoral Liturgy* [New York: Herder & Herder, 1962], 72-73). Jungmann later describes how the work of Christ was no longer seen as something present to the believer, but simply a past event which must be meditated on "by means of some such laudable devotion as the Way of the Cross or the Rosary" (78).

[89]Luther, "A Treatise on the New Testament, that is, the Holy Mass" (*LW* 35, 81).

The clearest thing for Cranmer to do was to remove and displace those consecratory prayers which, by their words and rituals (fraction,[90] elevation, signs of the cross), would draw any attention to the elements. It is not too strong to say that, in Cranmer's view, no ritualistic consecration should take place at all. This is evidenced by the 1552 rubric (shocking to medieval sensibilities) that allowed for the curate after the service to take any remaining bread and wine home to "have it to his own use."[91] The bread and wine remained bread and wine.[92] But this excision served a double-purpose. Not only did it remove the consecratory spectacle from view, it also dramatically shortened the Communion liturgy as a whole. In this way, it would function similarly to how Cranmer shortened the Daily Offices: there would simply be less for the worshiper to do before receiving the grace of God. In fact, it

---

[90] An unceremonious fraction was discussed in the final rubrics of 1549:

> For avoiding of all matters and occasion of dissension, it is meet that the bread prepared for the Communion be made, through all this realm, after one sort and fashion: that is to say, unleavened, and round, as it was afore, but without all manner of print, and something more larger and thicker than it was, so that it may be aptly divided in divers pieces: and every one shall be divided in two pieces, at the least, or more, by the discretion of the minister, and so distributed. (Ketley, *Liturgies,* 97)

By 1552, no mention of breaking the bread remained in the rite.

[91] Ketley, *Liturgies*, 283. It is noteworthy that this practice is not completely without early Christian warrant, whether or not Cranmer was aware of it. One of the earliest liturgical orders, the so-called *Apostolic Tradition* 38.1-2 (third to fifth century AD) makes provision for what Paul Bradshaw calls "the less common custom of taking consecrated wine home to be consumed daily there" (Bradshaw, *The Apostolic Tradition Reconstructed: A Text for Students* [Norwich: Hymns Ancient and Modern, 2021], 34n63). Almost certainly, the theology of consecration in the *Apostolic Tradition* is different from Cranmer's, and it is ambiguous whether this practice is tied to an at-home blessing of the cup of the faithful or of the catechumens (Paul F. Bradshaw, Maxwell E. Johnson, and L. Edward Phillips, *The Apostolic Tradition: A Commentary* [Minneapolis: Fortress, 2002], 184-85), but it is an interesting parallel which may indicate that the practice does not lack at least some precedent in the tradition.

[92] Andrew Atherstone ("The Lord's Supper and the Gospel of Salvation: Grace Alone and Faith Alone in the Book of Common Prayer," in *Feed My Sheep: The Anglican Ministry of Word and Sacrament,* ed. Lee Gatiss [Watford: Lost Coin Books, 2016], 97) notes the irony of this in the 1662 Prayer Book:

> The rubrics of the 1552 Prayer Book directed that if any bread and wine was left over, "the Curate shall have it to his own use"—that is, he could take it home to consume with his family for lunch. This was the natural corollary of Cranmer's theological principle that no eucharistic consecration had taken place. However, the 1662 Prayer book again took a step back from this bold position, not in its liturgy, but in its rubrics. The institution narrative is now titled "The Prayer of Consecration" and only "unconsecrated" bread and wine is given to the curate to take home. All the consecrated elements are to be "reverently consumed" immediately after the service.

It appears that the seeds were sown for this as early as 1604 when supplementary consecration was codified in the canons of that year (Atherstone, "Supper," 96).

would have been nearly startling (as grace always is) to the observant worshiper that the "liturgical distance" between the words of institution ("In the same night that he was betrayed") and the reception of the elements was cut down to *nothing*. "Drink it in remembrance of me" was followed by the people coming forward and receiving. In fact, even the absence of one little word should not be missed: the words of institution end with no "Amen." Figuratively, Cranmer would have no comma, no punctuation, no separation between the gracious words of Christ through Paul, and the spiritual feeding upon that very Word by faith through reception. It would be all one, continuous, prayerful act. "Amen" would only make an appearance after the post-Communion prayer. Colin Buchanan's influential booklet, *What Did Cranmer Think He Was Doing?*, illustrates visually the experiential shift and resulting theological impact (see fig. 6.8).

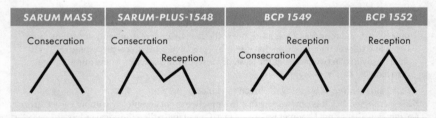

Figure 6.8. Theological-experiential shifts in consecration and reception through successive liturgical revisions (Colin Buchanan)[93]

It is critical to understand that in the medieval way of thinking, consecration and reception would have been extremely unlikely bedfellows, if not diametrically opposed. The whole thrust of medieval eucharistic practice drove toward consecration particularly because the principal act of the worshiper was not reception, but *adoration* of the Host.[94] It is telling that, when medieval mass books instructed the laity to pray vernacular "levation prayers" during the elevation of the host, "the most common and distinctive feature of levation prayers is the inclusion of a vocative 'hailing' in the opening salutation:

---

[93]Colin Buchanan, *What Did Cranmer Think He Was Doing?*, 2nd ed. (Bramcote: Grove Books, 1982), 23. These diagrams are reproduced here with the permission of the author.

[94]J. A. Jungmann describes how medieval liturgical life centered its piety around the moment of consecration, which often became "the very reason that people did not want or did not dare to communicate—and the pastoral attitude put people off rather than encouraged them" (*Liturgy*, 70).

'Hail,' 'Ave,' or 'Welcome.'"[95] It is clear that the medieval worshiper was led not so much to focus on the sacrifice of Christ on their behalf, but to worship Christ as present among them in the sacrament. In other words, the posture was not one of thankfulness and gratitude (dispositions of reception), but awe and wonder (dispositions of adoration).[96] Eamon Duffy describes the postconsecratory moment in the medieval rite, known as the "pax," when "the priest kissed the corporas on which the Host rested, and the lip of the chalice, and then the paxbred, a disk or tablet on which was carved or painted a sacred emblem." This pax was then taken to the congregation, outside the rood screen, where some (not all) were to kiss the pax. This action was, in Duffy's words, "clearly a substitute for the reception of communion."[97] It would have indeed therefore been shocking in Cranmer's liturgy not only that the *priest's* elevation and reception were ceremonially uneventful, but that the *people* actually ate the bread. The climactic shift of emphasis could not have been more dramatic, which raises the question: Why? The Archbishop himself answers:

> Our Saviour Christ hath not only set forth these things most plainly in his holy word, that we may hear them with our ears; but he hath also ordained one visible sacrament of . . . spiritual nourishment in bread and wine, to the intent that, as much as is possible for man, we may see Christ with our eyes, smell him at our nose, taste him with our mouths, grope him with our hands, and perceive him with all our senses. For as the word of God preached putteth Christ into our ears; so likewise these elements of . . . bread, and wine, joined to God's word, do after a sacramental manner put Christ into our eyes, mouths, hands, and all our senses.[98]

---

[95] Katherin Zieman, *Singing the New Song: Literacy and Liturgy in Late Medieval England* (Philadelphia: University of Pennsylvania Press, 2008), 86.

[96] "Levation prayers were thus an act of subjection in which one acknowledged and submitted oneself to God's authoritative power" (Zieman, *Song*, 86). Thinking further through the Pauline and Reformation filter, awe-filled adoration is ultimately indicative of encounter with the law, while thankful reception is ultimately indicative of encounter with the gospel. This exposes another reason why transubstantiation was a "gospel-issue" for Cranmer—it elevated encounter with the law over reception of the gospel. As with the Old Testament title "Immanuel" (cf. Is 7:14; 8:8), Christ present among us is by no means a comfort until we know and hear clearly what he is present to do and to give. "God with us" is only good news when it is spoken alongside a clear gospel (Mt 1:22-23).

[97] Duffy, *Altars*, 125.

[98] Cranmer, "Defense," in Henry Jenkyns, *The Remains of Thomas Cranmer*, vol. 2 (Oxford: The University Press, 1833), 302.

At stake for Cranmer in the ceremonial shift from consecration to reception is the proclamation of the gospel itself. Reception enacts ritualistically what the gospel proclaims theologically—Christ comes to us as an unconditioned, unmerited, categorical *gift*. We firstly experience this gift by receiving, not adoring. True adoration—worship borne of grace and not of works—follows reception.[99] The grammar of *sola fide* is no more clearly at work than here.

We now understand why Cranmer thus was compelled to alter the words of distribution from "The body of our Lord Jesus Christ" and "The blood of our Lord Jesus Christ" (1549),[100] to "Take and eat *this*, in remembrance that *Christ died for thee, and feed on him in thy heart by faith*," and "Drink *this*, in remembrance that *Christ's blood was shed for thee*" (1552).[101] Compared to the gospel proclaimed *through* them ("Christ died for thee," "Christ's blood was shed for thee"), the elements are relatively insignificant. In and of themselves, they deserve no reflection or focus. The bread and the wine are not even named. They are simply "this." For Cranmer, what is important—yes, of life and death importance—is what is going on in "thy heart."

This is furthermore what is behind the removal of the Benedictus from the end of the Sanctus in 1552. If we were only thinking of Cranmer as a biblicist, we would rightly be puzzled by this removal, for the Benedictus is simply a quotation of the biblical accounts of Jesus' triumphal entry on Palm Sunday (Mt 21:9; Mk 11:9; Jn 12:13). Cranmer's concern appears to have been how that verse was misused[102] to assist the vision of the consecratory moment when Jesus "entered into" the elements much as he entered into Jerusalem at the start of Holy Week.[103] The Benedictus had become a

---

[99]Which, again, confirms the point made earlier, that Cranmer's placement of the Gloria *after* Communion was not haphazard or expedient.

[100]Ketley, *Liturgies*, 92.

[101]Ketley, *Liturgies*, 279; emphasis added. Calvin too emphasized, "And, indeed, we must carefully observe that the very powerful and almost entire force of the Sacrament lies in these words: 'which is given for you,' 'which is shed for you'" (*Institutes*, 1362 [IV.17.3]).

[102]Though he would not see it as "misuse," Matthew S. C. Olver observes how "juxtaposition" of biblical texts to liturgical moments serves as interpretation and then notes, "The use of the *Benedictus qui venit* just before the *Te igitur* in the Roman Rite (and many other rites) may be interpreted as an allusion to the sacramental manner in which Christ will soon come to the gathered assembly, despite its non-eucharistic scriptural source" (Matthew S. C. Olver, "A Classification of a Liturgy's Use of Scripture: A Proposal," *Studia Liturgica* 49, no. 2 [2019]: 244.)

[103]Geoffrey Cuming, *A History of Anglican Liturgy* (London: MacMillan, 1969), 108: "The *Benedictus* was removed from the *Sanctus*, presumably because it might suggest corporal presence." Again, on our reading it is a little too simplistic to say that Cranmer's disagreement with

ceremonial distraction-point, where worshipers could be led to focus more on adoring the elements themselves than the Christ who would inhabit those very worshipers.

To be clear, therefore, it is not that Cranmer disavowed the idea of consecratory change during Holy Communion. It is rather that, ceremonially, the Archbishop recentered the *locale* of consecratory change away from the elements and onto the human heart. "Cranmer's focus was not a change in, or even instrumental use of, the bread and wine, but rather the transformation of the recipients, who by the power of the Spirit were linked afresh to the saving efficacy of Christ's Incarnation and Passion."[104]

This shift from transformation of the elements to the transformation of the people is evidenced, as well, in Cranmer's removal of the *epiclesis* of 1549.[105] Jeanes insightfully notes a shift in Cranmer's theology here in relationship to the Archbishop's interaction with John Damascene. In the 1530s, Cranmer's underlining and marginalia around Damascene's treatment of the "word" and the "Holy Ghost" in relationship to the transformation of the bread and wine reveal a view much more in line with the *epiclesis* of 1549: the Holy Spirit and word sanctify and transform bread and wine. The same passage of

---

transubstantiation was *the* reason for the removal of the Benedictus. His concern would have (at least) equally been for the way adoration of the host would have taken the spotlight off the "for you" character present in the moment of reception. Additionally, I am indebted to a reviewer of this manuscript who pointed out that during the singing of the Sanctus and Benedictus in some sung masses, the canon would have been said silently by the priest, along with accompanying actions of elevation of the host. Cranmer may have been trying to avoid this scenario, as well.

[104] Ashley Null, "Thomas Cranmer," in *Christian Theologies of the Sacraments: A Comparative Introduction,* ed. Justin S. Holcomb and David A. Johnson (New York: New York University Press, 2017), 227. This is similar to Gordon Jeanes's conclusion about Cranmer's mature sacramentology, namely, that "[Cranmer] seems genuinely to believe that he has preserved a sound notion of sacramental instrumentality. However, as we look more closely at his theology, symbolic parallelism rings more true" (Gordon Jeanes, *Signs of God's Promise: Thomas Cranmer's Sacramental Theology and the Book of Common Prayer* [London: T&T Clark, 2008], 186). Andrew Atherstone says, similarly, "The Roman church teaches that change takes place at the eucharist, by the power of the Holy Spirit transforming the bread and wine. The Prayer Book agrees that change does indeed take place, but by the power of the Holy Spirit transforming the hearts of communicants as they put their faith in Jesus Christ" ("Supper," 86).

[105] This most certainly means that despite the apparent East-West "ecumenical consensus" around the invocation of Word and Spirit, even this widespread agreement and attestation in Cranmer's mind was still subordinate to his more basic gospel-criterion we are observing at work. This further corroborates the argument made in the introduction about Cranmer's liturgical criteria and also questions further whether *BCP 2019* can unequivocally claim to be faithful to Cranmer, as we noted above in n55 of the introduction.

Damascene is again invoked by Cranmer in 1550, but this time with a completely different focus. From the *Defence:*

> And as Almighty God by his most mighty word and his Holy Spirit . . . brought
> forth all creatures in the beginning, and ever sithens hath preserved them; even
> so by the same word and power he worketh in us, from time to time, this
> marvellous spiritual generation and wonderful spiritual nourishment and
> feeding, which is wrought only by God, and is comprehended and received of
> us by faith.[106]

This observable shift in the *object* of consecration is precisely what we are recognizing in the structural changes of the eucharistic prayers between 1549 and 1552. Therefore, with tongue only slightly in cheek we could say that Cranmer *does* believe in transubstantiation at Holy Communion. Except that it is not the bread and wine that are transformed into the body of Christ, but believers.[107] Ashley Null summarizes it best:

> Since Cranmer considered the sacraments as "visible words" of God's biblical
> promises, the ultimate expression of Cranmer's vision of God's gracious love
> inspiring grateful human love was the 1552 Holy Communion service. In what
> he intended to be the central act of English worship, Cranmer wove together
> his great themes of free justification, on-going repentance, communal fellow-
> ship, and godly living and placed them in a sacramental setting which clarified

---

[106]See discussion, which includes this quote from the *Defence*, in Jeanes, *Signs,* 212-213.

[107]Though not recorded verbatim in my notes, I believe I heard Dr. Null say something quite similar in class (Knox Theological Seminary, "DM826: The Theology of Cranmer and the Book of Common Prayer," January 12-16, 2015). Null does publish this statement: "The sacrament's proper focus was not the transformation of the elements, but of the human will, by means of union with Christ through spirit-empowered faith" ("Thomas Cranmer's Reputation Reconsidered," in *Reformation Reputations: The Power of the Individual in English Reformation History,* ed. D. J. Crankshaw and G. W. C. Gross [London: Palgrave Macmillan, 2021], 208). Interestingly enough, Heiko Oberman observes this doctrine of the "transubstantiation of the people" as a feature of Zwingli's sacramentology, as well: "It may surprise us that Huldrich Zwingli . . . formulated this operation of the Holy Spirit so succinctly that there is reason to say that he taught a doctrine of transubstantiation— not the medieval doctrine of transubstantiation of the elements, but the Apostolic doctrine, mentioned in the *Didache of the Twelve Apostles*—according to which the dispersed congregation is assembled and changed into the Body of Christ" (Oberman, "Preaching and the Word in the Reformation," *Theology Today* 18, no. 1 [1961]: 21). Even Orthodox theologian Alexander Schmemann attests to this idea at the conclusion of his investigation of the origins and eschatological nature of the eucharistic liturgy, when he says; "It is precisely to this mission 'to proclaim the Lord's death and confess His resurrection' that the Sacrament of the Church bears witness. This Sacrament 'consecrates' Christians to this mission" (Schmemann, *Introduction to Liturgical Theology* [Crestwood, NY: St. Vladimir's Seminary Press, 1966], 74).

God's incomprehensible sacrificial love for the unworthy as their sole source. Cranmer made the reception of the elements the immediate response to the words of Institution. As a result, receiving the sacramental bread and wine, not their prior consecration, became the liturgy's climax. Now the sacramental miracle was not changing material elements but reuniting human wills with the divine.[108]

---

[108] Ashley Null, "Thomas Cranmer's Theology of the Heart," *Anvil* 23, no. 2 (2006): 216.

"NOT I, BUT CHRIST" DEVOTIONALLY AND HOMILETICALLY

SOLA FIDE IN CRANMER'S LITURGICAL PIETY AND PREACHING

WE HAVE EXAMINED the content of the liturgy thus far by analyzing words and ceremonial acts and tools. It is important to remember, however, that surrounding the worship services of the people of God was a piety, a devotional life, of the people. In a way, this devotional life served as the imaginative universe in which the words and ceremonies of the worship services orbited. Medieval piety created the plausibility structures that allowed liturgical words and actions to hang together. Though less concrete than words and ceremonies, devotional piety was therefore an equally important context for reform for the Archbishop of Canterbury. Let us examine how *sola fide* would inform this sphere of the liturgical life of sixteenth-century England before looking, finally, at Cranmer's reform of preaching.

"NOT I, BUT CHRIST" DEVOTIONALLY

When it comes to how the Prayer Book sought to shape the public devotional life of the people of God, few have observed *sola fide* as a possible unifying factor for much of Cranmer's decision-making. Why did the Archbishop simplify disparate regional liturgies to "but one use" and the Daily Offices to two? Some say that the motivation was political, congruent with Henry's agenda of kingdom-wide unity and loyalty. Why was devotion to the saints and praying for the dead eliminated? Some say that it was Cranmer's dogmatic biblicism or his early modern concern about superstition over against a more rational approach to religion. While, as noted in the introduction, elements of truth reside in all these assessments, less noticed is that justification by faith alone would insist on distinctions that would make such practices of public piety untenable and therefore recast the *devotional* content of the liturgy in a "not I, but Christ" framework.

Sola fide *and liturgical simplification.* Marion Hatchett expounds well that the political motivation in Cranmer's simplification of the liturgy to "but one use" was to establish uniformity with ease and cost-effectiveness.[1] The Prayer Book's preface more or less testifies to this. Elsewhere Hatchett points out that antiquity was another motivator behind some of the more specific simplification: "Cranmer greatly simplified the Church Year . . . based on a false assumption that days commemorating principal New Testament saints were older than Black Letter Days."[2] In other words, Cranmer's simplification was motivated by his favoritism toward older liturgical forms (be they historically accurate or not).[3] From another angle, while some correctly point out that Cranmer's Erasmian humanist training and medieval English affective piety would prompt the Archbishop to expand Prayer Book language[4]—that is, turn single words into doublets, or pairs into triplets—it would be C. S. Lewis's eye for medieval Latin that would notice Cranmer's penchant for linguistic contraction. Cranmer "tended to smooth out what was epigrammatic and to reject whatever might by the severest standards be thought exuberant. . . . Of all things, the Prayer Book dreads excess."[5]

But for Cranmer, was his work of liturgical contraction even simply an aesthetic conviction expressed through economy of words? We find an

---

[1]Marion Hatchett, "The Anglican Liturgical Tradition," in *The Anglican Tradition,* ed. Richard Holloway (Wilton: Morehouse-Barlow: 1984), 51. See n37 in the introduction for the quotation.
[2]Hatchett, "Tradition," 53.
[3]Hatchett does not there entertain the idea that another criterion of scripturality (i.e., fidelity to the Bible) could be at play, as well.
[4]Bryan Spinks, "Renaissance Liturgical Reforms: Reflections on Intentions and Methods," *Reformation and Renaissance Review* 7, no. 2–3 [2005]: 268-82; Ashley Null, "Comfortable Words: Thomas Cranmer's Gospel Falconry," in *Comfortable Words: Essays in Honor of Paul F. M. Zahl,* ed. John D. Koch, Jr. and Todd H. W. Brewer (Eugene, OR: Pickwick, 2013), 228-29; Null, "Thomas Cranmer and Tudor Church Growth," in *Towards a Theology of Church Growth,* ed. David Goodhew (New York: Routledge, 2016), 206-7.
[5]C. S. Lewis, *English Literature in the Sixteenth Century Excluding Drama* (New York: Oxford University Press, 1944), 220.

interesting note in the Archbishop's hand that helps here. In his study of Basil of Caesarea, Cranmer appears to have been influenced by the church father's desire for ordinary workers to attend morning and evening services where there would be Bible exposition. Cranmer's marginalia reveals him looking favorably on how simplification of the Daily Offices could help make the Bible-based piety of monasticism accessible to the average person's workday.[6] With this in mind, we can now see Paul Bradshaw's insight helping us closer to our thesis: "The major problem with the pattern of daily offices imposed on [worshipers] in the course of the Middle Ages was that it was excessively time-consuming and therefore *burdensome*."[7] What we want to argue is that, amidst other credible reasons for simplifying many regional liturgies into one, or paring down the Daily Offices from eight to two, or even contracting the "excess" of Latin liturgical phraseology, one very compelling reason for all of these moves is Cranmer's desire to place less of the burden of the work of faith on the worshiper. In other words, the doctrine of justification by faith alone offers a helpful explanation for Cranmer's simplification of liturgical devotion for the commoner: that worshipers would be less likely to fashion worship itself into a meritorious work, burdensome not only to the average person's schedule, but to their conscience.

That the Daily Office routine was tied up with one's standing before God is evident in Luther's own testimony:

> When I was a monk I was unwilling to omit any of the prayers, but when I was busy with public lecturing and writing I often accumulated my appointed prayers for a whole week, or even two or three weeks. Then I would take a Saturday off, or shut myself in for as long as three days without food and drink, until I had said the prescribed prayers. This made my head split, and as a consequence I couldn't close my eyes for five nights, lay sick unto death, and went out of my senses.[8]

---

[6]Cranmer's note, "*Horatur opifices ut cotidie sacris adsint contionibus*" was made in his copy of D. Erasmus, ed., *En amice lector thesaurum damus D. Basilium sua lingua loquentem* (Basel: H. Froben, 1532): 18, now held in the John Rylands Library, Manchester University, catalog number 18173. See Null, "Church Growth," 208 (including K. J. Walsh, "Cranmer and the Fathers, especially in the Defense," *Journal of Religious History* 11 (1980): 236, where this reference is originally noted).

[7]Paul F. Bradshaw, "The Daily Offices in the Prayer Book Tradition," *Anglican Theological Review* 95, no. 3 (Summer 2013): 447; emphasis added.

[8]Quoted in Bradshaw, "Daily Offices," 448.

As Bradshaw analyzed Luther, "This experience must have contributed to his questioning of the idea that such practices were 'works' necessary to satisfy God when his reading of St. Paul suggested that Christians were on the contrary justified by faith alone."[9] It is interesting to note that simplifying the Daily Office from eight to two was something proposed by Luther before it was enacted by Cranmer,[10] and all this compels us toward the conclusion that liturgical simplification was a value of Cranmer's precisely because the grammar of *sola fide* would press devotional piety to make less, not more, of the worshiper. Cranmer would agree with Luther's liturgical outlook that "one must not overload souls or weary them, as was the case until now in monasteries and convents,"[11] for the overloading of souls runs roughshod over the gospel of the *finished* work of Christ. Excess in worship becomes tantamount to an excess of works. We further see this principle of simplification at play throughout the Prayer Book, beyond Morning and Evening Prayer, in Cranmer's compression of the pastoral offices of marriage, burial, and visitation of the sick.[12]

In a sense, then, Cranmer's simplified liturgies were an attempt to enact devotionally what *sola fide* distinguishes theologically: God is approached by faith, apart from works.[13] Corroborating this understanding of Cranmer's agenda is a strong clue in his preface to the Prayer Book where, in a list of the vices of medieval worship, he includes "vain repetitions."[14] This connection

---

[9]Bradshaw, "Daily Offices," 448.

[10]Andrew Atherstone, "Reforming Worship: Lessons from Luther and Cranmer," *Churchman* 132, no. 2 (Summer 2018): 117: "[Luther] proposed to reduce the monastic hours in Wittenberg to two daily services—a morning assembly at 4 or 5am, and an evening assembly at 5 or 6pm—plus a midday service if desired."

[11]Luther, "Concerning the Order of Public Worship" (*LW* 53, 12).

[12]See Kenneth W. Stevenson, "Cranmer's Pastoral Offices: Origin and Development," in *Thomas Cranmer: Essays in Commemoration of the 500th Anniversary of His Birth,* ed. Margot Johnson (Durham: Turnstone, 1990), 83-86.

[13]It is also worth noting that at the time of the Reformation, the simplification of the Daily Office offered a critique of another important issue of the gospel we argued in the previous chapter—the intercession of priests. It was understood in medieval piety that priests and monks who prayed the eight offices of the breviary did so *on behalf of* others, "that the clergy might make propitiation to God for the people through their prayers" (Bradshaw, "Daily Offices," 449). If this is true, then Cranmer's simplification of the breviary was an attempt to take out the middleman, so to speak. Justification by faith alone grants direct access to God through Christ's propitiation and mediation.

[14]Joseph Ketley, ed., *The Two Liturgies, A.D. 1549, and A.D. 1552* (Cambridge: Parker Society, 1844), 18.

to Christ's criticism of the long-winded prayers of the Pharisees (Mt 6:7)—namely, those in Jesus' day who preached justification by works—reveals a likely perspective of Cranmer's: lengthy liturgies tend to aid and abet works-righteousness.[15]

Sola fide *and weekly communion.* Though weekly communion of the people is largely commonplace in twenty-first-century Anglicanism, it was not in sixteenth-century England. Indeed, back then the mass was performed more often than once a week, but as we have noted it was performed by the priest. It was not a communion of the people. Reception by the laity was rare. We observed above how, in Cranmer's mature sacramental understanding, the Lord's Supper paralleled the effect of preaching. What preaching does for our ears, the bread and wine do for "our eyes, mouths, hands, and all our senses." For Cranmer, the Eucharist is a multi-sensory proclamation and reception of the good news. What other conclusion could such a robust, evangelical theology of the table have but to urge weekly reception by the people of God? And this is precisely the innovation of the first English Prayer Books: Holy Communion was intended to be the principal Sunday service of the people[16] in order that, devotionally, the people of God would experience the gospel in all their senses on a regular basis. Indeed this was the intent, even if it did not achieve reality in Cranmer's day.[17]

---

[15]Note even further corroboration of this point below under sec. 5, where Cranmer's Morning Prayer confession places those confessing in the "character" of the Publican, who simply says, "Have mercy on me," over against the Pharisee, who prays in prolix eloquence (Lk 18:9-14).

[16]Unfortunately, the wonderful recovery of the centrality of the Eucharist in Christian worship, largely realized by the twentieth-century ecumenical and liturgical movements, has apparently come at the expense of the centrality of preaching. Even if not in intention, in *effect*, this emphasis on Holy Communion as "the principal act of Christian worship on the Lord's Day and other major Feasts" (the language of the *BCP 1979* opening preface, "Concerning the Service of the Church" [13]) has largely supplanted the preaching of the Word in some, if not many, Anglican and mainline contexts in North America. As we will see below, Cranmer never viewed preaching and sacraments at odds but instead insisted that both were necessary to faithfully minister the one Word of the gospel.

[17]Perhaps surprising to us, many English worshipers voted with their feet, and royal injunctions like those from Cranmer to the diocese of Norwich (explored more fully in our next section), called them out, inquiring "whether every Sunday at the least, you have a communion in your parish church" (Injunction xxxvi, recorded in Paul Ayris, "The Public Career of Thomas Cranmer," *Reformation and Renaissance Review* 4 [2000]: 123). MacCulloch interestingly notes the reasoning of the people: "The Edwardian Church failed as badly as John Calvin in Geneva in its efforts to establish the eucharist as the community's chief weekly service. The royal letter to the bishops on Christmas Day 1549 already complained about this, and admitted that one of the main problems was widespread resentment at the requirement that householders should provide bread and wine

Sola fide *and praying to the saints.* Cranmer's duties as Archbishop included visitations of the various dioceses under his watch care. These visitations were often accompanied by injunctions—official written statements and inquiries into the goings on of a given region. Visitations and injunctions were particularly useful for enforcing laws, and certain documents contained within the registers at Lambeth dating to the times in and around the ratification of the Prayer Books are especially telling for the Archbishop's understanding of the relationship of theology to practice. In line with our discussion, we find a clear connection in Cranmer's thinking between the practice of praying to saints and the doctrine of *sola fide* in the 1549 injunctions to the diocese of Norwich: Cranmer desires "that none maintain purgatory, *invocation of saints*, the six articles, bede-rolls, images, relics, rubric primers, lights, *justification by works*, holy bells, [etc.]."[18] Though prayer to the saints and justification by works are listed here among many other liturgical and doctrinal vices, even the fact that they exist in a list together should tell us something, especially given the weight of evidence already and still to be argued. We again make the point that it is not mere humanist-modernist allergy to superstition which accounts for Cranmer's concern over praying to the saints. Nor is it fully satisfactory to say that it was the Archbishop's biblicism which caused him to eschew the *Sanctorale* calendar, true as this may be.[19]

Duffy describes the contents of a medieval manual, the *Golden Legend,* which offers several reasons for the veneration and invocation of the saints. One reason listed is "to procure our own honour, 'for when we worship our brethren we worship ourselves, for charity maketh all to be common.'"[20] If this indeed was the common sentiment, one can see how the grammar of *sola fide* steps in to confront this not-gospel which, by "worshiping ourselves"

---

for the whole parish on a rotating basis" (Diarmaid MacCulloch, *Tudor Church Militant: Edward VI and the Protestant Reformation* [London: Penguin, 1999], 107).

[18]Cranmer, "Articles to be Inquired of in the Visitation to be had in the Bishopric of Norwich" (1549), printed in Ayris, "Career," 124. English modernized, and emphasis added.

[19]For this line of argumentation, see especially Shawn Strout, "Thomas Cranmer's Reform of the *Sanctorale* Calendar," *Anglican and Episcopal History* 87, no. 3 (September 2018): 307-24; see also James A. Devereux, "Reformed Doctrine in the Collects of the First *Book of Common Prayer,*" *Harvard Theological Review* 28, no. 1 (January 1965): 64-65.

[20]Eamon Duffy, *The Stripping of the Altars: Traditional Religion in England 1400-1580* (New Haven, CT: Yale University Press, 1992), 170.

(i.e., "honoring ourselves") attempts to undermine the negated "I" which the doctrine of justification by faith distinguishes. Put another way, the popular theology clarified by Duffy has far too high a view of the self, a spiritual and devotional outlook at odds with the clear declaration of the law, "No one is righteous."

Yet praying to the saints posed an even more direct threat to the clarity of the gospel. Popular devotion elevated the saints as moral exemplars (a good and biblical notion), but it was precisely their moral rectitude, according to Roman theology, which would qualify them to be intercessors and mediators for believers yet on earth. The Sarum rite (in line with all other Latin eucharistic liturgies) explicitly connects the saints' intercession to their virtue in the prayer after the Sanctus which states, "Communicating and venerating the memory . . . of all thy saints: by whose *merits and prayers* grant that in all things we may be defended."[21] According to Duffy, popular devotion viewed the prayers of the virtuous saints as "a source of power to be tapped."[22] Cranmer would no doubt see this in stark contrast to Paul's articulation of where "power" comes from— namely, in the gospel of Christ alone, by grace alone, through faith alone (Rom 1:16). That the saints could somehow mediate intercessory power *because* of their merited status obscured and confused faith's only rightful object—*solus Christus*. Cranmer would argue this very point with Henry's corrections to the Bishops' book. Whereas the king desired to maintain devotional appeal to the mediation of the saints, Cranmer insisted that while we can still believe that the heavenly saints indeed do offer ongoing prayers (Rev 8:4), we in no way seek them out for mediation because it nullifies the mediation of Christ. Cranmer quotes in particular Paul's clear word of the sole mediation of Christ in 1 Tim 2:5.[23] It is clear that "rejection . . . of the intercessory power of the saints" was indeed a "consequence of the reformed doctrine on justification."[24] And so it would be

---

[21]"By whose merits and prayers" (Latin: *quorum meritis precibusque concedas*). English translation from justus.anglican.org/resources/bcp/Sarum/English.htm, accessed September 30, 2019. Latin from Maskell, *Liturgy*, 130.

[22]Duffy, *Altars*, 175.

[23]Cranmer, "Corrections," in John Edmund Cox, ed., *The Works of Thomas Cranmer*, vol. 2 (Cambridge: The University Press, 1846), 93.

[24]Devereux, "Collects," 55.

that Cranmer would not only alter the *Sanctorale* calendar, but he would remove prayers to the saints from their traditional locations within the liturgy, such as in the Great Litany.[25]

Sola fide *and prayers for the dead.* Similarly, prayers for the dead became untenable for Cranmer ultimately, not only because they were shrouded in superstition or because they had no biblical precedent, but because they undermined the assurance, comfort, and confidence which *sola fide* provided. Cranmer would no doubt have agreed with Martin Bucer's argument from the *Censura* regarding the prayers for the dead which follow the Sanctus in the Communion liturgy:

> It is a true word of the Lord which says that they who hear him, and believe in him who sent him, have eternal life, they do not come into judgment but have passed from death into eternal life (John 5). But when prayer is offered for the dead that the Lord will grant them his mercy and everlasting peace, the common man supposes that this implies that the departed still feel the want of that peace and therefore of that full mercy of God by which he pardons their sins, and that the primary purpose of our prayers is to gain these things for them. No occasion must be given for this error.[26]

As Leuenberger comments on this passage, the grammar of *sola fide* exposes the lack of assurance implicit in prayers which intercede for the salvation of the dead: "Faith must lead to the certainty of salvation."[27] On this point, Cranmer would be meticulous in filtering out all references to prayers for the dead in the Communion liturgy, even to the point of changing the preface to the Prayers of Intercession from the potentially vague, "Let us pray for the whole state of Christ's church," to the doubly clear, "Let us pray for the whole state of Christ's Church *militant here in earth.*"[28] Obviously, therefore, not only does this affect the Communion liturgy, but the burial rite. Any prayers for the dead remaining in the 1549 liturgy ("Grant . . . that the sins which he

---

[25]Though present in shortened form in the English litany of 1544, prayers to the saints disappeared entirely in the litany reproduced in 1549. See H. C. G. Moule, *Our Prayer Book: Short Chapters on the History and Contents of the Book of Common Prayer* (London: Seeley and Co., 1898), 71.

[26]E. C. Whitaker, *Martin Bucer and the Book of Common Prayer* (Great Wakering: Mayhew-McCrimmon, 1974), 52.

[27]Samuel Leuenberger, *Archbishop Cranmer's Immortal Bequest: The Book of Common Prayer of the Church of England: An Evangelistic Liturgy* (Eugene, OR: Wipf & Stock, 1990), 36.

[28]Ketley, *Liturgies,* 87 and 270, respectively; emphasis added.

committed in this world be not imputed unto him, but that he . . ."[29]) are removed from 1552, such that the only intercessions remaining are for the living. Even more so, not only are prayers for the dead excluded, but prayers *to* the dead. Notice the difference (see fig. 7.1).

BOOK OF COMMON PRAYER, 1549	BOOK OF COMMON PRAYER, 1552[30]
Then the priest casting earth upon the corpse, shall say:	*Then while the earth shall be cast upon the body, by some standing by, the priest shall say:*
I commend thy soul to God, the father almighty,	**For as much as it hath pleased almighty God of his great mercy to take unto himself the soul of our dear brother here departed:**
and thy body to the ground,	**we therefore commit his body to the ground,**
earth to earth, ashes to ashes, dust to dust, in sure and certain hope of resurrection to eternal life, through our Lord Jesus Christ, who shall change our vile body, that it may be like to his glorious body, according to the mighty working whereby he is able to subdue all things to himself.	earth to earth, ashes to ashes, dust to dust, in sure and certain hope of resurrection to eternal life, through our Lord Jesus Christ, who shall change our vile body, that it may be like to his glorious body, according to the mighty working whereby he is able to subdue all things to himself.

Figure 7.1. Cranmer's 1549 and 1552 burial rite compared

Sola fide *and biblical characterization in the liturgy.* When the devotional piety of the Prayer Book is considered, it is scarcely observed that Cranmer creatively places the worshiper in the skin of various biblical characters, particularly when those characterizations serve to dramatize[31] the distinctions made according to the grammatical rules of *sola fide.* Two dramatic scenes stand out in Cranmer's liturgical role-play—the Syrophoenecian woman, and the Pharisee and the Publican. In the former, Cranmer's original

---

[29]Ketley, *Liturgies,* 147.

[30]Ketley, *Liturgies,* 145 (1549), 319 (1552).

[31]This dramatization usage of Scripture may be categorized most closely in Matthew Olver's taxonomy under "allusion" and further subcategory of "imitation" (Olver, "A Classification of a Liturgy's Use of Scripture: A Proposal," *Studia Liturgica* 49, no. 2 [2019]: 229, 234). However, this kind of dramatization does not seem to fit cleanly there, which makes me wonder, if I understand Olver correctly, whether there is not another category of biblical usage in the liturgy for us to explore.

Prayer of Humble Access liturgically dramatizes the scene of the woman who is found answering back Jesus' testing words by saying, "Yes, Lord, yet even the dogs eat the crumbs that fall from their masters' table" (Mt 15:27; Mk 7:28). And so we pray, "We be not worthy so much as to gather up the crumbs under thy table."[32] That Cranmer sees this as a tangible moment where *sola fide* makes distinctions is evident in both the context and the words of Jesus in the Gospel accounts. The context emphatically paints a picture of a meritless suppliant: she is a woman; she is not a Jew; she is even less than a child; she even in confession agrees with Jesus that she is a "dog." In other words, the Syrophoenecian woman finds her own identity completely negated and valueless ("not I"). And yet it is precisely *in* her "not I"–confession that Jesus by his words commends in particular not her boldness, not her courage, but her *faith*. The Markan account highlights that it is *because* of her faith (διὰ τοῦτον τὸν λόγον; Mk 7:29) that her daughter has been healed. It is highly significant and suggestive of Cranmer's understanding of *sola fide* that at one of the most tender and vulnerable moments in the Communion liturgy—the moment after the Sanctus where we are faced with the raw holiness of the living God—we would find ourselves in the character who in the Gospels perhaps represents the most stark distinction between faith and works.

Less obvious, but possibly intentional, is Cranmer's characterization present in the Morning Prayer Confession. There he alludes to Jesus' parable of the Pharisee and the Publican in Luke 18, imploring us to approach God as the Publican, rather than the Pharisee. We pray at the center of the Confession, "O Lord, have mercy upon us miserable offenders," which is the Publican's very prayer, commended by Jesus, "God, be merciful to me, a sinner" (Lk 18:13).[33] Here, too, is another significant place where our Lord distinguishes faith from works. The Pharisee is found commingling faith and works in their backhanded self-boast, "God, I thank you that I am not like other men" (Lk 18:11). And yet Christ commends the Publican not for

---

[32]Olver, "Classification," 92, 278.

[33]Massey Shepherd recognizes the Lk 18 reference in the Morning Prayer Confession (*The Oxford American Prayer Book Commentary* [New York: Oxford, 1950], 5-6). Interestingly Marion Hatchett does not follow suit (*Commentary on the American Prayer Book* [New York: HarperCollins, 1979], 101). Preceding both of them, F. E. Brightman, *The English Rite: Being a Synopsis of the Sources and Revisions of the Book of Common Prayer,* vol. 1 (London: Rivingtons, 1915), 130, does not recognize Lk 18 as source material for this original prayer of Cranmer's.

his feigned righteousness, but for his confession of unrighteousness ("not I"). Luke records these specific (Pauline) words in Jesus' response, "I tell you, this man went down to his house *justified* (δεδικαιωμένος)" (Lk 18:14). Again, we are caught up in a liturgical role-play that puts us in the Gospels' characters, who most starkly illustrate the distinctions made by the grammar of justification by faith alone. In these two characterizations, we see the doctrine of *sola fide* woven into the spirituality of the liturgy. The net effect of all these observations above is a picture of just how thoroughly Cranmer applied the filter of *sola fide* to the liturgy. Not only would justification govern and guide the theological language of the liturgy; it would decidedly impact the very devotional piety in and around the Book of Common Prayer. And it would go further still.[34]

Sola fide *and Scripture words in the Prayer Book.* Though a simple observation, we should note that even the Prayer Book's scripturality is itself a witness to the grammar of *sola fide* working itself out in devotional form. Many have observed how much of the verbiage of Cranmer's liturgy is not merely scriptur*al*, but Scripture. This is not to say that preceding liturgies did not also richly weave Scripture into their verbiage (especially in the Daily Office),[35] but it is to point out that in Cranmer's condensation of the liturgy and introduction of new material, the concentration of Scripture appears to have risen in percentage throughout. The Archbishop was very concerned to put the actual Word(s) of God on the lips of the people of God. If one of Luther's central cries was that "the whole of Scripture shows that the Word should have free course among Christians,"[36] then Cranmer's liturgy was very much in line with this commitment to let the Word do its work. In

---

[34]Before departing from the theme of biblical characterization, worthy of mention are the Opening Sentences of Morning Prayer (see Ketley, *Liturgies*, 217-218), three of which place the worshiper in the skin of adulterous David (Psalm 51:3, 9, 17), one places the Prodigal Son's confession on our lips (Luke 15:18-19), and one places us in the shoes of Daniel confessing on behalf of Israel (Dan 9:9-10). See Samuel L. Bray, "The Prayer Book Sentences, Pt. 2: Commonplaces of Contrition," *Ad Fontes Journal* online, accessed June 17, 2022, https://adfontesjournal.com/liturgy/the-prayer -book-sentences-pt-2-commonplaces-of-contrition/.

[35]Here is a good place to point out Olver's observations regarding just how rich the "scripturality" of historic liturgies actually is ("Classification," 220-45). His taxonomy reveals that historic liturgies' scriptural expression transcends mere quotation and allusion, and to his concluding point, this may mean that further study of liturgies Western and Eastern (not merely the English Prayer Books, as we are doing here) will yield more scripturality to appreciate and analyze.

[36]Luther, "Concerning the Order of Public Worship" (*LW* 53, 14).

"liturgizing" the Scriptures, Cranmer was offering yet another experiential way to engage a denial of the self. It is as if the liturgy is set up to tell us that not even our prayers and responses to God are of our own doing. The very words we use to speak to God are his own gifts to us. The liturgy then becomes not our words to God, but Christ's words to the Father through us. This is perhaps a devotional "not I, but Christ" in its most literal sense.

The scripturality of the Prayer Book taps into another vein of Cranmer's thought mentioned earlier—namely, that the Scriptures are a "reliquary" of the Holy Spirit. In medieval thought, a reliquary was something so filled with the Holy Spirit that it radiated God's own power and presence wherever it physically went. This is why the bones of saints, for instance, were cherished and sought after as "relics," for the saints were so filled with the Spirit that their bodies continued to radiate that presence, even after death. It is no small statement, then, when Cranmer claims in his 1540 preface to the Great Bible that the Scripture itself is "the most precious jewel, and most holy *relic* that remaineth upon earth."[37] Quoting Gregory of Nazianzus, Cranmer insists that knowing the Scriptures gives us the "illumination of the Holy Ghost."[38] Just as we cannot speak without breath, so the Word cannot go forth apart from the Spirit. Therefore, in Cranmer's mind, when he loads the Book of Common Prayer with the Bible, he is opening up for every believer direct access to the powerful presence of God through the Word.[39]

Also, it should not be missed that in the late Middle Ages it was an established idea that the church through the priesthood should be the primary arbiters of the Scriptures. Especially in England after the Lollard movement of the fourteenth century, having the Scriptures in the hands of the people was seen as a dangerous thing which threatened to destabilize not only the church, but society. And so it was that priests and clerics should handle the Word of God on behalf of, even for the safety of, the people. A Prayer Book filled with the Bible, then, would be yet another clear statement from Cranmer that Christ was the only mediator needed between God and humanity. One

---

[37]Cox, *Works,* vol. 2, 122; emphasis added.

[38]Cox, *Works,* vol. 2, 124.

[39]This adds further weight to our earlier defense against accusations that Cranmer's liturgies are devoid of the Holy Spirit (see chap. 3, n48). In Cranmer's mind, a scriptural Prayer Book *is* a Spirit-filled Prayer Book.

commentator on Cranmer's Homily on Scripture would remark, "Clearly Cranmer is angling some of the thrust of this homily against the Roman emphasis on the priest as mediator of what the believer needs to know, and saying instead that it is Scripture that holds this place."[40] Indeed, the Homily on Scripture could be seen in this regard as Cranmer's defense for a liturgy filled with the Bible—nothing but faith alone should stand between the Word of Christ and his people.

One example of Cranmer's ability to load the Bible naturally into the liturgy is found in his newly-composed Morning Prayer Confession. Within this short prayer, Cranmer references fourteen different passages of Scripture (see fig. 7.2).

GENERAL CONFESSION, MORNING PRAYER, 1552	SCRIPTURE REFERENCES[41]
Almighty and most merciful father,	
we have erred and strayed from thy ways, like lost sheep.	Isa 53:6; Ps 119:176; 1 Pet 2:25
We have followed too much	
the devices and desires of our own hearts.	Prov 19:21; Jer 18:12
We have offended against thy holy laws.	2 Chron 28:13
We have left undone those things which we ought to have done, and we have done those things which we ought not to have done,	Matt 23:23
and there is no health in us:	Ps 38:3
but thou, O Lord, have mercy upon us miserable offenders.	Luke 18:13

---

[40]Richard S. Briggs, "The Christian Hermeneutics of Cranmer's Homilies," *Journal of Anglican Studies* 15, no. 2 (June 2017): 177. Again, we see how the solas of the Reformation hang together. Especially in its original context, *sola scriptura*, properly understood, is a way of saying *solus Christus, sola gratia,* and *sola fide.*

[41]See Shepherd, *Commentary*, 5-6; and Hatchett, *Commentary*, 101. Note that with these Scripture references, it is especially helpful to read them in the English versions that Thomas Cranmer employed (the Matthew Bible of 1537 and the Great Bible of 1539), as subsequent English translations obscure the obvious nature of the allusion and/or quotation.

GENERAL CONFESSION, MORNING PRAYER, 1552	SCRIPTURE REFERENCES
Spare thou them, O God, which confess their faults.	Neh 13:22
Restore thou them that be penitent,	
according to thy promises declared unto mankind, in Christ Jesus our Lord.	Rom 15:8
And grant, O most merciful father, for his sake,	1 John 2:12
that we may hereafter live a godly, righteous, and sober life,	Tit 2:11-12
to the glory of thy holy name. Amen.	John 14:13

Figure 7.2. 1552 Morning Prayer Confession and its Scripture references

The Absolution to follow likewise quotes and alludes to seven different passages of Scripture (Ezek 33:11; Jn 20:22-23; Lk 24:47; Acts 2:38; Mk 1:14-15; Ezek 36:26-27; Lk 11:13). Throughout the liturgy, we find Cranmer's new compositions following this pattern of Bible-loading. We also see his redactions of other received liturgies attempting to add more Scripture than was there before, such as prescribing all rather than some Comfortable Words, as we noted above, or in his addition of Scripture sentences around the Offertory. It is clear that, for Cranmer, worship is at its best when we fill our prayers not with our words, but God's.

"NOT I, BUT CHRIST," HOMILETICALLY

The Reformation affirmation of preaching was not simply the result of humanist emphasis on the rhetorical arts, nor was it just a convenient platform for either political persuasion or the promulgation of the tenets of Protestant teaching. Underneath these real motivations[42] was the doctrine of justification by faith alone. It is most certainly in the 1547 Book of Homilies where we find Cranmer's vision for the pulpit in England. Cranmer no doubt would

---

[42]With regard to the English Reformation, Ashley Null outlines these motivations well in "Official Tudor Homilies," in *The Oxford Handbook of the Early Modern Sermon*, ed. Peter McCullough and Hugh Adlington (Oxford: Oxford University Press, 2011), 348-63.

have seen the implications of Paul's theology for preaching, and we can observe in what follows echoes of Paul's own homiletical method recorded in the book of Acts. For instance, in Acts 13, after preaching through a series of Psalm texts, the apostle's sermon climaxes with a declaration of full justification by faith through Christ alone, employing an explicit and categorical distinction of law from gospel: "Therefore let it be known to you, brothers, that through [Christ] forgiveness of sins is proclaimed to you, from everything of which by the law of Moses (ἐν νόμῳ Μωϋσέως) you were unable to be justified (δικαιωθῆναι), by this man, all who have faith (ὁ πιστεύων) are justified (δικαιοῦται) (13:38-39)."[43] Cranmer's agenda for the Book of Homilies bears this same theological and homiletical imprint.

We can start by observing first what the homilies were attempting to replace, and when we do so, we encounter once again Cranmer's concern about the priesthood as it was critiqued by the doctrine of *sola fide*. The priesthood of the Middle Ages was not homiletically oriented. In fact, as Duffy attests, "Everyone agreed that the average priest was by and large ill-equipped for preaching."[44] Indeed, preaching was unimportant then because the role of the clergy was sacerdotal and mediatorial. A priest's principal duties were to offer the sacrifice of the mass and to be a confessor. Manuals for priests in this era therefore placed their training emphases upon the words and techniques of procuring confessions and dispensing absolutions.[45] That the Reformation would press these clerical duties more toward the margins and replace preaching at the center would be a sign of *sola fide* at work. A minister is *not* a mediator. A minister's job, through preaching, is to point *to* the one Mediator, Jesus Christ. Even in sacramental discussions, Cranmer was found promoting proclamation of the gospel as the priest's most important task:

> The priest should declare the death and passion of Christ, and all the people
> should look upon the cross in the mount of Calvary, and see Christ there

---

[43] Author's translation. Two things make the translation of this awkward Greek sentence difficult. First, the language surrounding the verbs (such as the presence of the preposition ἀπὸ) press the translation of δικαιόω toward "free" rather than "justify" (so ESV, NIV, NASB, NRSV). Second, translating the wording fluidly often obscures the ordering and parallelism of the sentence (law of Moses // [unable to be] justified . . . faith // justified). While a more pleasing syntax results in more fluid English translations, in my opinion the theological force and rhetorical punch are lost.

[44] Duffy, *Altars*, 58.

[45] Duffy, *Altars*, 58-63.

hanging, and the blood flowing out of his side into their wounds to heal all their sores; and the priest and people all together should laud and thank instantly the chirurgeon (surgeon) and physician of their souls. And this is the priest's and people's sacrifice, not to be propitiators for sin, but . . . to worship continually in mystery that which was but once offered for the price of sin.[46]

It therefore appears to be an outworking of the grammar of *sola fide* that the first published manual for priests in the Reformation era, the Book of Homilies, is neither about sacramental priestcraft nor how to receive confessions and absolve. *Sola fide* would insist that ministers were preachers first.[47]

It is telling of the centrality and importance of preaching for Cranmer that of all liturgical reforms to be rolled out in England, preaching reform was first. The Book of Homilies was mandated for English pulpits two years before the first Prayer Book. This very well could signal that, for Cranmer, all true liturgical formation in the gospel cascades down from the pulpit. Even before the Book of Homilies, though, we see Cranmer making room for this rediscovered liturgical function of the minister. Possibly as soon as 1538,[48] Cranmer writes these notes into one of his early unpublished revisions of the Breviary:

Whenever any speech of exhortation is to be made to the people or preaching done, then the incumbent may leave out Te Deum, the Fourth Lesson and the creed *Quicunque vult* in those public prayers when the people are present, so that the people, kept too long and wearied by too lengthy a reading, should not attend keenly enough, or should not have enough time to hear the preaching of the gospel and clear showing-forth of the Spirit of Christ.[49]

---

[46]Cranmer, "Answer," in Cox, *Works*, vol. 1, 359.

[47]Corroborating this is the discussion on fig. 6.7 above regarding the giving of the Bible at ordination and the words of the bishop to the priest: "Take thou authority to preach the word of God."

[48]This document is known, among Cranmer's two early Breviary revisions, as "Scheme A." The dating of these revisions has been contested, but the most recent scholarship has as our best conjecture 1538 for "Scheme A" and 1543 for "Scheme B." For a good summary of the evolution of dating these documents, see Geoffrey Cuming, *The Godly Order: Texts and Studies Relating to the Book of Common Prayer* (London: SPCK, 1983), 1. The study of these schemes owes a great debt to the painstaking work of J. Wickham Legg, *Cranmer's Liturgical Projects* (London: Harrison & Sons, 1915), which enabled a much wider readership and analysis.

[49]Published in Cuming, *Godly Order*, 18.

The Archbishop desired to see preaching not draw the short straw amidst liturgical constraints of time and energy.[50] Note, too, that Cranmer clearly understands the homiletical enterprise to be particularly for "the preaching *of the gospel.*" Compare this with Cranmer's injunctions to Norwich, over a decade later, which include inquiries to find out whether any priests in the diocese have been preaching "justification by works."[51] From his earliest liturgical experiments, through the Book of Homilies, and into his Prayer Books, Cranmer has a consistent vision for what the pulpit exists to do. We also learn from his final sentence something of Cranmer's pneumatology as it relates to preaching and worship. Of the many ways the presence of the Holy Spirit is manifested in a worship service, preaching is one of the liturgy's primary vehicles—a "*clear* showing-forth."[52]

Yet the homilies would go further in not only emphasizing the preaching office of the priest, but even outlining the content of that proclamation. Ashley Null describes how Cranmer would deftly work the politics of including both conservative and Reformation contributions to the Book of Homilies. Conservatives John Harpesfield and Edmund Bonner would write the second Homily on Sin and the sixth Homily on Love, respectively. The remaining homilies, which were most critical for the Reformation distinction of faith and works, were left to the evangelicals.[53] "Cranmer brought theological consistency to the Homilies by carefully structuring the first six dogmatic topics," Null comments.[54] After the introductory Homily on Scripture, the

---

[50]This stands in contrast to Richard Hooker, the so-called father of Anglicanism, for whom it appears that preaching was a somewhat dispensable function of the priest's ministry of the Word. Hooker said, "The external administration of his word is as well by reading barely the Scripture, as by explaining the same when sermons thereon be made" (Richard Hooker, *Of the Laws of Ecclesiastical Polity*, vol. 2 [London: J. M. Dent, 1907], 80 [5:21.5]). In fact, Hooker equates Scripture reading and preaching in effect: "Our usual public reading of the word of God for the people's instruction is Preaching" (5:21.4). Apparently not taking Cranmer and the other English Reformers into account, Leonel Mitchell and Ruth Meyers insist that "the whole Anglican tradition" shares Hooker's perspective (Mitchell and Meyers, *Praying Shapes Believing: A Theological Commentary on the Book of Common Prayer* [New York: Seabury, 2016], 389n14). To be fair to Hooker, in context, the thrust of his argument seems to be directed more toward the idea that bare reading of the Scriptures can *also* be a form of "preaching," but his statements nevertheless seem clear enough of his view.

[51]See Ayris, "Career," 124.

[52]Cranmer's pneumatological understanding of preaching further corroborates our defense above in chap. 3, n48 against those who argue that Cranmer's liturgies downplay the Holy Spirit. To the contrary, for Cranmer preaching is a charismatic event.

[53]Ashley Null, "Official Tudor Homilies," in *The Oxford Handbook of the Early Modern Sermon*, ed. Peter McCullough and Hugh Adlington (Oxford: Oxford University Press, 2011), 354.

[54]Null, "Homilies," 355.

homily on "the misery of all mankind" by Harpesfield would naturally function as a strong word of condemnation preceding the homilies on Salvation,
Faith, and Good Works. Given that the Book of Homilies was intended to be
preached in succession in local parishes, it appears that Cranmer intended
the *ordering* of the sermons to proclaim the Word according to the grammar
of *sola fide.* We could say that the first six doctrinal sermons are structured
thus (see fig. 7.3):

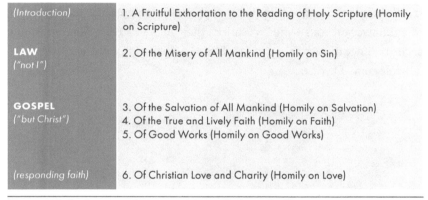

Figure 7.3. The law-gospel structure of the Book of Homilies[55]

Homiletically, we observe a clear distinction between law and gospel in
order that works might be sifted out so that the gold of *solus Christus*
remains clear and brilliant. Null observes a return to this law-gospel cycle
in the eighth and ninth sermons: "Of the Declining from God" preaches
the wrath of God only to be followed up by "An Exhortation Against the
Fear of Death," preaching the grace of God.[56] Therefore, even nestled in
the remaining six homilies which deal with ethical issues and are exhorta-
tive in nature, we find the grammar of *sola fide* at work. All this points to

---

[55]Null ("Homilies," 355):

    According to Melanchthon, to preach the law meant to point out "sin and its penalty" which
    included corruption and death. Thus, Harpesfield's erudite Erasmian, but still thoroughly
    traditional Catholic, homily became through Cranmer's placement of it in the book a Prot-
    estant proclamation of the law immediately preceding his own three sermons expounding
    the gospel. According to Melanchthon, preaching the gospel meant presenting the benefits
    of Christ and clarifying that they were received by faith. Such was the message of Cranmer's
    next three homilies.

[56]Null, "Homilies," 357.

the conclusion that *sola fide* governed Cranmer's homiletical philosophy. The pulpit's purpose is singular: proclaim Christ and Christ alone, by grace alone, through faith alone.

This chapter especially drives home what we should have sensed throughout the entirety of part two. For Cranmer, commitment to the centrality of the gospel in worship was not merely a theoretical exercise, but rather it was the heartbeat of the life of faith for believers. The Archbishop would not go to such extreme lengths nor take such painstaking care if he did not think that the kinds of changes instituted actually made a difference to the well-being of a follower of Jesus—their vocation, their relationships, their emotional security. Since the day the gospel grabbed a hold of him, Cranmer always was a theologian of the heart.

DEFINING AND IMAGINING GOSPEL-CENTERED WORSHIP IN THE TWENTY-FIRST CENTURY

WE BEGAN OUR JOURNEY by drilling down to the bedrock of Paul's theology. From there we traced upward through the layers of reception history, and back to the surface of Cranmer's theology, navigating the thick jungles of his liturgical method while ever mindful of the bedrock into which its roots are sunk. To summarize it all: what we learn from Paul is that the gospel is clearly proclaimed when faith and works are distinguished; what we learn from Cranmer is how thoroughly and effectively this can function when applied to the form and content of worship services, including in our meaning of "content" the ceremonies, practices, architecture, and ritual tools. As we peered over the Archbishop's shoulder we observed him, time and again, making editorial decisions that pointed to that chief evangelical concern. Cranmer's method gave us a vision for how worship services can be shaped so that they are gospel-centered. We determined therefore that remaining faithful to the gospel in worship is not simply filling our content with the good news of Jesus Christ but also being "gospel-grammared" in the *way* that content is delivered.

With Paul's vision, Cranmer teaches us that worship services need to oper-ate like an evangelical gold-pan to sift faith from works so that only the pure gold of the gospel remains as faith alone remains. The gospel's clarity is manifested *in* and *by* this sifting work. This critical filtering happens con-cretely for Cranmer as the "I" is negated and Christ is exalted in every aspect of worship—from its structure, to its words, ceremonies, aesthetics, devotional piety, and preaching. We now turn to the question of whether Cranmer's method has anything of value to share with those of us who some five centuries later strive to plan and lead gospel-centered worship services. Certainly the answer is yes, but first let us pave the runway.

DEFINING CRANMER'S VISION FOR GOSPEL-CENTERED WORSHIP

We arrive at this admittedly narrow and somewhat technical definition of gospel-centered worship: *Gospel-centered worship is worship that operates according to the grammatical rules of justification by faith alone in order that the good news of the finished work of Jesus Christ might be proclaimed as it is set apart from non-gospels.* Sola fide *does this work particularly through distinguishing faith from works and law from gospel. For this vision of gospel-centered worship to be thorough, these distinctions must be made on two levels: the liturgy's form and the liturgy's content. And with regard to the latter, we must recognize that liturgical content includes not only words, but their accompanying actions, assisting tools, aesthetic surroundings, and devotional piety.*

In contrast to this definition's narrowness, its application can be as broad and diverse as the church is broad and diverse. This is because gospel-centrality in this definition is less concerned with the *expression* of the form and content of worship and far more concerned with the *grammar* that norms how that form and content is conveyed.[1] To be clear, as we have observed, the expressions of worship services (their aesthetics, ceremonies, rituals, tools, and words) are not neutral and are subject to the rules of the grammar insofar as what they communicate either clarifies or obscures the distinctions drawn by *sola fide*. But the application of the grammar's rules in any culture need not flatten that culture's expression. Therefore, this understanding of

---

[1]It is ironic that one of the Reformation's best expressions of gospel-centered worship, the English Book of Common Prayer, has been one of the least culturally flexible liturgies as it traveled the globe and embedded itself into nonwhite, non-Western cultures. It is doubly ironic that as twentieth-century liturgical leadership attempted to undo this cultural rigidity by creating contextualized forms of the Book of Common Prayer, very little attention was paid to preserving the grammar of *sola fide*. I am certainly grateful, in this regard, that the 1662 Book of Common Prayer, which bears close resemblance to 1552, has been freshly platformed by InterVarsity Press with their recent International Edition edited by Samuel L. Bray and Drew N. Keane. One can only hope that this new exposure might have an effect on worshipers and liturgical revisers alike.

gospel-centered worship is culturally pliable even as it offers a transcultural liturgical logic for relating to God in corporate worship.[2]

This exposes an irony particularly in the history of Anglican worship, which often has a reputation among Protestant expressions for being the most rigid and unchangeable in its language and accompanying liturgical forms and ceremonies. Thankfully, with Anglicanism's globalization in the twentieth century along with the growth of its vitality and influence in non-Western contexts, enough pressure has been applied to the hardened layers of its form and expression that emerging fissures may indeed break open new life.[3] But talks of inculturation can have the tendency to ignore, or worse come at the expense of, the centrality of the gospel's transcultural liturgical logic. In fact, modern liturgical theologians who emphasize the need for Anglican liturgical inculturation often argue in such a way that makes the reader wonder whether there are any normative aspects of Anglican liturgy to be inculturated. There appears to be so much emphasis on theology as something locally created and "culturally constructed" and on the fact that "claims to universality [of Anglican liturgical theology] must be re-examined,"[4] that one often struggles to find any universalities identifiable after such a process of deconstruction. This book has argued that the universal norm of liturgical theology requiring preservation and inculturation is the same universal norm of the Scriptures—the gospel of Jesus Christ. Again, this gospel *is* the liturgy's transcultural, universal logic,[5] and for this reason Cranmer's labor and insights here apply well beyond the walls of

---

[2]I heard Glenn Packiam make this observation, paraphrased, "We can employ the *logic* of the liturgy even if we don't use the *language* of the liturgy" (Samford Worship Exchange, Samford University, October 22, 2019).

[3]See especially Juan Oliver's heartening discussion of inculturation and particularly his interaction with the "York Statement" of 2009 (Oliver, "Worship, Forming and Deforming," in *Worship-Shaped Life: Liturgical Formation and the People of God*, ed. Ruth Meyers and Paul Gibson [Norwich: Canterbury Press, 2010], 12-15).

[4]Oliver, "Worship," 22, 24.

[5]Of course, not all agree on this, at least in the sense of "gospel" as we have defined it throughout this book. It is not uncommon to hear argumentation that some aspects of biblical soteriology fundamental to our understanding of gospel, such as substitutionary atonement, are decidedly *not* transcultural but occasional to premodern times and places, such as first-century Palestine or the ancient Near East. This line of thinking often leads to radically different understandings of what the gospel is. For a helpful and comprehensive survey and analysis of the theme of substitution, see Fleming Rutledge, *The Crucifixion: Understanding the Death of Jesus Christ* (Grand Rapids, MI: Eerdmans, 2015), 462-535.

Anglicanism and have implications for the worship of all of Christ's holy, catholic, and apostolic church.

We have a powerful example of this logic at work (in a non-Western context and predating the English Reformation) right in the middle of the Scriptures in that famous showdown between Elijah and the prophets of Baal (1 Kings 18:20-40). Though the setting is not a formal worship service, we have set before us two ways of approaching and appealing to God—indeed, two worship ceremonies offering two competing liturgical theologies. The prophets of Baal, on the one hand, offer exhaustingly long prayers, "from morning until noon" (v. 26), and progressively more urgent pleas of sincerity, culminating in cutting themselves to the point of shedding blood (v. 28). The idea here is not simply that the prophets serve a deaf god. The underlying logic of the way they approach Baal—the *grammar*—is a showcase of works-righteousness: "Baal, look how serious we are! Look how surrendered and sold out we are!" Not unlike some sectors of evangelical worship today, what we have is a picture of a community of faith believing that if they present themselves in all their mustered faithfulness, then god will act and "bring the fire down."[6] Elijah, on the other hand, offers a brief and simple prayer (vv. 36-37), going so far as to douse the sacrificial altar with water in order to clarify, "If the fire consumes this sacrifice, there's no way of construing this as being caused by anything I've done." In other words, Elijah verbally and ceremonially declares a firm, "not I." Instead of proving himself to God, the prophet chooses to recount and remember God's past deeds as the "God of Abraham, Isaac, and Israel" (v. 36), appealing not to his own faith, but to God's very promises and faithfulness. In short, Elijah approaches God by distinguishing faith and works, not allowing any question that the victory is the Lord's *alone*.[7]

---

[6]This is my concern with well-meaning and passionate pleas for more "purity," "surrender," and "wholeheartedness" for worshipers and worship leaders, recently typified in a book like former Bethel worship leader Jeremy Riddle's *The Reset: Returning to the Heart of Worship and a Life of Undivided Devotion* (Anaheim, CA: Wholehearted Publishing, 2020). Again and again throughout the book, Riddle punctuates that God and heaven are "waiting" for our wholehearted devotion to be manifested in purity: "There is a spiritual authority waiting to be released on earth . . . but it waits for the wholehearted ones to rise . . . heaven will begin to respond to you . . . heaven has taken notice of your life, decision and consecration. . . . Don't hold anything back. Place it all on the altar. And watch. Fire will begin to fall" (48-49, cf. iii, 9, 39, 55, 66).

[7]Recent research bears out that the critique of evangelical worship here is not of something aberrant or on the fringes of the modern worship movement. In fact, this mode of liturgical theology—the dependence of God's actions based on our prior action—is embedded in the historical and

Inspired by the free gift made possible by faith alone: this is what we are after in gospel-centered worship. It can be expressed as Elijah on a mountain, Israelites in a temple, medieval Londoners in a cathedral, or twenty-first-century Chinese Christians in a living room. Still, the above definition and the idea of "liturgical logic" are yet quite theoretical and abstract, as we have taken the vat of Cranmer's work and boiled out its essence. But Cranmer's labors offer us a way back into the concrete details of how to pursue gospel-centered worship in our own contexts in the twenty-first century.

APPLYING CRANMER'S VISION FOR GOSPEL-CENTERED WORSHIP

If we were to summarize Cranmer's objective in a single sentence, it would be this: the Archbishop was attempting to create a liturgy whose chief objective was to create hearing aids for the gospel. To unpack this, we somewhat artificially broke down Cranmer's comprehensive work into observable portions in order to make sense of the data and more systematically argue a cumulative case. We must admit that analysis through those discrete categories may be just as antiseptic and technical as the definition for gospel-centered worship offered above. It appears that Cranmer was operating far more out of an instinctive, subterranean grammar, and far less from a prefabricated agenda with overt strategies and objectives. Nevertheless, breaking down Cranmer's moves allows us to employ similar analytical categories to apply constructively to worship today. Cranmer offers us five spheres in which to explore the gospel-centrality of our worship and therefore five ways we can evaluate how our services function as "hearing aids" for the gospel: (1) service-structures; (2) theological

---

theological origins of what historians Lim Swee Hong and Lester Ruth call the "contemporary praise and worship movement." They trace in particular the theology and teaching of 1940s and 50s Latter Rain movement leader, Reg Layzell, who "saw the sacrifice of obedient praise as the key to maintaining revival." With Ps 22:3 and Heb 13:15 as the centerpiece texts for his liturgical theology, Layzell taught that when we have "high praises in our mouths," we are able to "produce or release the presence of the captain of the Lord's army." In other words, God's blessing and presence rely upon our prior fervent acts of praise. This teaching would be a constant thread woven into the growing tapestry that has become the twenty-first-century modern worship movement. See Lester Ruth and Lim Swee Hong, *A History of Contemporary Praise & Worship: Understanding the Ideas that Reshaped the Protestant Church* (Grand Rapids, MI: Baker Academic, 2021), 18, 22. More on this below.

terminology; (3) rituals, actions, and architecture; (4) devotional piety; and (5) preaching.

1. Analyzing our service-structures. The grammar of *sola fide* presses us to think carefully about the ordering of content. Who God is and what he has done must precede and set the stage for any expression of self-offering. If we are serious about the clarity of the gospel, language of self-surrender, self-consecration, self-giving, self-sacrifice must most often be placed after language about how God has given himself in the person and work of Jesus Christ. It is not that there is nothing to say about "me" at the beginning of a worship service. On the contrary, justification by faith alone urges us that there is something very specific to say: "*Not* I." Before the face of God Almighty, these are words we can pray: "God, be merciful to me, a sinner" (Lk 18:13). Before the face of God Almighty, these are the things we can offer: our sinfulness, our brokenness, our need. Songs, prayers, and liturgies which construct this *order* of events—(a) God's glory, attributes, and law; (b) our inadequacy, sin, and need; (c) God's provision of Jesus' life and death for sinners; (d) our grateful response of self-offering—whether they be in one liturgical arc or in cycles as Cranmer did it, can rightly be said to be "in step with the truth of the gospel" (Gal 2:14), charged with "the power of God" (Rom 1:16; 1 Cor 1:18), and "filled with the Spirit" as "the word of Christ dwells in you richly" (Eph 5:18; Col 3:16).

This is where we must reckon with contemporary attempts to encourage a reappropriation of the "gospel-story" or the "narrative of the gospel" in our worship services.[8] Such voices, including my own,[9] can give the perhaps unintended impression that merely enacting and retelling the story of redemptive history, in and of itself, will ensure the gospel-centrality of our worship services. Though this is a necessary step, Cranmer would urge us further. We must recognize within that broad shape the subtleties that may undercut the

---

[8]E.g., Bryan Chapell, *Christ-Centered Worship: Letting the Gospel Shape Our Practice* (Grand Rapids, MI: Baker, 2009); Mike Cosper, *Rhythms of Grace: How the Church's Worship Tells the Story of the Gospel* (Wheaton, IL: Crossway, 2013), esp. 117-50; Constance M. Cherry, *The Worship Architect: A Blueprint for Designing Culturally Relevant and Biblically Faithful Services* (Grand Rapids, MI: Baker, 2010), esp. 19-122; Robbie F. Castleman, *Story-Shaped Worship: Following Patterns from the Bible and History* (Downers Grove, IL: InterVarsity Press, 2013), esp. 77-94.

[9]See Zac Hicks, *The Worship Pastor: A Call to Ministry for Worship Leaders and Teams* (Grand Rapids, MI: Zondervan, 2016), 143-72.

story's clear proclamation of the gospel. It is one thing to tell and participate in the story of creation, fall, redemption, and consummation in the liturgy. It is another thing to hear the gospel for oneself and receive that Word by faith alone, apart from works. This is why Cranmer's voice is so important in our contemporary attempts at liturgical retrieval.[10] Merely reviving ancient liturgical forms and structures that are more gospel-shaped does not ensure that the gospel will be clearly proclaimed or that the gospel's logic has been faithfully employed. These retrieved liturgies must speak the story by constructing its sentences according to the grammar of *sola fide*. If not, we may be in danger of utilizing gospel-shaped liturgies which take back with the left hand the very gospel that has been given with the right.

Here we can share a hopeful aspiration with the liturgical movement of the past century—namely, an achievable way forward for liturgical unity across ecumenical lines. The influence of Dix's *The Shape of the Liturgy* gave positive momentum to the idea that adherence to the structure of the ancient eucharistic liturgy, despite variance in the actual verbiage, could be a richer way to give liturgical expression to the unity of the one holy catholic and apostolic church. Though Dix's conclusion of what that structure actually is has been weighed and found wanting,[11] the principle is sound: structural fidelity may be the most important path toward doxological unity. Where the argument of this book diverges from those in the liturgical movement is in the structure itself proposed. The liturgical movement chiefly values antiquity and consensus in practice, hence the ongoing quest for the oldest eucharistic forms and a tracing of their patterns of commonality across the centuries.[12] This book argues that beneath those liturgies are the operations of the living and active Word, moving across church history by the power of the Holy

---

[10]For more on theology as retrieval particularly with reference to worship, see W. David Buschart and Kent D. Eilers, *Theology as Retrieval: Receiving the Past, Renewing the Church* (Downers Grove, IL: InterVarsity Press, 2015), 117-54.

[11]See summary and references in Bryan D. Spinks, "Mis-Shapen: Gregory Dix and the Four-Action Shape of the Liturgy," *Lutheran Quarterly* 4, no. 2 (1990), and Leonel Mitchell and Ruth Meyers, *Praying Shapes Believing: A Theological Commentary on the Book of Common Prayer* (New York: Seabury, 2016), 148-50.

[12]That antiquity takes precedence over gospel-logic is betrayed in comments such as these (plentiful in modern liturgics), regarding the 1979 Prayer Book's option of front-ending the general confession: "Many feel that the general confession should regularly be included in the service at this point [i.e., the beginning of the service], although there is no ancient precedent for a general confession of sin at any point in the eucharistic liturgy" (Mitchell and Meyers, *Praying*, 152).

Spirit to lead believers to worship the Father by Christ alone, by grace alone, through faith alone. And these operations necessitate and propel a structure more primal and fundamental than the iterations of any generation's and culture's liturgical expression. Cranmer's vision offers a helpful way forward toward unity well beyond the mere borders of Anglicanism,[13] which provides contextual freedom within the blessed boundaries of the gospel.

2. Analyzing our theological terminology. The grammar of *sola fide* creates in worship planners, worship leaders, songwriters, liturgists, and pastors a strong sensitivity to words and phrases and how their use may either promote or undermine the gospel. We become experts not just in vocabulary itself, but in the *effects* of words on hearers. Cranmer urges us to be sensitive to at least eight things in the words we employ in our singing, praying, preaching, and liturgical leadership. First, we become aware of the use of conditional language. We pay attention to how words like *if* are used in connection with statements or phrases about God's grace and mercy. Paraphrasing one worship song I heard not long ago: "Your grace is mine, if I only believe." In one sense, theologically, this is soundly biblical. The only "condition" of God's grace is the non-work of faith to believe it is true. But even here, we are compelled by the gospel to think through what might be the possible effects of these words. Conditional phrases such as these could turn faith into a work. We are concerned to leave the grace of God *un*conditioned precisely because, as the grammar insists, it is in the gospel's unconditionality that the good news is clearly proclaimed. A conditioned gospel is no gospel at all. We are aware of even how potentially unconditioned phrases might be heard as conditions, such as "Come to us, O Lord, as we put our faith in you." One interpretation of this might certainly be that in the act of expressing God's gift of faith, he comes to us. This is true enough. But this is not the only possible interpretation. Even if we do not change every word or phrase, the grammar makes us sensitive to both actual and potential conditionality.

---

[13]Prayer Book commentators Leonel Mitchell and Ruth Meyers get close to this vision when they identify, along with the 1995 International Anglican Liturgical Consultation, that there is something fundamental to the structure of the eucharistic rite which is the baseline for Anglican unity (Mitchell and Meyers, *Praying,* 150). However, Mitchell and Meyers do not see what we are seeing—that the structure of the liturgy must be most fundamentally architected according to the logic of the gospel.

Second, we would do well to take a cue from Cranmer by employing passive constructions in speaking about ourselves outside of our sinfulness. When we come to the point in our services where we are offering or committing ourselves to God in grateful response, even there, the grammar of *sola fide* might urge us to employ verbs in the passive form: "Make us to be holy," "cause us to be committed," "move us to keep your word," "guide us to be faithful," "turn our hearts to your Word," "help us want to walk in your ways." Whether these constructions are passive grammatically ("to be [adjective]") or conceptually ("move us to [verb]"), they do the work of *sola fide* by insisting that the action is God's alone to do. This is how the grammar of justification would urge us to construct prayers that pertain to our obedience, work, consecration, discipleship, offering, surrender, laying ourselves down, and following Jesus.

Third and similarly, even our active verbs and actions can be nestled in language of the work of God. We recall Cranmer's liberal use of phrases like "through the merits of Jesus Christ." Prepositional phrases are key tools for surrounding statements of our action with the work of God: "By the inspiration of your Holy Spirit," "in your grace," "by your power," "in response to your work," "in gratitude for your faithfulness," "through your mercy." Phrases of God's activity that precede verbs of our action are likewise useful: "Fill us with your Spirit to [verb]," "strengthen us to [verb]," "empower us to [verb]."

Fourth, we can with Cranmer add even more clarity to our songs, prayers, and proclamation through the employment of terms which qualify actions—whether divine or human—in a categorically exclusive way. Cranmer here reminds us of powerful words like "alone" and adverbs like "only," "solely," "wholly," and "completely." These words can be added onto many of the kinds of phrases offered above: "By your power *alone*," "*only* through your grace," "as we trust in you *alone*," "*only* as we rely on you," "while we depend on you *solely*," "*wholly* by your mercy," "through your finished work *completely*." Terms such as these add theologically emphatic punctuation to phrases already charged with the expression of *sola fide*.

Fifth, we are urged to apply language of our sin and weakness liberally throughout all points of the service. Whereas twentieth-century liturgical scholarship largely sought to erase from Cranmer's liturgy all negative anthropology in order to highlight the dignity of humanity and not cast the whole of worship in too much of a "penitential" light,[14] Cranmer would have us see statements of sin and weakness not as extreme but as a gospel-centered way of merely "calling a thing what it is."[15] To be committed to the grammar of *sola fide* means a perpetual acknowledgment that indwelling sin remains and self-righteousness is ever a threat for the Christian. Therefore, songs, prayers, and proclamation highlighting our frailty, unworthiness, weakness, need, and dependence throughout the service pave the gospel's runway. Indeed, so-called penitential liturgies and expressions such as Cranmer's should not be relegated to certain seasons of the church year which call for humility but should characterize every Christian gathering. As Luther's first thesis of 1517 states: "When our Lord and Master Jesus Christ said, 'Repent' (Matt 4:17), he willed the entire life of believers to be one of repentance."[16] Worship planners and leaders serious about the clarity of the gospel help us to wear our sin on our sleeve, not for the purpose of morbid self-loathing or downplaying human dignity, but that the powerful grace of Christ might be on display in most vivid fashion, in unshared spotlight.

Sixth, we can transpose statements of our work for God into statements of Christ's work for us. Taking some editorial cues from Cranmer, we can analyze our songs and prayers similarly to how he transposed the Collects. Such work can be useful both as an analytical tool for existing songs and prayers and as a grid to think through future songwriting and prayer composition. As an exercise, we could look at a transposition of a classic evangelical invitation hymn such as Judson W. Van de Venter's "I Surrender All" (see fig. 8.1).

---

[14]Classic examples include *BCP 1979*'s edits to the Morning Prayer: the elimination of the original sentences to the call to confession, and the removal of the phrases "miserable offenders" and "there is no health in us" in the following general confession. *BCP 2019* also eliminates "miserable offenders" and blunts Cranmer's sharp edge with the appendage, "*apart from your grace*, there is no health in us" (12).

[15]Luther, "Heidelberg Disputation" (1518), thesis 21.

[16]*LW* 31, 25.

I SURRENDER ALL[17]	CHRIST SURRENDERED ALL[18]
All to Jesus I surrender, All to him I freely give; I will ever love and trust him, In his presence daily live.	All, Lord Jesus, you surrendered, All to me you freely gave; All my sin you bravely shouldered, All for me, my life to save.
I surrender all, I surrender all; All to thee, my blessed Savior, I surrender all.	Christ surrendered all, Christ surrendered all; All for me and my salvation, Christ surrendered all.
All to Jesus I surrender, Make me, Savior, wholly thine; Let me feel thy Holy Spirit, Truly know that thou art mine.	All, Lord Jesus, you surrendered, All your rights you left behind; Trading might for humble weakness; For the good of all mankind.
All to Jesus I surrender, Humbly at his feet I bow, Worldly pleasures all forsaken; Take me, Jesus, take me now.	All, Lord Jesus, you surrendered, All for me, your enemy; Worldly pleasures I was seeking, Still, Lord, you were seeking me.
	All your life is all my merit; All Your death my ransom paid. Now I feel no condemnation, Just a love that cannot fade.

Figure 8.1. "I Surrender All" transposed

We could look at another common invitation hymn, "I Have Decided to Follow Jesus" (see fig. 8.2).

I HAVE DECIDED TO FOLLOW JESUS[19]	GOD HAS DECIDED[20]
I have decided to follow Jesus . . . No turning back, no turning back.	God has decided to save my lost soul . . . No turning back, no turning back
Though none go with me, I still will follow . . . No turning back, no turning back.	Christ has decided to die in my place . . . No turning back, no turning back.
The world behind me, the cross before me . . . No turning back, no turning back.	The Holy Spirit now lives inside me . . . No turning back, no turning back.

---

[17]"I Surrender All," by Judson W. Van De Venter (1896). Public Domain.
[18]"Christ Surrendered All," by Zac Hicks (2014). ©2014 Unbudding Fig Music (ASCAP).
[19]"I Have Decided to Follow Jesus," by Anonymous (c. nineteenth century). Public Domain.
[20]"God Has Decided," by Zac Hicks (2013). ©2013 Unbudding Fig Music (ASCAP).

I HAVE DECIDED TO FOLLOW JESUS	GOD HAS DECIDED
	The love of God will forever hold me . . . He won't let go, he won't let go; No turning back, no turning back.

Figure 8.2. "I Have Decided to Follow Jesus" transposed

We should keep in mind that the above transpositions are not criticisms of the power or truthfulness of the original songs, or even of their appropriateness and value in certain liturgical moments. Nor are we saying that the transposed versions of the songs are necessarily better. Rather, they simply serve as examples of the kinds of creative work that can be done when we develop sensitivities along the lines of the grammar of *sola fide*. On the ground in local churches, transposition work of this sort might more often be of lines and phrases, rather than whole songs.[21] The above examples can also guide us in new endeavors of song- and prayer-writing, which is almost certainly pastorally preferable to tinkering with songs (as I admittedly have done here) which may be imprinted deeply in a person's nostalgia or significant past experience.

Seventh, in the moments of the proclamation of the gospel itself, we can employ the language of direct address to punctuate the certitude of the good news. Though "there is therefore now no condemnation" (Rom 8:1) is certainly a strong, bald declaration of the gospel, Cranmer would have us be aware that, in the liturgical moment, there is a clarifying power in employment of the second personal pronoun: "There is therefore now no condemnation *for you*"; "*Your* sins are forgiven"; "Take and eat this, in remembrance that Christ died *for you*"; "Drink this in remembrance that Christ's blood was shed *for you*"; "May God have mercy on *you*, pardon and deliver *you* . . . confirm and strengthen *you* . . . and bring *you* to everlasting life."[22]

---

[21]We will not here get into the subject of intellectual property and copyright infringement for songs not in the public domain, but such considerations must of course factor into this kind of work.

[22]This, in conjunction with our first point above about the language of conditionality, poses a lingering question I have for Cranmer about the language of the Morning Prayer Absolution. It avoids direct address and can be conceived as conditional: "He pardoneth and absolveth all them [third personal address] which truly repent and unfeignedly believe his holy Gospel [could be perceived as a conditionality]" (Joseph Ketley, ed., *The Two Liturgies, A.D. 1549, and A.D. 1552* [Cambridge: Parker Society, 1844], 219). Given how sensitive Cranmer was to conditionality and direct address elsewhere, the only conclusion I have is that the Archbishop, as we have well noted, was avoiding

Eighth and finally, we might follow Cranmer's lead regarding the sheer quantity of talk about "me" and what "I" do versus that of what God does in Christ. The grammar of *sola fide* insists that the power of faith, transformation, and growth lies in the yes about Jesus ("but Christ") which follows the no about us ("not I"). If the power lies in that word about Christ, then frequency and emphasis really do matter. It would be a healthy exercise to quantify all talk of Christ and his finished work alongside the talk of our offerings, response, and obedience in order to see where the scales tip. Convinced that our good works will flow *from* the good news, we want to load our services, as Cranmer did, with the language of God's love, grace, and mercy.

Some may view the analyses in this section as excessive, exaggerated, or splitting theological hairs—a hypercriticism of words and phrases. Turning our attention to the modern worship movement, however, Cranmer would urge us toward such critical reflection. Historians Lim Swee Hong and Lester Ruth have well outlined the liturgical theology embedded in the history of teaching and practice of the contemporary praise and worship movement. Coded into the DNA of modern worship is a particular theological orientation, the heart of which is built on an Old Testament sacrificial typology that emphasizes the worshiper's ability to "produce or release the presence" of God through the fervent expression of *their* "sacrifice of praise," which God would eventually "come and consume" when the praise reaches a certain level.[23] Several early teachers would call this typological worship pattern the "divine order."[24] Needless to say, this *ordo*—this offering first a sacrifice of praise in order to release the powerful presence of God—does not speak the Christian faith according to the grammar of

---

the confusion which could be created by priestly absolution. Even though Cranmer makes clear that "Almighty God" is here doing the absolving, perhaps Cranmer wanted to be one step removed from any perception that the priest stood in the way of the mediatorial work of Christ. We also note that the latter half of the Absolution doubles back on what might be perceived as conditions by beseeching God to "grant us true repentance and his Holy Spirit" in order that the repentance might be real and fruit might be borne.

[23]Ruth and Lim, *History*, 22, 26. Lim and Ruth characterize this emphasis as "the causal instrumentality of praise" (Ruth and Lim, *History*, 93, 94). On the movement's Old Testament typology, see esp. 37-42, 46-73. Early teachers would emphasize "'praising-through for victories' (i.e., engaging in praise long enough until some sort of spiritual 'victory' was experienced)" (Ruth and Lim, *History*, 37).

[24]Ruth and Lim, *History*, 41, 57. Ruth and Lim describe this order's eventual codification as a "God-given pattern for worship" (Ruth and Lim, *History*, 127).

sola fide.[25] And downstream from such an order, over the generational branching of successive tributaries of contemporary and modern worship, comes a steady flow of songwriting emphasizing the worshiper's fervent action—surrender, sacrifice, laying down, wholeheartedness, commitment, zeal, decision.[26] Of course all these concepts are biblical and in their isolation find linguistic parallels in the Psalms and elsewhere. But in practice along its reproductive history, as the family tree of contemporary praise and worship has branched out across regions, traditions, and denominations, such songwriting emphases remain coded with that early DNA, and the deep and complex formational power of such coding requires more than superficial analyses and solution-offering that are often put forward in response to the "problems" of modern worship. What we are exposing is that the grammar of *sola fide* may be helpful to frame conversations of reforming the *lex orandi* of modern worship, if indeed modern worship can take seriously its own liturgical-theological genealogy.

3. Analyzing our rituals, actions, and architecture. In the twenty-first century, it is mostly in sectors of Anglicanism (and other areas of mainline Protestantism) where we find issues regarding ritual, action, and architecture potentially obscuring the clarity of the gospel in a fashion similar to that of the sixteenth century. In those places, it just may be that Cranmer's perspective needs no translation but can speak for itself just as well and as plainly as it did five hundred years ago.[27] That said, there are a host of ways that

---

[25]This stands despite the kind of teaching in the contemporary praise and worship movement which describes praise as "an act of *faith* creating the atmosphere for the presence of God" in contrast to worship as "the expression of our response to his presence" (Charlotte Baker in 1979, quoted in Ruth and Lim, *History*, 43; see a similar quote on 56). As we have established, faith by biblical definition is that which trusts God's work *solely*, to the exclusion of our work. Manifestations of God's presence, according to *sola fide*, cannot be bound by or based on our previous action, and therefore the idea of "activating," "creating," or "releasing" God's presence is simply not the right way of describing what is taking place, as though the blessings and benefits of Christ and the Holy Spirit were locked until we ourselves opened the door. However we might describe manifestations of the presence of God during singing, justification boundaries such descriptions to exclude language which promotes human causality of divine blessing.

[26]In using the imagery of a river, I am borrowing Ruth and Lim's apt metaphor that pervades the structure and language of their *History*.

[27]This is a major concern I have for much of even conservative Anglicanism in North America. The fact that many modern Anglicans can simultaneously claim fidelity to the gospel and yet engage in liturgical practices which serve to undermine, if not directly contradict, what we have outlined from Cranmer's work (see chap. 6, n105 and Introduction, n14 in the conclusion for concrete

Cranmer's analysis of his time might speak into the evangelical present in North America and beyond. Let us explore five possible avenues of inquiry.

First, we might examine how many of the current rituals associated with modern worship produce a similar kind of congregational passivity that the rituals of medieval worship did. We remember that in the sixteenth century, the passive laity was contrasted with a ritualistically dense and performative spectacle "up front." The job of the average worshiper was to remain silent, to pray and ponder in an individualistic manner, all the while staying in tune with what was happening front and center. Perhaps, then, with Cranmer, we can evaluate those elements of our modern worship services which may be prone to excluding or minimizing the participation of the people—everything from songs in singable keys, to downplaying "special music," to minimizing the featuring of highly performative, virtuosic music, drama, and other art.

Closely related is a second observation about architecture. The goal in the sixteenth century was to minimize the distinction between the congregation and the "platform." *Sola fide* causes us to step back and ask how today's platforms, stages, and chancels elevate and separate a unique set of ministers for the work of worship. Similarly, as we think about modern worship space design, we become aware of the way that similar structures in concert venues naturally lend themselves to passive receptivity. We become sensitive to the ways people might walk into a space which looks like a concert venue—elevated stage, sophisticated sound system, multimedia production, stacked lighting—and understandably slip into dispositions that one would feel and engage if one were at a concert, whether rock, jazz, pop, or classical. Perhaps it is not that we must totally do away with these helpful aesthetic means, but we become sensitive to their liabilities. Here we are careful not to let bias cloud objectivity. Many traditionalists eschew the rock stylings of multicolored lights, haze, and droned ambient music, not recognizing that the church in generations past used similar means of stained glass, incense, and melismatic chant to excite the senses and turn people Godward. *Sola fide* encourages us to be less concerned with the aesthetic means in and of themselves and more aware of how they and the formational contexts they engender either

examples) exposes considerable blind spots. It is my hope that this study of Cranmer might be some small contribution toward an awakening of this incongruity.

strengthen or deter from the proclamation and apprehension of the gospel. I find helpful here David Taylor's language about how "church architecture inescapably opens up and closes down possibilities for the formation of Christ's body on earth."[28] Especially over time, certain kinds of spaces "open up" or "close down" people's understanding of God, themselves, worship, mission, and more. For our purposes, we have observed that certain architecture carries that same potentiality, in a narrower sense, with regard to our apprehension of and formation in the gospel. Cranmer gives us cues to ask fresh questions about our spaces, especially when their "material fixity" may permanently send messages or direct formation away from a clear gospel.[29]

Third, perhaps Cranmer's work with liturgical nomenclature has something to say to us today. We might think specifically here about how the relatively new title of "worship leader" might not analogously raise similar concerns as "priest."[30] The term, though ubiquitous and probably here to stay, requires a caveat lest we begin to think that a worship leader is someone who mediates the presence of God for the people of God or somehow stands in the place of Jesus, who himself alone is given Scripture's closest parallel to the title of worship leader—τῶν ἁγίων λειτουργὸς, "minister in the holy places," or "liturgist in the sanctuary" (Heb 8:2). Similarly, certain sectors of evangelicalism are known to use the adjective *anointed* to describe leaders who appear to have a unique charisma in being able to guide groups of people into special encounters with God. The term, quite literally loaded with messianic overtones, might betray some of the ways we have allowed our leaders in worship to serve in mediatorial roles that obscure the access we have to the Father through Christ by the Spirit.[31] Worship leader Jeremy Riddle reveals some of this problem when he writes:

---

[28] W. David. O. Taylor, *Glimpses of the New Creation: Worship and the Formative Power of the Arts* (Grand Rapids, MI: Eerdmans, 2019), 113.

[29] Taylor, *Glimpses*, 106-7.

[30] On the connection between the modern worship leader and the priestly office in the history of teaching in the contemporary praise and worship movement, see Ruth and Lim, *History*, 126-27, 133-34.

[31] The idea underneath this understanding—namely, that the worship leader, while leading, might prioritize their own intimate encounter with God—is not part of the ethos of modern worship by happenstance. Along with the idea of "anointing," it is embedded into the liturgical theology and biblical teaching of the forerunners of the modern worship movement. See, for instance Ruth and Lim's outline of Charlotte Baker's 1981 conference talk later called, "The Eye of the Needle," where, upon receiving "a special anointing of the Holy Spirit," she urged worship leaders to abandon

Many times, I have sensed a strange, inappropriate relationship beginning to form between worship leaders and the people they're leading. I've observed when people become increasingly pulled into the tractor beam of someone's personal charisma, and when that leader begins to feed on that (I believe mostly unknowingly), they begin to lead people into intimacy with "themselves" instead of intimacy with [God].[32]

Riddle is exposing an irony in Protestant modern worship leadership—there has been a circling back to medieval Christianity's worship leadership as priestly mediation between God and his people.

Fourth, we might recognize that our evangelical "special ceremonies" are also in need of conformity to the gospel. We might think, for instance, of how for funerals in Cranmer's day the liability existed in prayers for the dead and masses for souls in purgatory. Where are our liabilities? It tends to be commonplace today at funerals for people to spend considerable amounts of time eulogizing the deceased, which often involves recounting their virtues in sentimental and idealized ways. The question is not whether this practice is edifying or comforting to the bereaved family members—indeed, it can be. Such testimonies are therapeutic and full of comfort. The question is whether, in a public worship service, they serve the gospel of *Christ's* righteousness. Especially in death, Cranmer would urge us to ask why we gather. If there is any time to attest to and proclaim the meritorious death and resurrection of Jesus Christ, it is at the hour of death. We might ask similarly about how other unbiblical national "ceremonies" have crept into our public services. For those in my country, could it be that the Hallmark calendar (Mother's Day, Father's Day) and the national holidays of the United States (the Sunday nearest Independence Day, Veterans Day) take our eyes off the international and adoptive family that Christ's blood has ransomed us into, and of which we are "very members incorporate"?

Fifth, we might with Cranmer inquire into the "priestly ceremonial" of modern pastoral and worship leadership. Could our platforms and positioning front and center have similar (even if unintended) mediatorial messaging

---

"ministering to men" in exchange for ministering to God alone in the act of worship. This ministry to God alone through music is the "gate" of true worship, "the eye of the needle" (Ruth and Lim, *History,* 117).

[32]Riddle, *Reset*, 30.

as a priest standing between the altar and the people? Could our musicianship as vocal leaders be so superb, could our vocal flourishes or instrumental stylings be so beautiful and virtuosic, that they shut the mouths of the singing congregation which instead stands in awe of the spectacle of the great performers up front, who are doing the work on behalf of the people? Though this draws an admittedly ambiguous and culturally relative line, perhaps those of us who lead people with our countenance and emotional expression could be more aware of the boundary between helpful emotional shepherding through example[33] and overly intensified expressions of personal worship (however authentic they may be) which cause people to marvel at us rather than the Christ we are all worshiping. Similar to issues surrounding our title, worship leader, the grammatical rules of *sola fide* might have us pause over common bullet points in standard job descriptions for worship leaders, such as "able to usher the church into the presence of God."[34] Might there, too, be modern worship "sacramentals" as sacrosanct as the medieval church's holy water? Of course, there is a fine line between a useful affective tool and a sacramental, but we could note here modern worship's ubiquitous keyboard pad. If somehow our people are trained that the presence of the Holy Spirit is contained or governed by ambient synths or a strategically placed key change (the inquiry into which must be local, not universal), then perhaps we are due for another stripping of the altars, so that we might return to the only Word that can mediate between God and humanity.[35] In fact, gospel-centrality would behoove us to question some sectors of modern worship which, in the sacramental vacuum of song-heavy services, attribute a sacramentality to music itself—that music, rather than the Word of God preached and proclaimed in sermon, the Lord's Supper, and baptism, has become the *locale* of Christ's presence through the power of the Spirit.[36] It

---

[33]I attempt to tease out what I mean by "emotional shepherding" in Hicks, *Pastor*, 143-55, 183-92.

[34]Hicks, *Pastor*, 37-38.

[35]Satirical Christian website, *The Babylon Bee*, certainly points to this liability in its article, "'Outpouring of the Holy Spirit' Coincides with Key Change," accessed November 22, 2019, babylonbee .com/news/outpouring-of-holy-spirit-coincides-with-key-change.

[36]This observation is made by two leading contemporary worship historians: "Understanding that sacramental notions have been attached to music helps us understand why baptism and the Lord's Supper have been relatively unimportant aspects of most forms of contemporary worship. If God was encountered in the music, they were not needed" (Lester Ruth and Lim Swee Hong, *Lovin' on Jesus: A Concise History of Contemporary Worship* [Nashville: Abingdon, 2017], 123).

is important to be nuanced about this, because Scripture certainly affirms that God acts in special and powerful ways as the people of God engage together in singing,[37] but perhaps we find the grammar of *sola fide* challenging not the music itself, but its excess as a substitute for other ordinary means of grace.

4. Analyzing our devotional piety. The grammar of *sola fide* likewise helps us to parse the way we approach and relate to God in our assumptions about devotional piety in worship. Certainly, for modern evangelicals, we are not likely to be praying to saints or praying for the dead,[38] but could there be other ways our corporate piety is marred by works-righteousness? Perhaps just under the surface some of our expressions of worship is a kind of transactional piety that attempts to muster and signal a sincerity and wholeheartedness in worship that in turn prompts God to act and pour himself out powerfully. Repeated statements or emphatic singing about *our* fervency, *our* surrendered life, *our* given-over will, *our* single-mindedness, *our* faith—all of this can teeter on the brink of sounding like the worshipers of Baal who go to increasing lengths to display their sincerity that the fire might fall. God becomes a vending machine receiving the currency of our virtue: we put in our righteousness, and he gives us his presence.[39] Justification by faith alone helps us to see this kind of piety as a not-gospel precisely because it forgets to say, "*not* I," and fails to receive God's presence as a gift through his Son ("but Christ").

We also learn from Cranmer's method about how the saturation of the service with Scripture creates a devotional context where we are offering to God his own words, not ours. There are several things here for modern worship leaders to practically assess. We might begin by asking how our song selections mirror the breadth and depth of the Psalms. We might even go further and ask how we can actually *sing* those Psalms more often. If we create our liturgies, we might do well to link those liturgical words and phrases to scriptural ones. If we pray extemporaneously, we might do well to memorize

---

[37]See Hicks, *Pastor*, 35-36, for a brief scriptural defense.

[38]Though, oddly, this practice currently seems to be experiencing an unchecked renaissance in some sectors of Anglicanism.

[39]Again, see n7 above for how this theological outlook is deeply interwoven into the fabric of modern worship.

key scriptural passages which help frame various liturgical and theological moments.[40] All this certainly urges worship leaders to take more seriously studying and meditating on Scripture. It is probably the case for Cranmer, as we observed above, that his new liturgical compositions were not necessarily done with a Bible and concordance, but rather the Scriptures simply flowed out of him because he was so saturated by them. Perhaps then for us worship leaders, if our lives were so steeped in the Scriptures, the verbiage of the Bible would pour out of our speech in both our preparation and our leadership, and we would also be more eager to place those words, rather than our own, on the lips of God's people.

Along the same lines, we might ask even more basic questions of some Protestant worship expressions which hardly read any Scripture in their public gatherings apart from the preaching text. Others have pointed out this painful irony of the *sola scriptura* tradition. The Bible is studied in small groups, taught in Sunday school, and prized in core value statements: but where is it read and prayed in public worship, apart from quotations, allusions, and references in worship songs? Cranmer's concern in the sixteenth century was how worship services had been crowded with the "traditions of men." In many sectors of Protestantism today, though our traditions are hardly the same, they could still be crowding out the Word which leads us to Christ.

One final word of Cranmer's might be given to traditions which tend to minimize either the significance or frequency of the celebration of the Lord's Supper. Holy Communion is the God-ordained ritual which makes the preached word "heard" with our eyes, noses, hands, and mouths. If indeed the sacrament "putteth . . . Christ into our eyes, mouths, hands, and all our senses," the Protestant traditions which come to the table infrequently might reconsider experiencing this potent gospel-encounter more regularly. Similarly, traditions which celebrate in a more casual or peripheral manner (e.g., "We've set up communion stations along the sides and back, and when you're ready, feel free to receive on your own as we sing our next song") may be challenged to make more central and corporate the ceremony and piety of Holy Communion, such that people receive together, exchange bread and

---

[40]E.g., prayers of confession informed by Ps 51 or Neh 1; prayers of sending informed by Lk 2:29-32; prayers of thanksgiving informed by Lk 1:67-79; or prayers of praise informed by Rom 11:33-36.

wine from person to person, and partake in locations more visible to the whole congregation.

5. Analyzing our preaching. Finally, we with Cranmer might ask whether our preaching makes plain the proclamation of the gospel, with justification by faith alone operating as the principal measuring tool for homiletical assessment. It offers a word to the more therapeutic, lighthearted, and topical modes of preaching, and, perhaps surprising to some, it offers a word to some renderings of expository preaching. The grammar of *sola fide* asks of topical preaching which might lean toward being more practical or motivational whether its content engages in any meaningful diagnosis and deliverance of sinners. It presses encouraging words to ask the diagnostic question: does this thrust people back on themselves in a way that co-opts the "I" rather than negates it? If so, then such preaching is rightly parsed by the grammar as a not-gospel, devoid of the power of God unto salvation.

And yet on the other end of the spectrum we find a critique of those who advocate for some forms of expository sermons, dedicated to preaching through entire biblical texts, breaking them down into segments and series. One of the potential pitfalls of this homiletical model is that in sticking to the segment of the text we are to preach, we fail to bring to bear its contextualized whole. And we mean whole in two senses. First, we mean the whole of the biblical book itself, and, second, we mean the whole of the Scriptures. Christ himself exposited his own death and resurrection "beginning with Moses and all the prophets . . . in all the Scriptures" (Lk 24:26-27). The liability of this kind of expository model is that it can hermeneutically distance a passage from the singular communicative event that is the whole biblical book. Even more, segmented expository preaching can further distance that book from its context within that singular biblical "Communicative Event" of the death and resurrection of the Word made flesh. If we engage in an expositional walkthrough of biblical texts, we must still speak each text "justificationly," understanding that for the gospel to be clearly proclaimed, and for any one exposition to avoid becoming a not-gospel, the text must be preached in a way that distinguishes faith from works and is sensitive to how the Word is working as law and gospel. In this sense, gospel-centered preaching is always zooming out from any given specific word to how that word is connected to the Bible's double-revelation of our need and God's provision in Christ.

THE FRUIT OF THE GOSPEL'S WORK: HEARTS ON FIRE

If in worship we were to take seriously Cranmer's gospel-centered methodology, what can we expect will be its fruits? The Archbishop himself answers:

> If the profession of our faith of the remission of our own sins enter within us into the deepness of our hearts, then it must needs kindle a warm fire of love in our hearts towards God, and towards all other for the love of God . . . a good will and mind to help every man and to do good unto them, . . . and, *in summa,* a firm intent and purpose to do all that is good, and leave all that is evil. This is the very right, pure, perfect, lively, Christian, hearty, and justifying "faith, which worketh by love," as St Paul saith, and suffereth no venom or poison of sin to remain within the heart, *fide Deus purificans corda* (Acts 15:9).[41]

There we have it. The proclaimed gospel births faith. Faith cleanses the heart. The cleansed heart is freed up for true love of God and love of neighbor. In other words, the clear proclamation of the gospel is the only means that can transform the individual human heart and therefore, from that transformed heart, transform the world. This is, in fact, Cranmer's answer to modern liturgical theology's goal of establishing in worship "the connection between Christian formation and ethics" while avoiding "shaping a people who think they can be close to God while remaining far from the everyday world, or who expect the arrival of [God's] Reign to be only an interior event."[42]

If world-transformation is begotten of heart-transformation, this really does get to the core of all the worship issues that seem to occupy an endless circle of discussions about what it means to be a worshiping community faithful to the Scriptures. We might call these worship-and discussions: worship and mission, worship and justice, worship and diversity, worship and culture, worship and formation, worship and emotions, worship and theology, worship and ethics, worship and evangelism, and on and on. Nearly

---

[41]Cranmer, "Corrections" (1538), in John Edmund Cox, ed., *The Works of Thomas Cranmer,* vol. 2 (Cambridge: The University Press, 1846), 86.
[42]Oliver, "Worship," 2, 13.

always in these discussions, we are looking for worship to *produce* a certain kind of person who is (insert Christian virtue here). And in our desire to see worship produce this kind of person we craft services which employ certain persuasive or formational content.

For instance, if we want worship to bridge the chasm between being a disciple of Jesus Christ and seeking justice in the world—a real gap in many regions of conservative evangelicalism—we often embark on emphasizing those themes in the content of our worship service: a sermon series from the prophets, readings and prayers that voice the lamentation of the marginalized, songs which intone the justice of God and our responsive activism. Cranmer's work tells us that for there to be true transformation toward these good ends, we must differentiate in worship between the root and its fruits. The root, for Cranmer, is down at the level of the ever-repenting, ever-being-changed heart. The fruit of that changed heart is the resulting outflow of all good works, including compassion and advocacy toward justice in the world. Cranmer might therefore caution us through his vision of gospel-centered worship. In seeking to emphasize the *fruit* of the transformed life, we must be careful not to cut off the supply that waters the *root* of the transformed life—the gospel. The methodology of the grammar of *sola fide* gives us a way to analyze whether all our "fruit-addressing" in worship services is remaining connected to or deviating from those lifegiving headwaters.

Cranmer's passion was for a "hearty" liturgy.[43] Like "mercy," the term "heart" appears in Cranmer's rites far more often than is warranted by any of his liturgical sources.[44] This is because, as we said in the introduction, he understood fruit of the gospel's work to be that we would "be the more inflamed with the love of [God's] true religion."[45] When Cranmer made the Collect for Purity a public prayer and set it as the opening words for the Holy Communion service, he was setting forth his liturgical theology in a single sentence: a worship service is nothing short of open heart surgery through the killing and resurrecting work of the Word of God. It is no mistake that this opening prayer alludes to the well-known statement from

---

[43]See Stephen Sykes, "Cranmer on the Open Heart," in *This Sacred History: Anglican Reflections for John Booty*, ed. Donald S. Armentrout (Cambridge: Cowley, 1990), 1-20.
[44]See the introduction, n23.
[45]Cranmer, "Preface," in Ketley, *Liturgies*, 17.

the epistle to the Hebrews on the "living and active" Word, which discerns "the thoughts and intentions of the heart," and from which "no creature is hidden" (Heb 4:12-13). The liturgy exists so that, in the deepest sense, the Word of Christ—indeed, the Word which *is* Christ—might dwell in us richly (Col 3:16).

BIBLIOGRAPHY

Acolatse, Esther E. *Powers, Principalities, and the Spirit: Biblical Realism in Africa and the West.* Grand Rapids, MI: Eerdmans, 2018.

Alesius, Alexander. *Of the Auctorite of the Word of God Agannst the Bisshop of London.* 1537.

———. *De authoritate verbi dei liber Alexander Alesij, contra Episcopum Lundensem.* Strassburg, 1542.

Anglican Church in North America. The Book of Common Prayer (2019). Huntington Beach, CA: Anglican Liturgy Press, 2019.

Aristotle. *Nicomachean Ethics.* Translated by Terence Irwin. 2nd ed. Indianapolis: Hackett, 1999.

Atherstone, Andrew. "The Lord's Supper and the Gospel of Salvation: Grace Alone and Faith Alone in the Book of Common Prayer." In *Feed My Sheep: The Anglican Ministry of Word and Sacrament,* edited by Lee Gatiss, 71-99. Watford: Lost Coin Books, 2016.

———. "Reforming Worship: Lessons from Luther and Cranmer." *Churchman* 132, no. 2 (Summer 2018): 105-22.

Augustine. "Answer to the Two Letters of the Pelagians." In *Answer to the Pelagians, II.* Edited by John E. Rotelle. Translated by Roland J. Teske. New York: New City Press, 1998.

———. *Confessions.* Translated by Albert C. Outler. Nashville, Thomas Nelson: 1999.

———. *Confessions I: Introduction and Text.* Edited by James J. O'Donnell. Oxford: Clarendon, 1992.

———. "Faith and Works." In *On Christian Belief.* Edited by Boniface Ramsey. Translated by Ray Kearney. New York: New City Press, 2005.

———. *On the Spirit and the Letter.* Lexington, KY: Beloved Publishing, 2014.

———. "A Treatise on Grace and Free Will." In *Nicene and Post-Nicene Fathers, First Series, Volume V—St. Augustine: Anti-Pelagian Writings.* Edited by Philip Shaff. New York: The Christian Literature Company, 1887.

———. "A Treatise on the Merits and Forgiveness of Sins, and on the Baptism of Infants." In *Nicene and Post-Nicene Fathers, First Series, Volume V—St. Augustine: Anti-Pelagian Writings.* Edited by Philip Shaff. New York: The Christian Literature Company, 1887.

———. "A Treatise on Nature and Grace, Against Pelagius." In *Nicene and Post-Nicene Fathers, First Series, Volume V—St. Augustine: Anti-Pelagian Writings.* Edited by Philip Shaff. New York: The Christian Literature Company, 1887.

Ayris, Paul. "The Public Career of Thomas Cranmer." *Reformation and Renaissance Review* 4 (2000): 75-125.

———. "Thomas Cranmer and the Metropolitical Visitation of Canterbury Province 1533-4." In *From Cranmer to Davidson: A Church of England Record Society Miscellany,* edited by S. Taylor, 1-46. Woodbridge: Church of England Record Society, 1999.

Barbee, C. Frederick, and Paul F. M. Zahl. *The Collects of Thomas Cranmer.* Grand Rapids, MI: Eerdmans, 1999.

Barclay, John M. G. *Paul and the Gift.* Grand Rapids, MI: Eerdmans, 2017.

Bates, J. Barrington. "Expressing What Christians Believe: Anglican Principles for Liturgical Revision." *Anglican Theological Review* 92, no. 3 (2010): 455-80.

————. "On the Search for the Authentic Liturgy of the Apostles: The Diversity of the Early Church as Normative for Anglicans." *Journal of Anglican Studies* 12, no. 1 (2012): 37-58.

Bayer, Oswald. *Martin Luther's Theology: A Contemporary Interpretation.* Grand Rapids, MI: Eerdmans, 2003.

————. "Theology as *Askesis:* On Struggling Faith." In *Gudstankens aktualitet: Festskrift til Peter Widmann,* edited by Marie Wiberg Pedersen, Bo Kristian Holm, and Anders-Christian Jacobsen, 35-54. Copenhagen: Forlaget Anis, 2010.

————. *Theology the Lutheran Way.* Grand Rapids, MI: Eerdmans, 2007.

Belcher, Jim. *Deep Church: A Third Way beyond Emerging and Traditional.* Downers Grove, IL: InterVarsity Press, 2009.

Bell, Catherine. *Ritual Theory, Ritual Practice.* New York: Oxford University Press, 1992.

Blakeney, R. P. *The Book of Common Prayer in its History and Interpretation.* 2nd ed. London: Miller, 1866.

Bond, Roland B., ed. *Certain Sermons or Homilies (1547) and A Homily Against Disobedience and Wilful Rebellion (1570): A Critical Edition.* Toronto: University of Toronto Press, 1987.

Bradshaw, Paul F. *The Anglican Ordinal: Its History and Development from the Reformation to the Present Day.* London: SPCK, 1971.

————. *The Apostolic Tradition Reconstructed: A Text for Students.* Norwich: Hymns Ancient and Modern, 2021.

————. "The Daily Offices in the Prayer Book Tradition." *Anglican Theological Review* 95, no. 3 (2013): 447-60.

————. "The Rediscovery of the Holy Spirit in Modern Eucharistic Theology and Practice." In *The Spirit in Worship—Worship in the Spirit,* edited by Teresa Berger and Bryan D. Spinks, 79-98. Collegeville, MN: Pueblo, 2009.

Bradshaw, Paul F., Maxwell E. Johnson, and L. Edward Phillips. *The Apostolic Tradition: A Commentary.* Minneapolis: Fortress, 2002.

Bray, Samuel L., "Ashes in a Time of Plague." *The North American Anglican* (January 6, 2021). Accessed July 9, 2022. https://northamanglican.com/ashes-in-a-time-of-plague/.

————. "The Prayer Book Sentences, Pt. 2: Commonplaces of Contrition." *Ad Fontes Journal* online. Accessed June 17, 2022. https://adfontesjournal.com/liturgy/the-prayer-book-sentences-pt-2-commonplaces-of-contrition/.

Bray, Samuel L., and Drew N. Keane. *The 1662 Book of Common Prayer: International Edition.* Downers Grove, IL: InterVarsity Press, 2021.

Briggs, Richard S. "The Christian Hermeneutics of Cranmer's Homilies." *Journal of Anglican Studies* 15, no. 2 (2017): 167-87.

Brightman, F. E. *The English Rite: Being a Synopsis of the Sources and Revisions of the Book of Common Prayer.* 2 vols. London: Rivingtons, 1915.

Brook, Stella. *The Language of the Book of Common Prayer.* London: André Deutsch, 1965.

Brooks, Peter N. *Thomas Cranmer's Doctrine of the Eucharist: An Essay in Historical Development.* London: MacMillan, 1965.

Buchanan, Colin. *Background Documents to Liturgical Revision 1547–1549.* Bramcote: Grove Books, 1983.

————. *The End of the Offertory—An Anglican Study.* Bramcote: Grove Books, 1978.

————. *An Evangelical Among the Anglican Liturgists.* London: SPCK, 2009.

————. *What Did Cranmer Think He Was Doing?,* 2nd ed. Bramcote: Grove Books, 1982.

Buschart, W. David, and Kent D. Eilers. *Theology as Retrieval: Receiving the Past, Renewing the Church.* Downers Grove, IL: InterVarsity Press, 2015.

Calvin, John. *Institutes of the Christian Religion.* Edited by John T. McNeill. Translated by Ford Lewis Battles. Philadelphia: Westminster, 1960.

Carey, Hilary M. "Devout Literate Laypeople and the Pursuit of the Mixed Life in Later Medieval England." *Journal of Religious History* 14, no. 4 (Dec 1987): 361-81.

Castleman, Robbie F. *Story-Shaped Worship: Following Patterns from the Bible and History.* Downers Grove, IL: InterVarsity Press, 2013.

Chan, Simon. *Liturgical Theology: The Church as Worshiping Community*. Downers Grove, IL: Inter-Varsity Press, 2006.

Chapell, Bryan. *Christ-Centered Worship: Letting the Gospel Shape Our Practice*. Grand Rapids, MI: Baker Books, 2009.

Cherry, Constance M. *The Worship Architect: A Blueprint for Designing Culturally Relevant and Biblically Faithful Services*. Grand Rapids, MI: Baker Books, 2010.

Cosper, Mike. *Rhythms of Grace: How the Church's Worship Tells the Story of the Gospel*. Wheaton, IL: Crossway, 2013.

Cox, John Edmund, ed. *The Works of Thomas Cranmer*. 2 vols. Cambridge: The University Press, 1844–1846.

Cuming, Geoffrey J. *The Godly Order: Texts and Studies Relating to the Book of Common Prayer*. London: SPCK, 1983.

———. *A History of Anglican Liturgy*. London: MacMillan, 1969.

Cyril of Jerusalem. "The Five Mystagogical Catecheses." In *St. Cyril of Jerusalem's Lectures on the Christian Sacraments: The Procatechesis and the Five Mystagogical Catechesis,* edited by F. L. Cross. Crestwood, NY: St. Vladimir's Seminary Press, 1995.

De Mézerac-Zanetti, Aude. "A Reappraisal of Liturgical Continuity in the Mid-Sixteenth Century: Henrician Innovations and the First Books of Common Prayer." *Revue Française de Civilisation Britannique* 22, no. 1 (2017): 1-11.

Devereux, James A. "Reformed Doctrine in the Collects of the First *Book of Common Prayer*." *Harvard Theological Review* 28, no. 1 (January 1965): 49-68.

Dix, Dom Gregory. *The Shape of the Liturgy*. New York: Seabury Press, 1945.

Dowden, John. *Further Studies in the Prayer Book*. London: Methuen & Co, 1908.

Duffy, Eamon. *The Stripping of the Altars: Traditional Religion in England 1400-1580*. New Haven, CT: Yale University Press, 1992.

Dunbar, Gavin. "Like Eagles in This Life: A Theological Reflection on 'The Order for the Administration of the Lord's Supper or Holy Communion' in the Prayer Books of 1559 and 1662." In *The Book of Common Prayer: Past, Present and Future,* edited by Prudence Dailey, 85-105. New York, NY: Continuum, 2011.

Dunlop, Colin. *Anglican Public Worship*. London: SCM, 1953.

Ellis, Christopher J. *Gathering: A Theology and Spirituality of Worship in Free Church Tradition*. London: SCM Press, 2004.

Ellis, Henry. *Original Letters Illustrative of English History*. London: Richard Bentley, 1846.

Episcopal Church, The. The Book of Common Prayer and Administration of the Sacraments and Other Rites and Ceremonies of the Church. New York: Church Publishing Incorporated, 1979.

———. *Constitution and Canons, Together with the Rules of Order*. New York: Office of the General Convention, 2018.

Estcourt, E. E. *The Dogmatic Teaching of the Book of Common Prayer on the Subject of the Holy Eucharist*. London: Longmans, Green, Reader, and Dyer, 1868.

Evett, David. "Luther, Cranmer, Service, and Shakespeare." In *Centered on the Word: Literature, Scripture, and the Tudor-Stuart Middle Way,* edited by Daniel W. Doerksen and Christopher W. Hodgkins, 87-109. Newark: University of Delaware, 2004.

Fagerberg, David W. *On Liturgical Asceticism*. Washington, DC: The Catholic University of America Press, 2013.

Fincham, Kenneth, and Nicholas Tyacke. *Altars Restored: The Changing Face of English Religious Worship, 1547–c.1700*. New York: Oxford University Press, 2007.

Ford, David. *The Gospel of John: A Theological Commentary*. Grand Rapids, MI: Baker Books, 2021.

François, Wim. "Vernacular Bible Reading in Late Medieval and Early Modern Europe: The 'Catholic' Position Revisited." *The Catholic Historical Review* 104, no. 1 (2018): 23-56.

Frere, Walter Howard. *Some Principles of Liturgical Reform: A Contribution Towards the Revision of the Book of Common Prayer*. London: John Murray, 1911.

Fuller, Donald. "Sacrifice and Sacrament: Another Eucharistic Contribution from Peter Martyr Vermigli." In *Peter Martyr Vermigli and the European Reformations: Semper Reformanda,* edited by Frank A. James III, 215-37. Leiden: Brill, 2004.

Gelston, Anthony. "Cranmer and the Daily Services." In *Thomas Cranmer: Essays in Commemoration of the 500th Anniversary of His Birth,* edited by Margot Johnson, 51-81. Durham: Turnstone, 1990.

Gibson, Jonathan, and Mark Earngey. *Reformation Worship: Liturgies from the Past for the Present.* Greensboro, NC: New Growth Press, 2018.

Hall, Basil. "Cranmer, the Eucharist and the Foreign Divines in the Reign of Edward VI." In *Thomas Cranmer: Churchman and Scholar,* edited by Paul Ayris and David Selwyn, 217-58. Woodbridge: The Boydle Press, 1993.

Hardwick, Charles. *A History of the Articles of Religion.* Cambridge: Deighton, Bell, & Co., 1859.

Hatchett, Marion. "The Anglican Liturgical Tradition." In *The Anglican Tradition,* edited by Richard Holloway, 47-77. Wilton: Morehouse-Barlow, 1984.

———. *Commentary on the American Prayer Book.* New York: HarperCollins, 1979.

Hebert, A. G. *Liturgy and Society: The Function of the Church in the Modern World.* London: Faber and Faber, 1935.

Hicks, Zac. *The Worship Pastor: A Call to Ministry for Worship Leaders and Teams.* Grand Rapids, MI: Zondervan, 2016.

Holmer, Paul L. *The Grammar of Faith.* New York: Harper & Row, 1978.

Holmes, Urban T. "Education for Liturgy: An Unfinished Symphony in Four Movements." In *Worship Points the Way: A Celebration of the Life and Work of Massey Hamilton Shepherd Jr.,* edited by Malcolm C. Burson, 116-41. Greenwich: Seabury, 1981.

Hooker, Richard. *Of the Laws of Ecclesiastical Polity.* London: J. M. Dent, 1907.

Hubert, Friedrich. *Die Straßburger Liturgischen Ordnungen Im Zeitalter Der Reformation.* Göttingen: Vandenhoeck & Ruprecht, 1900.

Hunt, J. Eric. *Cranmer's First Litany, 1544 and Merbecke's Book of Common Prayer Noted, 1550.* London: SPCK, 1939.

Jasper, R. C. D., and G. J. Cuming. *Prayers of the Eucharist: Early and Reformed.* Collegeville, MN: Liturgical Press, 1987.

Jeanes, Gordon. "Cranmer and Common Prayer." In *The Oxford Guide to the Book of Common Prayer: A Worldwide Survey,* edited by Charles Hefling and Cynthia Shattuck, 21-38. Oxford: Oxford University Press, 2006.

———. "Liturgy and Ceremonial." In *Liturgy in Dialogue,* edited by Paul Bradshaw and Bryan Spinks, 9-27. London: SPCK, 1993.

———. "A Reformation Treatise on the Sacraments." *Journal of Theological Studies* 46, no. 1 (1995): 149-90.

———. *Signs of God's Promise: Thomas Cranmer's Sacramental Theology and the Book of Common Prayer.* London: T&T Clark, 2008.

Jenkyns, Henry. *The Remains of Thomas Cranmer.* 4 vols. Oxford: The University Press, 1833.

Jennings, Nathan G. *Liturgy and Theology: Economy and Reality.* Eugene, OR: Cascade, 2017.

Johnson, Margot, ed. *Thomas Cranmer: Essays in Commemoration of the 500th Anniversary of His Birth.* Durham: Turnstone, 1990.

Johnson, Maxwell. "Liturgy and Theology." In *Liturgy in Dialogue,* edited by Paul Bradshaw and Bryan Spinks, 202-25. London: SPCK, 1993.

Jungmann, J. A. *Pastoral Liturgy.* New York: Herder & Herder, 1962.

Kapic, Kelly M. "The Law-Gospel Distinction in Reformed Theology and Ministry." In *God's Two Words: Law and Gospel in the Lutheran and Reformed Traditions,* edited by Jonathan A. Linebaugh, 129-51. Grand Rapids, MI: Eerdmans, 2018.

Kavanagh, Aidan. *On Liturgical Theology.* Collegeville, MN: Liturgical Press, 1984.

———. "Response: Primary Theology and Liturgical Act." *Worship* 57 (1983): 321-24.

Ketley, Joseph, ed. *The Two Liturgies, A.D. 1549, and A.D. 1552.* Cambridge: Parker Society, 1844.

Kolb, Robert, and Timothy J. Wengert, eds. *The Book of Concord: The Confessions of the Evangelical Lutheran Church.* Minneapolis: Fortress, 2000.

Kracke, Gil. "Cranmer's Häuptartikel: Revisiting Thomas Cranmer's Theology Through a Lutheran Understanding of Justification." DMin diss., Knox Theological Seminary, 2017.

Krosnicki, Thomas A. "How Dark the Night: The 'Inlumina' Prayer," *Worship* 85, no. 5 (September 2011): 447-54.

The Lambeth Conference 1958: The Encyclical Letter from the Bishops together with the Resolutions and Reports. London: SPCK, 1958.

Legg, J. Wickham. *Cranmer's Liturgical Projects.* London: Harrison & Sons, 1915.

———, ed. *The Second Recension of the Quignon Breviary.* 1 vol. London: Harrison and Sons, 1908.

Leithart, Peter J. *Theopolitan Liturgy.* West Monroe, LA: Theopolis Books, 2019.

Leuenberger, Samuel. *Archbishop Cranmer's Immortal Bequest: The Book of Common Prayer of the Church of England: An Evangelistic Liturgy.* Eugene, OR: Wipf & Stock, 1990.

Lewis, C. S. *English Literature in the Sixteenth Century Excluding Drama.* New York: Oxford University Press, 1944.

Lincicum, David. "Philo of Alexandria and Romans 9:30-10:21: The Commandment and the Quest for the Good Life." In *Reading Romans in Context: Paul and Second Temple Judaism,* edited by Ben C. Blackwell, John K. Goodrich, and Jason Maston, 122-28. Grand Rapids, MI: Zondervan, 2015.

Lindbeck, George A. *The Nature of Doctrine: Religion and Theology in a Postliberal Age.* Philadelphia: The Westminster Press, 1984.

Lindsay, Mark. "Thomas Cranmer and the *Book of Common Prayer:* Theological Education, Liturgy, and the Embodiment of Prosper's Dictum." *Colloquium* 47, no. 2 (2015): 195-207.

Linebaugh, Jonathan A. "The Grammar of the Gospel: Justification as a Theological Criterion in the Reformation and in Paul's Letter to the Galatians." *Scottish Journal of Theology* 71, no. 3 (2018): 287-307.

———. "Introduction." In *God's Two Words: Law and Gospel in the Lutheran and Reformed Traditions,* edited by Jonathan A. Linebaugh, 1-11. Grand Rapids, MI: Eerdmans, 2018.

———. "'The Speech of the Dead': Identifying the No Longer and Now Living 'I' of Galatians 2:20." *New Testament Studies* 66, no. 1 (2020): 87-105.

———. "The Texts of Paul and the Theology of Cranmer." In *Reformation Readings of Paul: Explorations in History and Exegesis,* edited by Michael Allen and Jonathan A. Linebaugh, 235-54. Downers Grove, IL: InterVarsity Press, 2015.

———. "The Uglier Ditch: First-Century Grace in the Present Tense." In *The New Perspective on Grace: Paul and the Gospel after Paul and the Gift,* edited by Edward Adams, Dorothea H. Bertschmann, Stephen J. Chester, Jonathan A. Linebaugh, and Todd D. Still. Grand Rapids, MI: Eerdmans, 2022.

———. *The Word of the Cross: Reading Paul.* Grand Rapids, MI: Eerdmans, 2022.

Lloyd, Charles, ed. *Formularies of Faith Put Forth By Authority during the Reign of Henry VIII.* Oxford: Clarendon, 1825.

Lull, Timothy F., and William R. Russell, eds. *Martin Luther's Basic Theological Writings,* 3rd ed. Minneapolis: Fortress, 2012.

Luther, Martin. *The Babylonian Captivity of the Church* (1520).

———. *Disputation Against Scholastic Theology* (1517).

———. *Heidelberg Disputation* (1518).

———. "Lectures on Romans."

———. *Luther's Works.* Edited by Jaroslav Pelikan and Helmut T. Lehmann [American Edition, 55 vols.]. St. Louis: Concordia; Philadelphia: Fortress Press, 1955–1986.

———. "The Sacrament of the Body and Blood of Christ—Against the Fanatics" (1526).

———. *Three Treatises.* Minneapolis: Fortress Press, 1990.

———. "A Treatise on the New Testament, that is, the Holy Mass" (1520).

Lyons, Frank. "Critiquing Cranmer: *Ordo* and Ecclesial Identity." *Evangelical Theological Society* 66 (November 2014): 1-10.

MacCulloch, Diarmaid. *All Things Made New: The Reformation and Its Legacy.* Oxford: Oxford University Press, 2016.

———. "Cranmer's Ambiguous Legacy." *History Today* 46, no. 6 (June 1996): 23-31.

_____. *Thomas Cranmer: A Life.* New Haven, CT: Yale University Press, 1996.

_____. "Thomas Cranmer and Johannes Dantiscus: Retractation and Additions." *Journal of Ecclesiastical History* 58, no. 2 (April 2007): 273-86.

_____. *Tudor Church Militant: Edward VI and the Protestant Reformation.* London: Penguin, 1999.

Marsden, Richard. "The Bible in English in the Middle Ages." In *The Practice of the Bible in the Middle Ages: Production, Reception, and Performance in Western Christianity,* edited by Susan Boynton and Diane J. Reilly, 272-95. New York: Columbia University Press, 2011.

Mascall, E. L. *Christ, the Christian, and the Church: A Study of the Incarnation and Its Consequences.* London: Longman, Greens and Co., 1946.

Maskell, William. *The Ancient Liturgy of the Church of England,* 3rd ed. Oxford: Clarendon, 1882.

Maxwell, William D. *An Outline of Christian Worship: Its Developments and Forms.* London: Oxford, 1936.

McFarland, Orrey. "Philo of Alexandria and Romans 9:1-29: Grace, Mercy, and Reason." In *Reading Romans in Context: Paul and Second Temple Judaism,* edited by Ben C. Blackwell, John K. Goodrich, and Jason Maston, 115-21. Grand Rapids, MI: Zondervan, 2015.

Melanchthon, Philip. *Apology of the Augsburg Confession* (1531). In *The Book of Concord: The Confessions of the Evangelical Lutheran Church,* edited by Robert Kolb and Timothy J. Wengert, 107-294. Minneapolis: Fortress Press, 2000.

——. *Commonplaces: Loci Communes 1521.* Translated by Christian Preus. Saint Louis: Concordia, 2014.

Mitchell, Leonel, and Ruth Meyers. *Praying Shapes Believing: A Theological Commentary on the Book of Common Prayer.* New York: Seabury, 2016.

Mohlberg, Leo Cunibert, ed. *Liber Sacramentorum Romanae Aeclesiae Ordinis Anni Circuli (Cod. Vat. Reg. lat. 316/Paris bibl. Nat. 7193, 41/56). Sacramentarium Gelasianum.* Rome: Herder, 1960.

Moo, Douglas. *The Epistle to the Romans.* NICNT. Grand Rapids, MI: Eerdmans, 1996.

Moule, H. C. G. *Our Prayer Book: Short Chapters on the History and Contents of the Book of Common Prayer.* London: Seeley and Co., 1898.

Neil, Charles, and J. M. Willoughby. *The Tutorial Prayer Book: For the Teacher, the Student, and the General Reader.* London: The Harrison Trust, 1913.

Newman, John Henry. *An Essay in Aid of a Grammar of Assent.* London: Burns, Oates, & Co., 1870.

——. *An Essay on the Development of Christian Doctrine.* London: James Toovey, 1845.

Nichols, John Gough, ed. *Narratives of the Days of the Reformation.* London: Camden Society, 1859.

Norris, Frederick W. "Theology as Grammar: Nazianzen and Wittgenstein." In *Arianism After Arius: Essays on the Development of the Fourth Century Trinitarian Conflicts,* edited by Michael R. Barnes and Daniel H. Williams, 237-49. Edinburgh: T&T Clark, 1993.

Null, Ashley. "The Authority of Scripture in Reformation Anglicanism: Then and Now." In *Contesting Orthodoxies in the History of Christianity: Essays in Honour of Diarmaid MacCulloch,* edited by Ellie Gebarowski-Shafer, Ashley Null, and Alec Ryrie, 77-97. Woodbridge: Boydell, 2021.

——. "Comfortable Words: Thomas Cranmer's Gospel Falconry." In *Comfortable Words: Essays in Honor of Paul F. M. Zahl,* edited by John D. Koch, Jr., and Todd H. W. Brewer, 218-42. Eugene, OR: Pickwick, 2013.

——. *Divine Allurement: Cranmer's Comfortable Words.* London: The Latimer Trust, 2014.

——. "Divine Allurement: Thomas Cranmer and Tudor Church Growth." In *Towards a Theology of Church Growth,* edited by David Goodhew, 197-216. New York: Routledge, 2016.

——. *The Efficacious Word: Thomas Cranmer on Scripture,* Vol. 1, *Cranmer's Great Commonplaces.* Oxford: Oxford University Press, forthcoming.

——. "Official Tudor Homilies." In *The Oxford Handbook of the Early Modern Sermon,* edited by Peter McCullough and Hugh Adlington, 348-63. Oxford: Oxford University Press, 2011.

——. "The Power of Unconditional Love in the Anglican Reformation." In *Reformation Anglicanism: A Vision for Today's Global Communion,* edited by Ashley Null and John Yates III, 45-76. Wheaton, IL: Crossway, 2017.

——. "Salvation and Sanctification in the Book of Homilies." *The Reformed Theological Review* 62, no. 1 (2003): 14-28.

———. "Thomas Cranmer." In *Christian Theologies of the Sacraments: A Comparative Introduction,* edited by Justin S. Holcomb and David A. Johnson, 209-32. New York: New York University Press, 2017.

———. "Thomas Cranmer and the Anglican Way of Reading Scripture." *Anglican and Episcopal History* 75, no. 4 (2006): 488-526.

———. "Thomas Cranmer and Tudor Evangelicalism." In *The Emergence of Evangelicalism: Exploring Historical Continuities,* edited by Kenneth J. Stewart and Michael A. G. Haykin, 221-51. Downers Grove, IL: InterVarsity Press, 2008.

———. *Thomas Cranmer's Doctrine of Repentance: Renewing the Power to Love.* Oxford: Oxford University Press, 2000.

———. "Thomas Cranmer's Reading of Paul's Letters." In *Reformation Readings of Paul,* edited by Michael Allen and Jonathan A. Linebaugh, 211-33. Downers Grove, IL: InterVarsity Press, 2015.

———. "Thomas Cranmer's Reputation Reconsidered." In *Reformation Reputations: The Power of the Individual in English Reformation History,* edited by D. J. Crankshaw and G. W. C. Gross, 189-221. London: Palgrave Macmillan, 2021.

———. "Thomas Cranmer's Theology of the Heart." *Anvil* 23, no. 2 (2006): 207-17.

———. *The Word of God and its Efficacy in Thomas Cranmer: New Insights into his Sources and Mature Thought.* Oxford: Oxford University Press, forthcoming.

Oberman, Heiko. "Preaching and the Word in the Reformation." *Theology Today* 18, no. 1 (1961): 16-29.

Oliver, Juan M. C. "Worship, Forming and Deforming." In *Worship-Shaped Life: Liturgical Formation and the People of God,* edited by Ruth Meyers and Paul Gibson, 1-25. Norwich: Canterbury Press, 2010.

Olver, Matthew S. C. "A Classification of a Liturgy's Use of Scripture: A Proposal." *Studia Liturgica* 49, no. 2 (2019): 220-45.

———. "Confessions of a Penitential Orderer." *Covenant* (May 10, 2022). Accessed July 6, 2022. https:// covenant.livingchurch.org/2022/05/10/confessions-of-a-penitential-orderer/.

Packer, J. I. *The Gospel in the Prayer Book.* Downers Grove, IL: InterVarsity Press, 2021.

———. "Introduction." In *The Work of Thomas Cranmer,* edited by G. E. Duffield, x-xlv. Philadelphia: Fortress, 1965.

Parsons, Edward Lambe, and Bayard Hale Jones. *The American Prayer Book: Its Origins and Principles.* New York: Charles Scribner's Sons, 1937.

Power, David. "Theology of the Latin Text and Rite." In *A Commentary on the Order of the Mass of the Roman Missal: A New English Translation, Developed Under the Auspices of the Catholic Academy of Liturgy,* edited by Edward Foley, John F. Baldovin, Mary Collins, and Joanne M. Pierce, 259-78. Collegeville, MN: Pueblo, 2011.

Price, Charles P. *Introducing the Proposed Book.* New York: Church Hymnal Corporation, 1976.

———. *The Prayer Book in the Church.* Cincinnati: Forward Movement Publications, 1997.

Ratcliff, E. C. "The Liturgical Work of Archbishop Cranmer." *Journal of Ecclesiastical History* 7, no. 2 (1956): 189-203.

Rex, Richard. "The Crisis of Obedience: God's Word and Henry's Reformation." *The Historical Journal* 39 (1996): 863-94.

Riddle, Jeremy. *The Reset: Returning to the Heart of Worship and a Life of Undivided Devotion.* Anaheim, CA: Wholehearted Publishing, 2020.

Ridley, Nicholas. "Reasons Why the Lord's Board Should Rather Be After the Form of a Table, Than an Altar." In *The Works of Nicholas Ridley,* edited by Henry Christmas, 321-24. Cambridge: Cambridge University, 1841.

Ruth, Lester, and Lim Swee Hong. *A History of Contemporary Praise & Worship: Understanding the Ideas that Reshaped the Protestant Church.* Grand Rapids, MI: Baker Academic, 2021.

———. *Lovin' on Jesus: A Concise History of Contemporary Worship.* Nashville: Abingdon, 2017.

Rutledge, Fleming. *The Crucifixion: Understanding the Death of Jesus Christ.* Grand Rapids, MI: Eerdmans, 2015.

Schmemann, Alexander. *Introduction to Liturgical Theology.* Crestwood, NY: St. Vladimir's Seminary Press, 1966.

Serra, Dominic E. "The Roman Canon: The Theological Significance of Its Structure and Syntax." *Ecclesia Orans* 20 (2003): 99-128.

Shepherd, Massey Hamilton. *The Oxford American Prayer Book Commentary.* New York: Oxford, 1950.

Spinks, Bryan D. *Do This in Remembrance of Me: The Eucharist from the Early Church to the Present Day.* London: SCM, 2013.

———. "German Influence on Edwardian Liturgies." In *Sister Reformations (Schwesterreformationen),* edited by Dorothea Wendebourg, 175-89. Tübingen: Mohr Siebeck, 2010.

———. *Luther's Liturgical Criteria and His Reform of the Canon of the Mass.* Bramcote: Grove Books, 1982.

———. "Mis-Shapen: Gregory Dix and the Four-Action Shape of the Liturgy." *Lutheran Quarterly* 4, no. 2 (1990): 161-77.

———. "Renaissance Liturgical Reforms: Reflections on Intentions and Methods." *Reformation and Renaissance Review* 7, no. 2-3 (2005): 268-82.

———. "Treasures Old and New: A Look at Some of Thomas Cranmer's Methods of Liturgical Compilation." In *Thomas Cranmer: Churchman and Scholar,* edited by Paul Ayris and David Selwyn, 175-88. Woodbridge: Boydell, 1993.

Stacey, Caroline M. "Justification by Faith in the Two Books of Homilies (1547 and 1571)." *Anglican Theological Review* 83, no. 2 (2001): 255-79.

Stephens-Hodge, L. E. H. *The Collects: An Introduction and Exposition.* London: Hodder and Stoughton, 1961.

Stevenson, Kenneth W. "Cranmer's Pastoral Offices: Origin and Development." In *Thomas Cranmer: Essays in Commemoration of the 500th Anniversary of His Birth,* edited by Margot Johnson, 82-93. Durham: Turnstone, 1990.

Strout, Shawn. "Thomas Cranmer's Reform of the *Sanctorale* Calendar." *Anglican and Episcopal History* 87, no. 3 (2018): 307-24.

Sumner, George R. *Being Salt: A Theology of an Ordered Church.* Eugene, OR: Cascade, 2007.

Sweeney, Sylvia A. *An Ecofeminist Perspective on Ash Wednesday and Lent.* New York, NY: Peter Lang, 2010.

Sykes, Stephen. "Baptisme Doth Represente Unto Us Oure Profession." In *Thomas Cranmer: Essays in Commemoration of the 500th Anniversary of His Birth,* edited by Margot Johnson, 122-43. Durham: Turnstone, 1990.

———. "Cranmer on the Open Heart." In *This Sacred History: Anglican Reflections for John Booty,* edited by Donald S. Armentrout, 1-20. Cambridge: Cowley, 1990.

Targoff, Ramie. *Common Prayer: The Language of Public Devotion in Early Modern England.* Chicago: University of Chicago Press, 2001.

Taylor, W. David O. *Glimpses of the New Creation: Worship and the Formative Power of the Arts.* Grand Rapids, MI: Eerdmans, 2019.

Tchividjian, Tullian. *One Way Love: Inexhaustible Grace for an Exhausted World.* Colorado Springs, CO: David C. Cook, 2012.

Thompson, Bard. *Liturgies of the Western Church.* Philadelphia: Fortress, 1961.

Vajta, Vilmos. *Luther on Worship: An Interpretation.* Eugene, OR: Wipf and Stock, 1958.

Vogel, Cyril. *Medieval Liturgy: An Introduction to the Sources.* Translated and revised by William Storey and Niels Rasmussen. Portland, OR: Pastoral Press, 1986.

Wainwright, Geoffrey. *Doxology.* New York: Oxford, 1980.

Walker, Charles. *The Liturgy of the Church of Sarum.* London: Hayes, 1866.

Walsh, K. J. "Cranmer and the Fathers, especially in the *Defense.*" *Journal of Religious History* 11 (1980): 227-47.

Westerholm, Stephen. *Perspectives Old and New on Paul: The "Lutheran" Paul and His Critics.* Grand Rapids, MI: Eerdmans, 2004.

Whitaker, E. C. *Martin Bucer and the Book of Common Prayer.* Great Wakering: Mayhew-McCrimmon, 1974.

White, James F. *Introduction to Christian Worship*. 3rd ed. Nashville: Abingdon, 2000.

Williams, D. H. *Evangelicals and Tradition: The Formative Influence of the Early Church*. Grand Rapids, MI: Baker Books, 2005.

——. *Retrieving the Tradition and Renewing Evangelicalism: A Primer for Suspicious Protestants*. Grand Rapids, MI: Eerdmans, 1999.

Wittgenstein, Ludwig. *Philosophical Investigations*. Translated by G. E. M. Anscombe. New York: MacMillan, 1953.

Wordsworth, C., ed. *Horae Eboracenses: the Prymer or Hours of the Blessed Virgin Mary, According to the Use of the Illustrious Church of York*. Durham: Andrews & Co.; London: Bernard Quaritch, 1920.

Zahl, Paul F. M. *Grace in Practice: A Theology of Everyday Life*. Grand Rapids, MI: Eerdmans, 2007.

Zahl, Simeon. "On the Affective Salience of Doctrines." *Modern Theology* 31, no. 3 (2015): 428-44.

——. "The Bondage of the Affections: Willing, Feeling, and Desiring in Luther's Theology, 1513-25." In *The Spirit, the Affections, and the Christian Tradition*, edited by Dale M. Coulter and Amos Yong, 181-206. Notre Dame: University of Notre Dame Press, 2016.

——. *The Holy Spirit and Christian Experience*. Oxford: Oxford University Press, 2020.

——. "Incongruous Grace as Patterns of Experience." *International Journal of Systematic Theology* 22, no. 1 (2020): 60-76.

Ziegler, Philip G. *Militant Grace: The Apocalyptic Turn and the Future of Christian Theology*. Grand Rapids, MI: Baker Books, 2018.

Zieman, Katherine. *Singing the New Song: Literacy and Liturgy in Late Medieval England*. Philadelphia: University of Pennsylvania Press, 2008.

GENERAL INDEX

SCRIPTURE INDEX

DYNAMICS OF CHRISTIAN WORSHIP

Worship of the triune God stands at the heart of the Christian life, so understanding the many dynamics of Christian worship—including prayer, reading the Bible, preaching, baptism, the Lord's Supper, music, visual art, architecture, and more—is both a perennial and crucial issue for the church. With that in mind, the Dynamics of Christian Worship (DCW) series seeks to enable Christians to grow in their understanding of the many aspects of Christian worship. By harvesting the fruits of biblical, theological, historical, practical, and liturgical scholarship and by drawing from a wide range of worshiping contexts and denominational backgrounds, the DCW series seeks to deepen both the theology and practice of Christian worship for the life of the church.

TITLES INCLUDE

+ John Rempel, *Recapturing an Enchanted World: Ritual and Sacrament in the Free Church Tradition*

+ Glenn Packiam, *Worship and the World to Come: Exploring Christian Hope in Contemporary Worship*

+ Noel A. Snyder, *Sermons That Sing: Music and the Practice of Preaching*

+ Steven Félix-Jäger, *Renewal Worship: A Theology of Pentecostal Doxology*

ADVISORY BOARD

Constance Cherry, Indiana Wesleyan University
Carlos Colón, Baylor University
James Hart, Robert E. Webber Institute for Worship Studies
Todd Johnson, First Covenant Church, Seattle, WA
Trygve Johnson, Hope College
Glenn Packiam, Rockharbor Church, Costa Mesa, CA
Melanie Ross, Yale Institute of Sacred Music
Lester Ruth, Duke Divinity School
John Witvliet, Calvin Institute of Christian Worship